SURVIVING THE SHIPWRECK

SURVIVING THE SHIPWRECK

· WILLIAM McILVANNEY ·

MAINSTREAM
PUBLISHING

EDINBURGH AND LONDON

First published in Great Britain 1991 by
MAINSTREAM PUBLISHING COMPANY (EDINBURGH) LTD
7 Albany Street
Edinburgh EH1 3UG

ISBN 1 85158 359 9

A catalogue record for this book is available from the British Library

Typeset in 10/12 Times by Polyprint, 48 Pleasance, Edinburgh, EH8 9TJ
Printed and bound in Great Britain by
Butler & Tanner Ltd, Frome and London

For Siobhán and Liam, whose independence of mind and spirit is my sole vanity as a parent, and to the memory of Tony Finlay, formerly Executive Editor of the *Glasgow Herald* and a man of integrity, who – in a journalistic sense – first booked me on board.

Acknowledgments

Acknowledgment is made to the *Glasgow Herald, Scottish International, The Observer, Observer Scotland, Radical Scotland,* the *Sunday Standard, Departures* and the *Times Educational Supplement,* where some of this material first appeared.

Contents

Preface

As long as we have more to do, we have done nothing. So, now, let us add Moby
Dick *to our blessing and step from that. Leviathan is not the biggest fish; – I have
heard of Krakens.*

I HAVE USED THIS QUOTATION IN ONE PART OF THIS BOOK
and I suppose it could stand as epigraph to the whole. It was written by
Herman Melville in a letter to Nathaniel Hawthorne just after he had
finished writing *Moby Dick*. It seems to me apposite to these times of
shallow social aspirations when a drifting dust of pragmatism is obscuring
the view, like fallout that deforms our dreams. Captain Ahab having failed
in his quest to capture the great white whale, and, instead, having gone down
with it and lost his ship, Melville's response is not that we should give up the
hunt but that we should intensify it and go after an even more elusive quarry.
That seems to me an honourable reply to failed experience.

I believe that one disaster of our time has not been a physical event. It is
something much more widespread, more lasting, more crippling to our
subsequent aspirations. It is the perceived shipwreck of social idealism – the
loss of belief in our ability significantly to reconstruct society towards a more
justly shared community of living. The wreckage of its current failure has
washed up most conspicuously in the Soviet Union and Eastern Europe. But
debris can be found in many other parts of the world and has been noticed
in the recent history of Britain. It may be noticed but I don't think it is always
accurately identified. Picking up some of the pieces, many people remark
that socialism has failed. I would disagree. I think they are looking at the
fragmentation of Marxist-Communism. They have simply insisted that
socialism went down with the ship. But I believe it must resurface into
survival. That is one of the implied, if fugitive, themes of this book.

For Ahab read Marx. From my first acquaintance with Marxism, I felt it
was doomed in its own absolutist error. It does not seek so much to discover
human nature as to re-invent it. It does not seek merely to grow through time
but to negate it. It would liberate humanity into the contradiction of itself.
Formidably intelligent as Marx's arguments are, their conclusions seem to
me about as rational as achieving immortality by committing suicide.

11

For Kraken read socialism. What Marxism is after is certain and reachable and is supposed to be finitely realisable in a time-scale that is, in any humanly experienceable way, infinite (as the great white whale is finite in the infinity of the sea). Socialism is trying to move towards that which may never be finally found, like the Kraken, though we can imagine it. And if we can imagine it, I would think we demean ourselves by not at least trying to realise it. It seems to me one of the greatest nobilities of which our imagination is capable, because it is simultaneously the least selfish and the most fulfilling. While Marxism is a demand for absolute justice which our individual natures cannot honestly answer, socialism is an attempt to share as justly as we can with one another the terms of human existence. The first says: you must be other than you are and force other people to do likewise. The second says: you must be the most that you can be while still allowing others to be the most that they can be. Only one of these demands is human. The other is a denial of our humanity.

The great white whale of Marxist-Communism has gone somewhere dark and deep and taken a manic part of us, like Captain Ahab, with it. It has been the strange, dark waters of the 1980s that took it down – those times when countless conceptual paper-boats have been hailed as armadas of intellect and any more serious craft of human fulfilment has foundered. The search for Leviathan has failed, as perhaps it deserved to, for Marxism meant to kill him, not find him a habitat. To terminate history is to terminate humanity. Idealism realised is idealism dead. We must find a way to coexist justly with our dreams, to let them share our reality without trying to coerce them to be it. In the search for what may not be there, we will surely discover that we are not as much as we wish we were but just as surely that we are more than we thought we were. The Kraken is out there somewhere because we made him there, though we may never see him. Social idealism remains.

But first it is necessary to survive the shipwreck, to find the pieces we can cling to without going under, no matter how fragmentary they seem, or fragile or light – just as long as they float and help to bear our aspirations up with them.

My own pieces gathered here are fragmentary enough. They are journalism and essays and a speech and they incorporate some poetry. But they have some thematic coherence, as I've suggested. As a writer of journalism for some years, I have refused commissions that didn't relate to a need already in me to examine or try to understand some aspect of my life or the lives around me. Most of them were written for myself first before they were offered. Such journalism as I have done has simply been an extension of my preoccupations. Obviously, everything else in the book comes from the same source.

The source is located in Scotland, firstly because that is where I live. But there is another reason why, apart from a few foreign visits, all the material here relates to Scotland: I believe that the political and social experience of this country has importance beyond its borders. Scotland has existed for almost 300 years in a uniquely arrived at limbo in which a strongly shared sense of social and cultural values persists without the political means to express itself effectively. That makes Scotland – among other things – an interesting case-study. Here is held in embryo the possibility of some kind of socialism, a more just way of living with one another.

The accent in this book is Scottish but the voice, I hope, is trying to say things that matter beyond Scotland. As far as the Scots are concerned, I think our time is running out for listening. The Act of Union of 1707 was just the first of many attempts to abort the possibility of Scotland's realising its long and troubled dream of itself. I believe that those attempts are nearer to succeeding than they have ever been before. If Scotland does not soon begin to happen in terms of political power as well as dream, we will be left with the detritus of afterbirth and no baby.

For others who might read this book, there may be a problem of cultural style. The Scottish tradition, it seems to me, has always insisted that thought and feeling are only happy as a married couple. They should never be divorced. I think that is one reason why Robert Burns has come for so many Scots to incarnate the nation. He may seem to some academics who take intellect for a hobby as being a poet of the emotions. He is, I think, one of the most stringently intellectual of poets. It is the fierceness of his intellect that makes possible the awesome precision of his passion. In his finest work – like *A Man's A Man* – that Scottish tradition is almost perfectly expressed in the exact fusion of intellect and passion, each justifying the other.

The human honesty of such writing is something I believe in. It is by no means specific to Scotland. I have found it in the poems of Rilke, in the essays of Montaigne, in the work of Wilfred Owen. But it has for a long time been especially strong among Scots, so that, while we love ideas, we usually don't like to see them wandering about dangerously on their own, unchaperoned by experience. Perhaps that's one reason why Marxism – where the concept seems to exist in its own right beyond the intervention of individual witness (like some kind of intellectual parthenogenesis) – has achieved no serious popular support in a country that, nevertheless, has a fair history of radical socialism.

This trait certainly helps to differentiate our culture from that of England, where, it is my impression, ideas have tended not to be taken seriously enough, in case they interfere with the social plumbing. It may also help to differentiate our culture from, say, that of France, where ideas can be taken so seriously that they can lead to a phenomenon like the literary theory of structuralism, in which perceptiveness is translated into Mandarin so that a clique of intellectuals can commandeer the terminology of literary appreciation and act as if they've made a science.

13

The Scottish tradition, I believe, has long distrusted the concept for its own sake. I share that distrust. To follow the seductive logic of ideas in separation from the constantly re-earned reality of our daily, individual experience can lead the most powerful of minds into determinedly held positions that are humanly uninhabitable.

I still remember the conflicting sensations that came to me reading Rousseau's *Social Contract*. It wouldn't be easy to convey the intensity of my excitement as I started to read – such incisive perception, such clarity. At last, a way out of the wilderness of compromised truths and prevarication. But very soon, round about chapter five or six, a chilling dismay began to settle on me. I started to suspect that you couldn't trust Rousseau as far as the next sentence. We were being led by a half-blind Moses who could see hardly anything clearly but the inside of his head and even there the prevailing weather seemed to be fog. Obsessed with the destination of his dialectic, he refused to admit that he didn't honestly know how to get there. Urging us to follow, he was walking head-on into massive oak trees of observable human experience and pretending they didn't exist. I was left with a sense of the grandeur of the endeavour and the dangerousness of the result. I had opened the book like a window. I closed it like a tomb – interesting bones but where was the flesh?

I believe in the flesh. I believe that the idea must inhabit the person, not the person the idea. So these writings approach their common themes by indirections. They do not set out from a concept that seeks to superimpose itself on an existing reality. They look at people and places and situations and experiences and try to earn their thought from them. I also hope they may have lightness as well as seriousness, for where there isn't any laughter, or at least a smile or two, you'll find people hiding from themselves behind a mere idea of what they're supposed to be.

These pieces are mainly attempts, in specific and often confusing contexts, to take readings from the compass of a socialist conscience amidst the humanly featureless amorality of monetarism. They will have served their purpose if, besides hopefully passing the time, they can act as reminders of some of the shared ideals we have that go beyond the self-interest, greed and indifference to others that have so often lately been dressed in intellectual shoddy and presented as political theory.

Hitting the Reef

Before: February 1979 – Referendum

WEATHER APART, MARCH IN SCOTLAND LOOKS AS IF IT MAY come in like a lamb. If the indifference with which most of us seem to approach the impending referendum on devolution is an accurate gauge of our sense of national identity, the flag of Scotland might be a lion dormant, with mange. This is a strange mood, reminiscent of the awakening that can follow a night of bevvy-inspired vaunting and mead-hall proclamations, when self-doubt squats on your chest and says, 'What have you let us in for this time?' The signs of ego-withdrawal abound.

The most obvious signs relate to the Scottish National Party, without which there would be no referendum. A phenomenon always difficult to define, the SNP seems at least temporarily to have been designated by recent events as more route than destination, less command module than expendable booster. Three by-elections in 1978 found its fortunes in recession. At the January party conference in Perth, Donald Stewart stressed heavily the injustice of demanding the acceptance of at least 40 per cent of the total electorate for a National Assembly. Mr Stewart is, of course, making a perfectly valid point (it won't be enough for Scotland to *say* 'Yes', it will have to shout it), but his insistence on it might be taken to imply a certain loss of confidence, perhaps due to his awareness of the virile apathy with which so many Scots confront political issues.

This apathy functions by a tremendous displacement of energy into other areas. The most striking recent example was the B-picture remake of the Darien Scheme that was Scotland's World Cup sortie into Argentina. It's not that we went, but went with such naïve hopefulness. It's not that we lost but that it meant so much. Losing a football match shouldn't be confused with loss of identity. I suspect that the kind of commitment Scots invest in football means that there's less left over for more important concerns.

But although the Scottish tendency not to take politics seriously enough is a familiar fixture (we've had more than 200 years of practice), the current manifestation of it remains surprising. The muddy tide of patriotism that took us as far as the Scotland Act appears to have receded with a suddenness that makes the Solway seem leisurely. Why?

One possible reason is the shock of realising where that surging sense of identity had led us – to the parliamentary debate on the Devolution Bill. A confused but potent climacteric, roughly definable as orgiastic, found that its fulfilment has been to be clinically analysed, dissected by amendments, stored in clauses. Who needs to make love to a test-tube?

The Scottish proclivity for confrontation, that love of turning every occasion into an event, was baffled. The sensation conveyed by trying to follow the almost Kafkaesque ramifications of debate on the Devolution Bill, where every quibble was a Russian doll of other quibbles, was not so much that of being fitted for a new and more realistic national costume as of being measured for a coffin. Passion was neutered by boredom.

Then again, faced with the strangeness of where we had come to, we were perhaps more inclined to wonder about the strangeness of how we had got there. The single most powerful factor in bringing about the Scotland Act has been the Scottish National Party. And what is that? It is a strange thing which bears the same relationship to a political party as an identikit picture does to a human face. It has recognisable features but no coherent identity.

When the SNP were in full swing, before the prospect of devolution had crystallised into an Act, there was for me something contagious about their energy. It was like watching a vigorous eightsome-reel which made you clap your own hands and tap your feet. But as the music dies and the sweat cools, the wee sceptic who sits, half-turned away, at the back of a lot of Scottish heads begins to get a clearer hearing.

'Here, wait a minute,' he is saying. 'That wis a funny dance, wintit? Ah mean, if you saw Genghis Khan linkin' arms wi' Rosa Luxembourg, ye'd winner whit they were celebratin', widn't ye?' He has a point. You have to worry. But neither of these worries could adequately explain why so many Scots seem less than very enthusiastic about the chance they have to determine a significant area of their own future. After all, if the Scotland Act has less the aspect of Moses leading us dramatically to a new sense of identity than that of a confused policeman vaguely pointing us towards a place he has never heard of, it is still all we have at the moment.

It doesn't help to go in the huff with your opportunities because they don't seem big enough. Maturity means some kind of marriage between your ambitions and the actual context they have to inhabit. Whatever the Act is, it involves a real choice that every voter in Scotland should be concerned to make.

Similarly, if the policies of the SNP frequently suggest a convention of Hamlets, that in no way vitiates the opportunity they have been instrumental in bringing us. Whatever mists obscure their essential position in the political spectrum, the choice remains separable from them.

No, I would suggest what lies behind our hesitancy as March approaches is something else. Not to put too fine a point on it: I think a lot of us are feart. It's a feeling I share. What worries me most about this is that in such a

18

situation the natural reaction is either to abstain or to vote 'No', not as an act of assertion but as a passive endorsement of the status quo. 'Better the devil ye ken' – that great Scottish cliché that has so often been fitted like manacles round the prospect of change.

These fears, as I've said, are obviously more likely to afflict someone who is tempted to vote 'Yes'. If the referendum is to be an accurate representation of ourselves, it would be better to confront them rather than simply be intimidated by them.

One fear is, I think, that of administrative incompetence in Edinburgh; the Scots just aren't up to governing themselves. This seems to me a kind of naturalised bastard offspring of the old bogeyman that used to stalk the hustings like a latter-day Puritan – Socialists-lack-the-experience-to-govern. It found succinct expression in the *Scottish Daily Express* front-page leader of 26 January:

'Why put all this at risk? And for what? To allow wee Willie McTaggart, who might have made a passable councillor in Cumbernauld in a bad year, to prance and preen as a Scottish Assemblyman?'

The contemptuous patronage contained in that statement takes my breath away. That what purports to be a national daily offers its readers the fact of their own inevitable incompetence as a premise of how they must live says a lot about the weird state of the Scottish psyche. It's enough to make you want to picket their main offices, if it wasn't such a long journey. It amounts to being wished a happy inferiority complex.

The answer to the *Express* is the same as the answer to the whole question of Scottish administrative incompetence. And it's simple. If we're that bad, it's time we weren't. The only way we're going to improve is by the practice of government. After all, presumably the removal of government to Westminster didn't do a lot to make us less parochial.

This awareness of Scottish parochialism ushers in another fear. By voting 'Yes', will we not be taking a backward step, closing in on ourselves instead of opening out to Europe and some kind of internationalism? That troubles me. But then I would think healthy relationships depend on a clear sense of self for each of those involved. That isn't a qualification Scotland could meet at the moment. It would be like drawing up a contract with a schizophrenic. Besides the dubiousness of the EEC as at present conceived, seemingly not so much a mutual aid society as an elaborate game of economic strip poker, it seems at least possible that a heightened sense of our own identity would make us better able to relate to wider issues.

Then there is the related fear that by opting for an assembly we will be evolving a formula for confrontation with England, creating a context for intensifying argument between the two countries. 'Things won't stop there,' the logic runs. The separation between ourselves and England will widen. That seems to me something I wouldn't want and something which might possibly happen. But if it did happen, it would surely be because Scotland's attitude had changed in the interim, because the experience of a limited control of our own affairs had made us reach new decisions. Isn't that a necessary and healthy chance to take? To reject the assembly because it might lead further is equivalent to a refusal to engage in argument because you might have to change your mind – not the healthiest premise on which to base your thinking.

That other deep fear – of the economic non-viability of Scotland as a separate unit – can perhaps be left in the bank for a future orgy of dread, since the assembly on which we will be voting remains financially dependent on Westminster. In any case, both it and other fears I've mentioned do, I believe, merely serve as retinue for the Big Daddy Fear that must be haunting many a Scot's midnight hours. It has certainly appeared to me more than once. The thought of a Scottish Assembly should release in anyone who has seriously tried to understand this country of multiple contradictions The Great MacDread, the Behemoth of them all.

If the 40 per cent limit is passed, if the Scottish Second Coming takes place, what strange creature will it be that slouches towards Edinburgh to be born? Mine eyes dazzle. Strange shapes do haunt the edges of the mind. For how can we tell? There are certain likelihoods, of course. The present party polarisation, for example, will continue with Labour in the ascendancy. But that's like a weather forecaster announcing that tomorrow there will be weather. What will the weather be like? It should at least be psychologically less foggy. One thing an assembly should provide is the means for us to confront ourselves a little more honestly. For a country so long provincialised by England and still subject to the psychic tics that process has induced in us, the self-regarding narrowness, the torpor of frustration, the corrosive resentment of the English, the dead attitudes that fit the present like a catafalque and encourage us to applaud grotesquely simplistic images of ourselves rather than have the guts to explore our current reality, that could be quite a confrontation.

That refurbished building in Edinburgh might just give us a slightly clearer focus on what we're really like and allow us to unpack some of the contents of that obscure portmanteau-word 'Scottish'. I would admit that I can't contemplate what might emerge without some trepidation. After all, we have, I believe, spent well over two hundred years in a kind of limbo of nationhood. That does odd things to people. Imagine having the status of a guest in your own house. Imagine the confused repressions that must give rise to. I think we've endured a condition analogous to that, one that has left us trapped in a weird psychic shuttle that runs from bleak and sterile self-doubt to wild declarations of arrogance and back again, with not a lot of stops in between.

An assembly might begin to give us some of the confidence we need to start making some of those more rational intermediate steps. What we will find there has to be uncertain. For example, Scotland is a country nominally Socialist and blatantly conservative, not to say reactionary, in a lot of ways. Who knows which of the fiercely mixed elements in this country will come most strongly to the surface? I know some of those elements I wish would do so, but I feel no certainty that my wish will be granted.

Why then will I – as the astute reader will have gleaned by now – be voting 'Yes'? It won't be because I think there is no risk but because I think the risk is valid and necessary. It's valid because it's not a crazy risk. It's a measured step towards assuming more responsibility for the way we live. It's necessary because wilfully to go on as we are is to forego the right to what we claim to be.

If we're not prepared to take the responsibility for Scotland, we should acknowledge that most of our protestations of Scottishness should be taken as seriously as vaudeville. Furthermore, no matter what we might learn about ourselves that we'd rather not know in the process of trying to govern, I think acknowledged characteristics are always healthier than the repressed variety. Freud compares the work of translating id into ego to the reclamation from the Zuider Zee of solid ground. 'Where id was, there ego shall be.'

In those terms, I reckon Scotland, with its long history of deferred identity, has an id grossly out of proportion to its ego. Whatever we are, let's try to own up. Then maybe we can live in a more fruitful relationship with our own capacities.

Some time ago I was invited to a BBC Governors' dinner at Queen Margaret Drive. Since, with the exception of a good Scottish actress, everybody else belonged either to the upper reaches of the BBC hierarchy or to positions of importance in industry, my first problem was one of bafflement as to how I had come to be invited, unless I had been cast as the statutory darkie at the liberal establishment's table.

When Sir Michael Swann initiated the post-mastication chat, my bafflement was greatly increased to realise that among the BBC's guests there was unanimity minus one that Scotland should not have more control of its own broadcasting. I can understand some of the misgivings of the other guests. But I would repeat what I said then: I think maturity begins in having the nerve to make your own mistakes. I will be voting 'Yes' because I think it's time we had that nerve.

This is not to say that if we opt for an assembly all we will proceed to do is make mistakes. I don't think so. If I emphasise the risk involved, it's because I think it's a valuable element in the choice and something we need. It's a way of relating fresh to reality as opposed to hiding from it behind archaic masks. We've been good at the latter skill for far too long. Even if we were to decide for an assembly and then later choose to rescind the decision, I still think the experience would be worthwhile. We have ghosts that need laid.

That's why I hope we vote for change. If I might just mention one final wee fear, though: what if we get a bare majority in favour of the assembly but fall well short of the 40 per cent limit? Would that not be a peculiarly Scottish response, leaving us still in that limbo where emotional assertion does not quite connect with the practical demands of the situation?

If that happens, I'll remember a supporter I once saw emerging from a Scotland-England match, waving aloft his tartan banner and proclaiming, like the patron saint of Scottish ambivalence, 'We murdert them wan each.'

Unaccustomed as I am to public prayer: 'O Calvinist God, who givest with the right hand what Thou takest away very quick with the left, spare us a hung jury.' To try to avoid that, I will go on 1 March, jostling my way through my self-projected picket-line of misgivings, and make my mark. It may be shaky from years of nationally nurtured self-doubt but it will go down categorically opposite 'Yes'.

After: March 1979 –
The Cowardly Lion

THERE WAS A LION DORMANT, WITH THE MANGE.
Its roar was out of practice and its teeth
Were brown with eating scraps or something worse.
There was a smell of carrion on its breath.
Asleep, it dreamed a past that never was;
Awake, lapped spirit from a drinking bowl
The keepers had allowed it, walked its cage
In which a full length mirror was installed.
All day it watched itself and practised rage,
Whispered 'I am a lion', bared its fangs
And sometimes snarled so fiercely that it ran
In fear of its own image to the end
Of its small cage, and hid its head and then
Peeped out, approached the mirror once again.
'I can remember being strong,' it said.
Then it lay down again and licked the wounds
It didn't have and thought of all the cubs
The keepers took away and taught strange tricks.
Throughout the world those cubs had won great fame,
Performing always in the keepers' name.
And wondering where they were, where was its soul,
It would return to find it in the bowl
And gather strange, imaginary strength
And roar and fill itself with its own terror
And beat itself unconscious on the mirror.

But lions will be lions and one day
It saw behind it in the mirror keepers laughing
At its preposterous enactment of itself.
They giggled, winked and nodded and it turned
And in an instant lionhood was formed.
The roar was real. In the eyes a dark past burned.
It saw its own horizons without bars.

23

It saw that keepers only keep the past
And it was present and its powerful paws
Could free it from injustice of the laws.
It took its strength and ran and the bars shook.
The keepers were afraid. They mustn't lose
The cubs and revenues the lion gave.
It was a prize exhibit in their zoo.
They watched it lying down, ignore the mirror
And stare at them in hunger, leave the bowl.
They watched it gather strength from day to day
Towards when it would smash the bars away.

The keepers held a conference. A plan
Was needed or the lion would escape.
It wanted freedom. Why not give it some,
Extend its compound but still keep it trapped?
Some nodded sagely who were not asleep.
They would pretend to free it but still keep
It as their pet. And even some of those
Who loved the lion said the plan was good.
These in their cunning thought they understood
The lion would escape this half-way house.
This was a lion. It was not a mouse
To be content with just a little room.
The compound was constructed. Every stone
Was argued over fiercely. Like a tomb
It never would escape the thing was made.
Still those who loved it acquiesced. They said
In private, 'Things will work out very well.
Give it one sniff of freedom and we'll see.
The lion will be a lion and will be
True to itself again. Don't be afraid.'
Some sleepers wakened briefly and agreed.

The day of 'freedom' came. The cage-door creaked
Out on its ancient hinges and swung open.
In awe the keepers waited. What would happen?
Would the lion attack and had they been too bold
In their decisions? Would the compound hold?
The lion approached the door. Its head emerged
Noble and proud, its snout raised to the wind.
It smelt the terrible distances of freedom,
It felt the risk of being not confined,

24

AFTER: MARCH 1979 – THE COWARDLY LION

It knew the pain of hunger unassuaged,
It sensed the emptiness where self is found,
It heard the bitterness where life is waged.
Slowly the keepers relaxed into a smile
And giggled and nodded again, were winking while
Those who loved the lion had nothing to say.
For the lion had turned to its cage and slunk away
And lives still among stinking straw today.

Clutching at Straws

A Tale of Two Cities

IT WILL, OF COURSE, DEPEND WHEN YOU GO THERE, AND ON what terms. If you arrive during the Edinburgh Festival, the three weeks of the locust, with Mahler on your mind or with introductory notes to *Ane Satyre of the Thrie Estaitis*, you may be visiting your own hallucination. Most cities are street-wise enough to sell us back our preconceptions, usually at an inflated rate.

You may find living sculptures on the Mound, exotic dancers in the Royal Mile advertising a show which, if you miss it, will apparently leave you culturally anorexic all your life, the George Hotel sounding like an American Hilton fitted with a silencer, unlikely events occurring in unlikely places and buskers almost everywhere. The Assembly Rooms in George Street will offer you so many pamphlets and handouts and programmes of what you ought to see that you will feel a sinking of the heart, as if you have given yourself half an hour to visit the Prado. You will have fun, since only those who are dead but have not yet been informed of the fact can't find a way to enjoy the Edinburgh Festival. But you will miss the city. For these are deciduous impressions the city discards with the cultural tourists.

Edinburgh is more complicated than that. You don't relate to it like a one-night stand. You woo the city or your sense of it will have to sleep alone. And since not everybody can live in it and since not everybody can visit it often enough to learn to interpret its changing and frequently hypocritical moods, it might be as well to practise an approach.

At some time, for example, you're going to be in Princes Street and looking at the Castle. Don't succumb too quickly. Don't say simply, 'Beautiful!' Edinburgh expects you to say that. Most other people have. Edinburgh is aware of being beautiful. Like most of the beautiful, the city hides behind the fact and would be content to have you think just that. But the only interesting thing about beauty is what is behind it. Beauty is interesting precisely because it is never merely skin deep. Glamour may be but not beauty.

Look at the Castle carefully, say from the entrance to Castle Street. It is volcanic rock and battlements and lawns and a conspicuous building that looks oddly bland as part of such a forbidding castle. It is as if the ferocity of

29

the rock had been cultivated into gentle stone, as if the root of a thistle should nourish a rose. It's a strange castle. Visit it, read about it and you'll be aware of what a peculiar hybrid it is, necessity mingling with expediency. Come back and stand on Princes Street and look at it afresh. Between you and it are Princes Street Gardens, formerly the Nor Loch. At your back are the shops of Princes Street, now going down market with the occasional remainder bookshop and a Virgin Records store. The commercial and the mythic confront each other. Each, reflected in the other, distorts slightly.

If you are feeling unkind, you may begin to see the Castle as the biggest store overlooking Princes Street, selling a tourist image of Scotland. If you are feeling indulgent towards the city, and Edinburgh is beautiful enough to make it easy to feel like that, you may simply wonder what it is the Castle is defending these days. Either way, you will be between two of the basic contradictions of Edinburgh, whose element is contradiction. It is the most romantic of cities and the most commercial of cities. It is the contradictions of Scottish history set in stone.

Appreciating Edinburgh involves appreciating those contradictions. It is centrally the Old Town and the New Town, impaction and expansiveness, compulsion and deliberation. The contradictoriness of the city can be seen most vividly in the proximity of these two parts of it but its contradictions subdivide endlessly and subtly within themselves.

The core of the city is the Old Town and the core of the Old Town is the Royal Mile, that justly famous sequence of short streets from the Castle to the Palace of Holyroodhouse. The confused elements of whatever Scottish-ness is have fought one another for centuries up and down this thoroughfare and left some informative skeletons. There can't be many streets in the world where the history of a nation is so succinctly recorded, like a microchip housing a library.

You could browse there a long time. Among the many things you may notice, the contradictions will proliferate. The buildings are handsome; what they represent is frequently dark and brutal. John Knox's House looks merely pretty, the harmless vanity of some moderately successful man. The man who is said to have lived there helped to create – with the patrician peremptoriness of his belief in democratic forms of worship – schisms in Scotland's sense of itself that are still unresolved today. St Giles' Cathedral, symbolically combining church and crown in its architecture, has the structured calm of all old churches. In this case it is the still eye of the destructive hurricane of Scottish history. Many fierce antagonisms purport to be held in balance here. But even a casual sense of Scottish history may make you wonder if the stabilising force is anything greater than hypocrisy. Notice, for example, how James Graham, Marquis of Montrose, and Archibald Campbell, 8th Earl and 1st Marquis of Argyll, lie in statued dignity almost opposite each other. Argyll gloatingly watched Montrose hang and was later executed himself, partly to satisfy the vengeance of Montrose's admirers. It seems fitting that the heart of Montrose doesn't lie here with his gathered remains but is somewhere unknown. Nearby is Parliament House, surely the strangest monument to its own ambiguity any nation ever had. Here, in 1707, the Scottish Parliament sold itself to Westminster for a not very impressive cash settlement and the promise of jobs for the boys.

The sense Edinburgh frequently gives of things being perhaps not quite what they seem (what is the point of a Parliament House without a parliament?) is epitomised by one of the less impressive monuments in the Royal Mile – Brodie's Close. This was once occupied by Deacon William Brodie, a respectable citizen by day and eventually hanged for his criminal nocturnal activities. He was the original for Robert Louis Stevenson's *Dr Jekyll and Mr Hyde*. The story of the enlightened researcher, the rational seeker after truth, and the dark bundle of atavistic impulses he couldn't quite control has a special relevance to Edinburgh and Scotland. Before leaving the cluster of the Old Town, with its closes leading you're not sure where, to move into the airy perspectives of the New Town, perhaps you could entertain the possibility that Stevenson got the emphases wrong and that Mr Hyde has been given an unjustifiably bad press. Isn't it possible that Mr Hyde behaves in that spectacularly anti-social way precisely because he has been denied? Isn't it possible to see Dr Jekyll's boring rectitude as being another kind of crime against life? Such questions may help to provide a perspective on the connection between the New Town and the Old.

The first reaction to have to the New Town is to disagree with Ruskin, who thought it ugly. Only an architectural pedant who thinks he knows exactly what should be there and therefore can only see the disappointment of his expectations could find the New Town less than impressive. It is a triumph of town planning, spacious and beautiful. Charlotte Square is a marvel, George Street a recurring pleasure. But even as the beauty impinges, it can trouble. For there is something almost too self-conscious about the New Town. Such concentration on presenting an image implies the sacrifice of other, more complicated awarenesses. The New Town doesn't merely exist as itself but as a kind of wilful and deliberate denial of the muddle of the Old Town and what it stands for. Perhaps the New Town has pleased so many visitors partly because it is easy for them to feel at home there. It is more superimposition than development. It is arguably the least authentically Scottish place in Scotland.

The most obvious giveaway is the street names. You find the three main parallels of Princes Street, George Street and Queen Street with between them the narrower Rose Street and Thistle Street, and you realise that the very principle of the New Town is an abjuration of Scottishness as something significantly specific in itself, a placative insistence on Scotland as being

31

merely a part of the British Empire. The New Town is where the empty Scottish Parliament eventually went, a kind of Hanoverian clearing house of the Scottish identity en route to being upholders of the Empire and the professions. Goodnight, Mr Hyde. Good morning, Dr Jekyll.

If you want to check on that impression, visit Dean Cemetery in Dean Village, ten or fifteen minutes' walk from the west end of Princes Street. (Cemeteries are always a good way to understand a city. All cities are full of ghosts and you're as well to visit them at home. Père Lachaise, for example, will tell you more about Paris than a dozen tourist guides.) The headstones and memorial plaques and tombs in Dean Cemetery read like a coda to the symphonic architecture of the New Town or like the small print in the contract many leading Scots made with England after it had been decided that Scottishness was a bad investment. The names aren't those of the very famous or the original or the creative. They are mainly the names of the solidly respectable, the formidably well off, those who can measure their worth in social status and financial success. An awful lot of them have the profession appended to the name, like a translation of Scottishness into the esperanto of success. Here are merchants and newspaper owners and high-ranking soldiers who died in India and doctors and innumerable Writers to the Signet. Home is the Scotsman who has been on the make.

You may begin by this time to appreciate the nature of the fascinating contradictions of which Edinburgh is composed. It incarnates both the clearest features of Scottish history and their most effective disguise. It is simultaneously the most Scottish and the most English place in Scotland. If you sell your history, you create a vacuum in the nation's psyche. The easiest way to fill that vacuum is with a romanticised version of the history, although the unfulfilled force of that history will remain in the people, baffled and repressed, like Mr Hyde skulking ineffectually inside Dr Jekyll.

The process of trying to remodel the psychology of this historically tortured old city by cosmetic surgery has continued. It has made of Edinburgh an endlessly interesting gallery of complicated appearances so that, among the face-lifts and false noses and stucco masks, you're left wondering where the real Edinburgh is. Or has it emigrated and left only facsimiles of itself behind? Is it in the Old Town or the New, the villas of Morningside so loathed by Stevenson, the genteelly tatty tenements of Marchmont, in run-down Leith where trendy wine bars have begun to appear like found sculptures among debris?

The question is made more difficult to answer because what you thought you knew keeps changing. Edinburgh never runs out of disguises. Rose Street, for example, used to be one long, dim stagger of pubs (or perhaps it only seemed dim) where women were sometimes waiting, though no buses ran there. It was like a time-lock by which the Old Town had managed to infiltrate the New Town. Today it is very respectable. Not too long ago, the

Old Town was largely depopulated, the working classes – who perhaps too obviously offered proof of Edinburgh's unresolved argument with itself – being moved out to housing schemes on the city's edges, rather as if the evidence were being disposed of. Now the Old Town, refurbished and attractive, is being repopulated, though not, one supposes, by too many people from the council schemes of Pilton and Craigmillar and Sighthill. (A trip on a number 32 bus will show you some of these places not often mentioned in the brochures.)

Edinburgh remains an elusive place, founded on rock yet strangely shifting. I've just been trying to point you towards where I suspect it is. I'm not sure I've ever seen it clear myself but I have surely enjoyed looking. And I've certainly caught glimpses: conversations in old pubs that are like debriefing rooms for preconceptions; a sudden view that can temporarily confound private purposes (so that once taking a short-cut across Victoria Terrace, I turned it into the long way round, surprised by what I had found); times of being dazzled into a new sense of the place by the strange planes and clefts of light this high city makes.

The effect of such occasions can be to push you past your own assumptions. You've lost the courier and the city is mysterious around you, a stranger that is complex with a life no one has ever quite realised. It has been for me as if, among the well-rehearsed violins that are following the carefully orchestrated score of official attitudes, I could catch a lonely and slightly demented fiddle playing its own strange tune and impossible to silence, a part of Scotland refusing to be other than itself.

If you like cities, go to Edinburgh. And may you hear the fiddle.

Being Poor

I BELIEVE ONE OF THE HIGHLY DEVELOPED NATIONAL skills the Scots have is the ability to deny the reality of their own circumstances. In my more fanciful moments, I wonder if it doesn't relate to a central psychic need to hide from the painful truth of their own history, from the fact that they sold their independence and did it – clichés of Scottish tight-fistedness notwithstanding – very cheaply. Whatever the causes, the results can have a certain grand absurdity when expressed in comparatively unimportant areas, like football. In areas of importance, the results can be damaging to the development of a realistic sense of how we live.

One such damaging result is for me the Nelsonian attitude of many Scots to the deprivation around them. Putting to their eye a telescope with a ben and loch painted on the lens, they say, 'I see no poverty'. They have for long been aided in their illusion by the poor themselves. Scots pride, that formidable quality, has always tended to rebound upon itself. For generations the poor of this country have equated poverty with shame and have consequently hallucinated adequacy in a desert of deprivation.

When the sick man refuses to moan, the healthy are grateful. But their gratitude is a balm applied to themselves. It allows them, first of all, not to share the other's pain and soon to imagine that it isn't there. In the 1930s Edwin Muir was amazed at how effectively well-off Glaswegians failed to notice the city's destitution. But that comfortable blindness was never a Glasgow monopoly. And it has in recent years developed thicker cataracts of complacency, thanks to repeated applications of the phrase 'The Welfare State'.

Ours is a caring society, people think vaguely. Steps are being taken. Provision has been made. Such bromide thoughts minister as effectively to the conditions of our society as an aspirin would to cancer. The truth is that the Welfare State has become less a panacea for the poor than valium for the rich, more concept than reality, more psychic palliative than physical cure.

Scotland is still a society of chronic injustice. In some ways its condition has worsened precisely because the more superficial manifestations of poverty have been cosmetically treated while its root effects remain. We do not see children barefoot in winter now. But the disease of poverty is still rife enough among us in its subtler forms. Its effects aren't always dramatic but they are always destructive. Numerous statistics testify to its presence. For example, it has been estimated that 800,000 Scots live below the government's own poverty guideline (that is, a family of four on less than £56 per week).

The statistics are there. Unfortunately, they're not all that's there. For being poor is never merely statistical. It is specific and individual and sore enough, even in its milder forms.

Take as an example a woman living in Livingston new town, to whom I was directed by a social worker as representing an ordinary kind of hardship. I'll call her Kathy, because it isn't her name. Her circumstances are hardly exceptional. Stated baldly, they have a dull familiarity to them in the present epidemic of dissolving families, as arresting as a hyphen in a graveyard.

She is 41. Six years ago her husband, who was 29 at that time, left her, ironically, for an older woman. Their daughter was seven at the time, their son six. There followed one of those periods of social disorientation that tend to be experienced by such an amputated half of a couple, when you're living by braille. The nerve-ends seem to be on the outside of the skin and the hurts home in. Paranoia hovers near and the insensitivity of others feels like a plot.

Her own incredulity at the behaviour of others had its justifications. She remembers a couple of them with special clarity. During her first Hogmanay alone, her estranged husband and the woman he was living with arrived at the door at 2 a.m. on New Year's Day to wish her a Happy New Year. At another time her father-in-law turned up with a tenner to help her out. Wrapped in the note she found a durex, which he had apparently thought was a tasteful way of suggesting what he had in mind.

After almost a year of emotional confusion she moved to Livingston with the children, having come to the admission that she had to work out her problems for herself. She's still trying to do that. Central to the difficulty of doing so is simply lack of money.

Her ex-husband pays her nothing. But every week she receives £46.12 supplementary allowance, £13.80 child benefit and she is allowed to make £12 per week from part-time work. It's hardly the stuff of which a tear-provoking Victorian print might be made. There are hundreds of thousands far worse off than she is. It's all the more significant then that her life shows a lot of the corrosive effects of being even mildly poor.

One of these is the sense of defeat, of being trapped in a self-perpetuating set of circumstances. Her part-time work earns her £21.13 a week. She is allowed to make £4 clear. Beyond that, up to £20, she is allowed to keep a half of her earnings. Above £20, anything she earns is taken back. In other words, no matter how much part-time work she does, she can't earn more than £12 from it in any given week.

35

That sense of helplessness is exacerbated by some of the attitudes of others and by a conscience about as tractable as a piece of heavy engineering. A friend has remarked to her, 'You're nothing but a sponger.' ('If that's what a friend thinks of me, what are other people thinking?') Feelings of amorphous guilt grow like a fungus in the secretiveness the dread of such reactions promotes, choking off her natural sociability. Her only apparent indulgence, smoking, is something she's not keen to let other people see her doing.

The guilt that waits in ambush in some of the simplest actions has promoted in her a hypersensitivity to the complex and largely incomprehensible rules she feels governing her life. She mentions the thought of the police coming to her door, for a reason she can't and doesn't want to imagine, and the moment is like a child trying to contemplate the bogeyman.

Even the obeying of the rules can lead to guilt. When the family was moving to Livingston, she consulted with the housing authority to make sure it would be all right to bring the family pet, a golden labrador called Tanya. She was informed dogs were forbidden in the type of housing she was moving into. Advised by the vet that the dog would pine in another house, she had it put down and told the children, who had an extravagant affection for it, that it had been taken by other people. Arriving at Livingston, she found that several neighbours living in the same type of housing kept dogs. 'I can still cry for it.'

Breaking the rules certainly leads to guilt. About three years ago, she started doing extra shifts at her part-time job as a kitchen-assistant. The additional money she was making became addictive. 'It's not as if I was spending the money on drink and bingo,' she says, watching for a reaction. 'It was to get things we needed.' But she knew the money was more than she was allowed to make and the guilt grew like compound interest.

At the end of the year, she could cope with it no longer. Having confessed, she was greatly relieved not to be prosecuted. Instead, she agreed to pay back £327.13 at the rate of £6 per week. It took her just more than a year. Talking about it now, she has no self-justifying analogies to make with other people's financial fiddles, just an immense thankfulness that it's over and a determination not to do it again.

That determination seems to imply her acceptance of being immured indefinitely in her present circumstances. She can see no significant alleviation of them in the foreseeable future. The children, at 13 and 12, are at that stage when the young grow like the Incredible Hulk in a bad mood, with a corresponding need for new clothes, unfortunately not supplied magically by the props department. She says she gets no clothing grant. It looks as if they'll be outgrowing their mother's purse for a long time yet. Paradoxically, her ambitions for them threaten to lengthen that time. She is determined that if anything thwarts her daughter's desire to be a teacher or her son's desire to be a civil engineer, it won't be their financial situation.

Such long-term ambition by proxy seems to be the only kind Kathy can afford to indulge. Talking of herself, she gives the impression she has a horizon of about six inches. She hopes to hold on to her part-time job. She hopes, by scrupulous managing of money, to be able to let the children go on such school trips as are on offer. Asked what her greatest ambition is for herself, she claims it is to have the house redecorated. 'To get it the way I want it.' She admits how badly the paint and the furniture need renewing, but she's too used to them for her embarrassment to be more than token.

She has had a long education in learning by daily rote the acceptance of diminished dreams. Her father died when she was 13 and she can remember her partially blind mother going to collect her 13/6d. a week to keep them both. She expresses no bitterness about her circumstances, as if even that were something the rules perhaps don't entitle her to.

She simply stays at home except for the few hours she works each day and one night a week when the local amateur dramatic society is preparing its pantomime. On those nights she and the children go along to help in the rehearsals and perhaps get a small part. It's an economical activity, involving only the bus fares and the price of coffees.

Kathy's case is unremarkable. It is at least partly the result of personal experiences no one could have legislated for, but its most definitive element remains insufficient money to live anything like a reasonably fulfilling life and no apparent possibility of getting more. She is one of very many trying to fight a rearguard action of personal decency against the economic odds in a society where the principles behind the distribution of the available wealth have developed, it should be acknowledged, beyond the logic of the fruit-machine and the morality of a Monopoly board, but not far enough beyond them.

She and others like her are able to maintain a superficial appearance of sufficiency and to do it successfully enough, in many cases, to convince not only others but themselves. They may live in different types of areas. They will have little sense of sharing a common condition with one another. They will assuredly have no sense of a common voice. They're rather like a reservist army of the poor, uniform only in a discreet malnutrition of the spirit, not yet mobilised into an open acknowledgment of their shared state. For many of them perhaps their greatest pride is that they have not yet had to make such open acknowledgment. In a truly caring society it would be made for them.

Disco Kids

I ARRIVED TOO LATE AT THE DISCO. BY THE TIME DISCOS had become the popular place for male and female to meet, I was already pushing remorselessly towards middle age. My formative years related to 'the dancin''.

The disco, then, has to be looked at carefully by someone of my generation if its assault on the senses is to be resolved into any coherent impression. It is necessary to go beyond the initial self-protective nostalgia for the big-band sound, empty half-bottles of whisky in the toilets and the patiently acquired mastery of the fishtail. You have to try and make sure you're not seeing things through an old fogey darkly.

Even the moments of apparent familiarity are liable to stop the voyeur of the youth culture in his geriatric tracks. They aren't *quite* familiar. They are like traditions whose features have distorted in ways that are unexpected, so that the traveller from an antique land may have to stare at them a long time before he recognises them at all. Is that really the same thing as we used to do? It is as if Rip Van Winkle were trying to trace the lineaments of the people he used to know in the people he sees before him.

Take the age-old tradition of arriving late on the dance floor. That still applies, but with a difference. It used to be only certain boys who turned up late, rather chauvinist and trying not to puke up the beer they had been practising drinking in the pub. Now everybody turns up late. A disco before 11 o'clock looks like a tax inspector's birthday party.

Also, the reason some boys used to turn up late was that they were trying to inhabit two colliding male clichés and they couldn't do it simultaneously. They had to learn to wow the women and they had to learn to hold their drink. Dance halls were unlicensed. But every disco has a bar, and some of them more than one.

What began by looking familiar starts to take on a strangeness. The contemporary reluctance to come to the dance floor has no necessary cause. Having no such cause, it begins to savour of mere effect. It looks suspiciously like sophistication and, if that's what it is, it's a very different animal from the late arrival of the '50s. Then coming late was usually the result of a clumsy mixture of playing at being a hard man and the need for Dutch courage. Those who practised that method were rarely noted for their suavity. They often seemed no better than even money to know their right foot from their left. I had a cousin who once arrived at the dancing in such a state of mental disarray that he asked a girl to dance to God Save the Queen. (And that's another thing. God Save the Queen?)

To see the disco for itself, let's acknowledge what isn't there and then replace it by what is. There is no band, not even a group. As the name of the place tells you, there are records. These are played by one of the strange new craftsmen of our times, a disc jockey. A disc jockey is, as you know, a masseur of the ears, since a lot of people in our society seem to believe that they may die of silence. Like all pop music, the quality of the records varies. One of the great, vulgar strengths of popular music is the voracity of its appetite, its ability to ingest almost anything, the mind-numbingly twee, the banal, the stunningly good. You may wonder at the roughness of its palate and the frightening capacity of that enormous maw. You may even wonder sometimes just where, in that vast corpus, the brain is located. But nobody should be patronising about pop music. It is a cultural giant. Beside it, modern poetry looks like a seven-stone weakling.

But I think it would be fair to say that nobody whose ears are not made out of tin would go to a disco to hear the best of modern popular music. The kind of music roughly classified as 'disco music' is almost invariably bad: monotonous and hypnotically dull. If pop music is a giant, I know which part of the giant's anatomy is represented by disco music.

The one quality disco music does unmistakably have is its quite amazing loudness. I have a theory about this, though perhaps we shouldn't give it too much weight, since I believe it was a thought not so much arrived at as spontaneously generated on the throbbing eardrums. You have the disc jockey holed up there in his glass box, with his earphones, like some kinky experiment on the effects of human isolation. You have a lot of attractive girls passing before him like a eunuch's dream. You have a lot of young men mingling with the girls as he cannot. He is only human. He *attacks* them with the music. That's disco music for me: the DJ's revenge.

Unlike the situation in the old dance halls, there is no stag line. And since there is no stag line, there is no row of seated girls, some shyly judging, from the directions the feet of the approaching males are taking, whether they will get 'lifted' or not. We should feel no nostalgic pangs about that. That contrived cultural gap between the males and the females damaged both groups and frequently left their natural instincts signalling incomprehensibly to one another across a grand canyon of social engineering.

The stag line was a mental locker room where it was at least as unhealthy for men to be locked in as it was for women to be locked out. Things could get pretty foetid in there, with jokes as sterile as a nude centre-fold and the reek of stale chauvinism, and some of the mildewed attitudes that were passed around as props to male vanity stank like a boxer's jock-strap.

The etiquette of the old dance hall put both sides under pressure. I've known boys adopt various elaborate attitudes of what would later be called 'cool' to hide the fact that they couldn't face the long trek across the dance floor towards possible refusal. Some stood around all night, looking rough and talking tough and picking fights. One I knew used to sit up in the balcony every Saturday night, reading the *Sporting Pink*. He would have been better going to the reading room of the local library (they had lots of papers there) except that it would have spoiled his image. But at least the boys had a choice of how they would cope with the problem of their awkwardness and embarrassment.

The girls had no such choice. They had to meet the problem frontally. Even this comparatively short time later, the memory of their situation evokes in me a much milder form of the kind of disbelief I felt when I read that Chinese women used to have their feet bound. They paid the same money as the boys for what might be the chance not to participate in the dancing. They bought a passive ticket, the boys an active one. Given the role they were assigned, they should have been allowed in free. They were, after all, there to be on view and perhaps be graced with a dance or two.

It is true, of course, that a lot of girls enjoyed the dancing, as did a lot of boys, myself included. But we had the energy of youth to adapt and, given healthier conditions, we might have enjoyed it more. Also, the means to enjoy it were unfairly distributed. A boy could use his looks, his nerve, his patter, his brashness, his sheer persistence to get himself involved in proceedings. A girl essentially only had her looks. If she couldn't pull just by being there, she couldn't pull. I've heard boys it would have taxed a mother's love to call good looking disdain an attractive girl because her breasts weren't big.

The disco has, at least on the surface, moved beyond that conditioned nonsense. Even physically, it doesn't allow it.

Some old dance halls were simply a big open space with the line drawn up on either side, like a battleground. Discos are usually much more physically differentiated. There is a bar, there are tables and seats all round, there is a small area for dancing. The size of the dance floor is significant. It is indicative of the fact that your night doesn't live or die by whether you dance. In any case, at a disco a girl is as likely to ask as be asked.

This means, in accordance with the domino effect by which traditions die, another cultural dinosaur has become extinct. Hands up (if your rheumatism permits it) those of us who can remember . . . the Ladies' Choice. What did you do during the Ladies' Choice, Daddy?

I manfully stood my ground, trying to look nonchalant, wondering if the fragile flower of my ego would be watered into bloom or crushed in the stampede to get to other males and sometimes, when my nerve cracked, I went and hid in the toilets. For that was when, perhaps two or three times a night, the roles were reversed.

The Ladies' Choice: why did we never notice what a strange archaic ring it has to it? It comes to me quaintly now, redolent of musty lace mittens and old ball gowns. The Ladies' Choice: chauvinism's phoney liberal clause in a contract that bound women over, hand and foot, to male vanity. The Ladies' Choice: the moment when the feminine libido was briefly let out to play. But it wasn't, of course, what it purported to be. It wasn't so much the ladies' choice as the gentlemen's stocktaking. For what was the inevitable effect of it?

The women had at most three times in the night when they could actively choose, place a bet on the outcome of the game. The men had the rest of the time. They could place bets right across the board. All the Ladies' Choice achieved was a clarification of the odds for the man. This one definitely fancied him, that one he couldn't be sure about. It didn't weaken the tyranny of the man's position, it strengthened it.

What place could such outmoded conventions have in a disco? Male and female go there ostensibly on an equal footing. To this extent at least: hail to the disco.

Nevertheless, I have to admit that the longer I contemplate the disco, the harder I find it to get rid of some bleak reflections. Not all loud music is necessarily joyous and what we may carelessly regard as meaningless sounds are seldom quite meaningless. Like the muzak which these days in pubs and hotel foyers seeps round us like nerve gas, most social noises mean something, even if that meaning is as negative as the hypnotist's 'Empty your mind'. What is the disco saying?

The music, perhaps, is a clue. The absence of the band takes on a significance more than merely economic. The music is all pre-processed. The humanity of error or improvisation has been abstracted. It has all the piquancy and individual flavour of fast foods. The point of the music is more easily understood when you watch people dance to it.

Disco dancing looks like a kind of solipsism, a lonely celebration of the self. You may have a partner but he or she will have a separate orbit. You revolve round each other like planets. The nature of it comes close to being a-social. It is understandable that the music for such an activity should be an almost monochrome rhythm, a means for the ego to disport and pleasure itself, a kind of musical vibrator.

A pattern begins to emerge to the experience of the disco: egocentric and not significantly social. Other elements seem to me to bear this out. There is a welcome variety to the clothes compared with the boringness of the old days at the dancing. But the clothes don't seem to belong to anywhere in particular. A disco can look like the Hollywood canteen with, milling around there, people who might be extras from a dozen unrelated films.

Further, the loudness of the music doesn't encourage the development of conversation as an art. You might as well be in a welding shop. If Oscar Wilde had spent all his life in discos, no one would ever have known how witty he was. And then there are the lights. The strobe lights at a disco are often used to create a flickering, unreal, robotic effect. It is as if you were inside a magic lantern.

It all begins to fit together. Conversation is minimal; the genre here isn't patter but style and stance and attitude. The clothes are costume. The lighting is dramatic. You dance to yourself, inside your own dream. The music is a plastic rhythm you bend to suit yourself.

Disco is virtually an accentless medium, like a silent film in which your own imagination writes the script. You needn't go there as yourself. You can become someone else when you go there. You may be on the dole or have a father who has been two years redundant or a sister hooked on heroin but at the disco who would know? You're just another stylist in your clothes that come from nowhere. And if there are others there who do know the banal, external realities of your life, well, tonight they're playing their own disco role. Let's all just move together. Don't rock the dreamboat.

And why shouldn't it be like that? The young should enjoy. But modes of pleasure sometimes strand us in them. The heroin addict no doubt enjoys the addiction to begin with. But that doesn't make it a pleasure to be recommended. I'm not suggesting that discos are in any way as pernicious as drugs can be, just that even our pleasures define us and we should try to understand what they may cost.

The proliferation of discos in the run-down West of Scotland seems to me rather ironic. Young people can walk down a street that is like an irrefutable argument for change and, just by stepping through a door, pretend that they are not where they are. At least in the old dance hall you took your condition with you like an identity card. Now even the decor could be anywhere.

You have entered the fantasy-parlour. The rough dialect of your living conditions has been translated into a stateless smooth-speak. Subjecting yourself to the experience too often could be like volunteering for a political lobotomy.

Maybe I'm wrong. I may have arrived too late to see clearly what's happening here. But I hope at least some of the disco kids will leave early, before they have postured too much of their energy away in the places that are nowhere, the dream-machines. They are needed at home.

Anatomy of a Flapper

–N. Flapper, one who or that which flaps: a flipper: young wild duck or partridge: (slang) a girl nearing womanhood: a flighty young maid.

(*Chambers Twentieth Century Dictionary*)

WHEN SOMETHING MEANT TO BE AS SOLEMNLY COMPRE-hensive as a dictionary omits the most significant contemporary meaning of a word, you have to wonder why. Are our cultural overlords trying to rob us lower orders of the effective expression of our own experience? For 'flapper' is a word common enough in working-class usage.

And when those two flat syllables surface in the smoke of a pub or on a bus or around a shopping precinct (for hangers-about the modern equivalent of the old street corner), it's a safe bet the boys are not discussing partridges. Flighty young women may be part of the discussion but they probably use another word for them. What they are talking about, as the Chambers Dictionary might have said, is: (*slang*) a dog-track not officially registered with the National Greyhound Racing Council, where the rules are interestingly flexible.

In the absence of official clarification I've been doing my own research. I don't offer my findings as definitive, merely as initial and haphazard fieldwork in an inadequately documented area of working-class experience. Perhaps more rigorous definers will follow up my work. If they do, I must warn them that the funds required for effective research can be considerable. A flapping track (formal usage) won't cost you much getting in but it can be very expensive to get out.

For flappers are all about gambling. If you're not going there to put money on, stay at home. At the White City, you may have come just to give the Rolls an airing or for the aesthetic pleasure of greyhounds running on heraldic green or to enjoy a good meal and a drink. At some flappers there may be a pretty basic bar, but mostly not. There will be the dogs and the bookies and the punters.

Just about every flapping track gives out its early warning signal that the facilities you are about to make use of will be as plush as a bus-shelter. The approach road is almost sure to be pot-holed enough to suggest that it was laid before the tarmacadam process was fully developed. In a symbolic kind of way, this isn't entirely a wrong impression. The first thing to know about flappers is that they live in a time-lock. In flappers the Second World War didn't happen and we're still waiting to get to the moon.

To have the full effect, you must go in winter. You will be cold, of course, but so you should be. You aren't here for idle pleasure. This is serious business. The god of chance of the flapping track is a Calvinist god.

Consider his shrine. Most often it is a corrugated stand with a dais at the back where the bookies stand and chalk up their prices, numbers as mysterious in their origins as the Dead Sea Scrolls. As the time of the race comes nearer, prices are rubbed off and changed with bewildering speed. What was evens moves to two-to-one. Three-to-one plummets to six-to-four. The tick-tack man, signalling the changes in the odds, becomes a kind of manual dervish.

Meanwhile, the innocent inspirers of this activity are being paraded under the lights. Owners or relatives of the owners walk the greyhounds up and down the central grass of the stadium, inside the railing of the track. This is an informality not allowed at official tracks. There the walkers of the dogs are employed by the management.

Between the bookies and the greyhounds mill the punters, motley humanity caught between destiny and a muddied and perhaps illusory free choice. As with every religious event, the congregation are the most interesting part of it, given the tics and quirks with which their awareness of their own fallibility tries to take on the remorseless mysteries of fate. No wonder punters at a flapping track are a shifty lot, always on the move, eavesdropping on conversations, watching the bookies' boards, watching other punters. Time is passing and they must soon reach a decision which can never be changed. The number of such decisions they can make is strictly limited. The hip-pocket, that frequently one-way hourglass, may be running out.

The various ways of making your decision have their committed adherents, like separate schisms. You can study the dogs as they parade, trying to peer soothsayer-fashion into their entrails as if the future were expressed there. You can move around, sifting information from the other punters, who usually know much less than they say. You can watch the changing prices on the bookies' boards, wondering what inside knowledge they signify. You can crowd in behind someone who is obviously rushing for what he considers a good price and bet the same dog as he does before the price changes. You can pick a dog with a nice name. You can even, like an ecumenical movement of one, try to combine all these tenets into one act of faith.

Then the dogs run. They do not run for long. A dog race isn't an epic, it's a lyric, a short, sharp experience that often breaks the heart. It can happen that by the time the dog comes out of the traps you feel an immediate chill wind at the hip, seeing your favoured dog emerge as if it were still on a leash with a geriatric at the other end of it.

The process will be repeated maybe 12 times a night. As the losing tickets cover the ground in patches of white, like a sudden frost, the casual visitor may wonder why flapping tracks have kept their precarious place in working-class life. The single-sheet programme you are given in return for your admission money may afford some clues.

Some dogs' names suggest a determined attempt at sympathetic magic, a kind of 'Adam naming the beasts' moment. As ye call them, so shall they be. So you get Killer and Giant and Diesel Dan. Some suggest an almost primitive belief in first responses, as in those legends where the first person the hero or heroine meets will hold the key to their destiny. So you get She's Tiny, a name that evokes for me a hut somewhere late at night and a family summoned forth to witness the miracle of canine birth.

But perhaps that image only comes to me so forcefully because it belongs to my own boyhood, to the night when my father delivered the bitch of three strong pups by the light of a candle he'd found somewhere. It was a holy candle. Greyhound owners need all the help they can get. Prolonged and involved discussion took place among us, too, about what we should call them. As the youngest member of the family, I found my function essentially negative. I appeared to come up with a lot of ideal suggestions for what not to call a greyhound. I became an instant wastebasket of useless ideas. But I could appreciate the astonishing inventiveness of my elders. My favourite was what they called the big, black dog – Voodoo, subsequently renamed Blue Do by an old woman who had put money on it.

Browsing through any programme for a flapping track, that strange, fragmentary mythology of working-class life, you find one recurring factor among the variety. Whether the names are evocative magic or commemorative of anything from relatives to favourite songs, they frequently hint at one of the surviving traits of working-class life in a world of eroding traditions. The trait is most clearly recognisable in the number of times the dog's name makes it a part of the family: Homebred and Papa's Boy and Anne's Boy and Lynne's Pet and Sharon's Pet. It is the continuing tendency of working-class people never to quite separate purpose from sentiment. The dog is hopefully a means of making money but it is also often a focus of affection. To realise that, you only have to watch an owner come to the water-tray after a race and carefully bathe the abraded feet of a dog that has just run as it if weren't sure which way is forward.

That attitude seems to me central to the continuing existence of flapping tracks, the heart of their social anatomy. People go there to try and make a few quid. Whatever happens, they're never going to make an awful lot. Flapping millionaires are so far an undiscovered species. It's a weekly scuffle with the bleakness of the economy. Win or lose, it's a challenge, a pitting of the wits against imponderable factors and, anyway, they like the dogs.

A flapper is not a place where dreams of militancy will thrive. A social reformer might find it an exercise in despair to go and watch these people peering at the bookies' boards as if they were *Das Kapital*, listening furtively for inside information, dissecting parading dogs with their eyes and scrambling for the best price they can get, while the tick-tack man develops galloping St Vitus and the lights make an isolated dome of brightness in the dark and breath-clouds rise like incense and the dogs run in constant circles. Political progress is probably not what it most resembles.

But it expresses a real and abiding truth of working-class life, whether the theorists like it or not. It's like a found metaphor of the working class's sense of its own experience. That sense frequently fails to coincide with the political theorists' ideas of what it should be, for the truth is that most theorists of working-class life have been middle class in origin. Traditional working-class intelligence has never accepted the separation of mind and feeling. It has always tended to conform to Lazare Bickel's definition of intelligence: 'Intelligence is our faculty for not developing what we think to the very end so that we can still believe in reality.'

The working class's interpretation of its own experience emerges, I think, from that kind of intelligence, combining thought with feeling and instinct with analysis. No doubt, the kind of people who attend flapping tracks would fit Karl Marx's *lumpenproletariat*. But then I've always felt that there is no such thing as the *lumpenproletariat*, not as an absolute grouping within working-class life. I think there may be such a thing as 'lumpenproletariat-ism', an intermittent condition to which anybody in working-class life may be subject from time to time.

This must be a frustrating condition for the social reformer to be faced with, since it implies at least a distrust of political theory and, in its severest forms, a total rejection of it. But it would be an error to assume that it is a condition devoid of any rational or historical basis. It has strong roots in the realities of working-class experience. We live always in fact but governments frequently try to make us inhabit theory. It is logical that we shouldn't wish our present to be cannibalised by the past (as it was with feudalism) or by the future (as is threatened by dialectical materialism).

Alexander Herzen, the great 19th-century Russian, has made the point that there is a kind of obscenity in asking people to sacrifice such present as they have to an unknown, theoretical future. Working-class life has usually shown a reluctance to do that. It has preferred a distrust of theory, a daily pragmatism.

Flappers thrive on that pragmatism, although the roughness of the excitement they afford does make you wonder how long these small fortresses of the 1930s can hold out against the siege of modernity. Perhaps before 'flapper' has found its rightful place in all dictionaries, it will already be out of date, about as contemporarily relevant as 'Fletcher' – a maker of arrows. But even if that happens, I suspect that the quality of working-class life it represents will have found another mode of expression.

The punters will have moved elsewhere. But they will still be punters. I have heard more than one purist of language sniffily lament the adoption of the word 'punter' from racing into everyday speech to signify 'an ordinary person', as being a flabby use of words. They are wrong. It is a very precise piece of terminology. A punter is someone who tries to survive the fluctuations of chance and circumstances and finance without significant ownership of the wealth of society or reliable information as to how it is being deployed. It remains, as it always has been, a hard and uncertain business being a punter, as any flapping track will demonstrate.

Greenlea

LET'S CALL IT GREENLEA. THAT IS THE KIND OF NAME SUCH places are often given, words suggestive of tranquillity and comfort and rest. Those names are perhaps another expression of the impulse that makes our society call a lethal weapon an 'anti-personnel device', an all-out nuclear attack an 'unlimited response' and the annihilation of a workforce 'rationalisation'. Euphemism is one of the few expanding industries in Britain today.

Greenlea sits among trees in its own grounds. It is a big house built early in the century, an affirmation of social certainties that have long since eroded. The last private owner has moved on, presumably to investments new. Ironically enough, many of its present residents are probably much of an age with the building and they haunt it now like the ghosts of the inequality that built it. For Greenlea has become a home for the old.

Discretion is in the nature of such places. You will not know what small, sad incontinences take place, what mundane dramas are enacted during the night. A home for the old functions in part as a kind of social colostomy, drawing off, like emotional waste, the awkwardness of having to deal with the aged and letting us get on with our lives. All you will know is what you see when you visit and then you will be seeing only the best of it, reality with its nicest clothes on.

The large lounge where the visiting takes place gets a lot of sun. There is a big colour television set. The furnishings are good, mainly a scattering of floral armchairs and neat, oblong tables with magazines on them. Hardly anyone seems to read the magazines, though. Just occasionally you may see someone leaf absently through one, not reading so much as remembering the habit of reading, a formerly complex activity eroded to its tactile residue.

This indifference to the magazines isn't surprising. They are full of stunning places never to be reached, expensive objects never to be acquired, beautiful people of galactic remoteness and stories of lives whose intense problems, if they could be shared, would come as a relief. They are like free passes to everywhere in the world washed up on a desert island.

Also, although the funiture looks to the casual eyes of an outsider fine and suggestive of caring, closer familiarity shows small things more disturbing.

You notice a burn on a carpet, perhaps where the ash from a pipe has fallen. The welt of braid on the arm of a chair dangles, fretted by nervous, distracted fingers. A tea-stain mars a cushion. This is no more than the petty vandalism of forgetfulness but it can make you feel that the room perhaps doesn't mean for its residents what it means to their visitors, that its niceness has a purpose more related to those outside than in, like the carvings on a mausoleum.

A quality of abstractedness haunts the times of visiting. The residents are waiting. They are always waiting. But the sense you may have is that they are not waiting for people. They sit like a strange group sculpture, though to regular visitors familiarly placed.

There is the old woman with the walking-frame. Her hair is sparse yet tangled and her face time has buffed to the one placative expression, proferred constantly around the room, an alms-cup begging for attention. No one ever seems to visit her, although sometimes people visiting others will take a few minutes to talk to her. The moment after they leave can be a sore one. She will glance around the room, having briefly found a fierce complacency, hoarding what has happened to her from everyone else. That is a touching smugness.

There is the man who cries when his family visit him. Mostly it is a woman who comes. She looks like his daughter. She seems harassed, perhaps because she is having to fit him into a busy day, perhaps because she wants to convince herself that the day *is* very busy so that she won't notice this part of it so much, perhaps just because she knows he will cry.

Sometimes a man is with her and sometimes children, two teenagers and one very small, a girl of three or four. But the husband, if that's who he is, is always uncomfortable. He clears his throat a great deal and whistles aimlessly and smokes. He doesn't come much. The two teenage boys look out the windows and make faces at each other. Only the small girl seems at ease. She is curious about what is happening to the old man, talks at him and plays with his fingers as innocently as if he were a toy. But that makes him cry even more. There are others. Each is different, of course, but the shared condition imposes something like a common identity – the gnarled hands, the bodies that seem to have become no more than roosts for various illnesses, the way that breathing is often a conscious act and the haunting eyes, like sentient marble, last prolonged glimmerings of bewilderment that is hardening into death.

When you notice that someone is no longer there, there is always another to fill the place, different but not much more so than one sentry is from another.

Some visitors tend to arrive late and have to leave early. They exchange a lot of understanding glances with one another. They quickly adopt a special way of speech that is common to almost all of them. Its essential tone is one of heavy banter and exaggerated patience. The staff are expert in it, that slightly oblique way of talking as if the other person weren't quite present. In talking to them, you are communicating with yourself or perhaps with what you hope is other people's idea of you.

On the face of it, the residents remain almost undisturbed. The pre-occupation is, perhaps, with their own dying, but not in any transcendental sense. Far from any mystical implications, the impression they give is of dull pupils being taught something they will never understand. Dying, is, after all, as banal as the two-times table. Negotiating doorways, trying to walk, forgetting names, trying to hold a teacup, they are learning their dying by rote.

That's how it is in Greenlea and places like it. The depression that comes with us when we leave isn't difficult to understand. We have visited a hard and universal truth. We have seen ourselves as we may be, if we're lucky enough to live so long. But for me that general depression is always shadowed by a more particular one. That secondary bleakness isn't so easy to explain.

It's not that I have found anything to criticise seriously in the places themselves. I have no experience of maltreatment, no startling revelations of abuse of authority. All the Greenleas I have visited have impressed me, more or less. It's true I have occasionally found myself gritting my teeth at the way some members of staff talk with a kind of bullying condescension to the old, as if bodily decrepitude were some odd, private whim, or wear a constant smile the way a welder wears a mask. But casual visitors have no right to pass judgment on the mannerisms those who work in daily proximity with the old have had to acquire in order to cope. So it isn't that.

And when I consider what provision was made for the old in the past, our present institutions seem a huge improvement. The workhouse they are not. They are usually well-appointed and comfortable and they are humanely managed, as far as I can assess. Such places are necessary. There are old people who cannot look after themselves and who, if left on their own, would live miserably or die quickly. We can only be thankful that places like Greenlea exist, for they are needed.

But it's about here that my additional depression is located, I think. I wonder if the necessity of places like Greenlea isn't sometimes abused, if some of us with aged and troublesome relatives don't take advantage of their existence before there is any final justification for doing so. 'It's got to be impossible,' people say. But impossibility is usually a comparative term. 'The children were suffering.' Children commonly do and those who make a fetish of over-protection of children are usually protecting themselves, from the realities of where we live. 'They're happier there.' Anyone who is happier in an old people's home, no matter how well or kindly it is run, must have been having a very bad time outside.

Our old belong to us personally, as we belong to them. To depersonalise that essential relationship before it is absolutely necessary, while we still have a habitable area of option left, is to amputate a crucial part of ourselves. One of the sicknesses in our society is the preparedness to hand over too hastily to 'specialists' aspects of our lives that are crucially our own. Soon someone may set up a Ministry of Love. Love and caring are not things that can be very effectively institutionalised, although where it is necessary the attempt has to be made.

Where that necessity exists, let's be thankful for the progress that has been achieved and let's work to take that progress further. The 'Bield' housing project, for example, where old people live in a small community and retain a significant degree of independence within it, seems a real advance.

But whatever advances may be made, I think people should search themselves very carefully before deciding that an old mother or father or a mildly batty aunt or uncle must go into a home. Such places are, in my experience, orderly and clean and quiet and profoundly depressing. We should be very sure that we are not using them as euphemisms for our lack of humanity. We should try very hard to avoid the possibility that any old person who is in there is a casualty not so much of necessity as of gentility, the not uncommon desire to deodorise experience.

Journeys of the Magi

Glasgow–London

ENGLISHMEN AND THE SIMPLE-MINDED BELIEVE THAT Wembley Stadium is approached by a broad, straight avenue called Wembley Way. Scottish football supporters know different. From years of experience, they know that the Scottish route to Wembley is about as direct as the Hampton Court maze. The most difficult thing about any Wembley international has always been just getting there.

The scene is the compartment of a Wembley Football Special from Glasgow. Slumped in one of the window-seats is a man in his 30s. He is ruminatively drunk. Every so often his eyes rake the other passengers. But there's no cause for alarm. He's merely flexing his malice for London.

His mate comes in and sits beside him.

'Aye then.'

'Aye.'

'Whaur i' the rest' o' the boays then?' the man at the window asks.

'Faurer up the train. They've flaked oot like. The beer's a' by. It couldny last forever, eh? Only twa dizzen cans.'

'Aye. Right enough.'

The man at the window wipes the misted pane with his hand, peers out.

'Whaur's this we're gawn through onywey?' he asks.

'Crossmyloof.'

It is the following day, as the saying is, aboard another special train going from Euston to Wembley. The coach is incredibly crowded. People are folded against one another. It seems it will only take somebody to cough to create the first recorded case of communal rupture. But suddenly, miraculously, a man who has been sitting down shoots to his feet, his arms fully extended, and bellows, 'Sc-o-o-o-t-l-a-a-a-n-d!' His voice describes an enormous vocal loop, fading reluctantly like a skyrocket. He collapses back into his seat, his head rolling in terrible ecstasy, a mystical transport.

A tall Englishman hanging from a strap gives the impression that he's trying to climb up it. His laughter is a tentative question.

'Whit a fuck i' you laughin' et?' the mystic asks.

The Englishman is not laughing. His is the definitive non-laugher's expression. He is, in fact, involved in a thorough investigation of an unusual stain on the ceiling of the coach, a stain he apparently hadn't noticed before. That stain is becoming something of a passion with him.

The mystic repeats his performance several times, leaving a litter of injured eardrums in his wake. Then suddenly he goes calm. His eyes cloud with vision.

'Penicillin!' he screams.

It isn't, it transpires, an appeal for medical attention. For he goes on.

'Taur MacAdam! Steam Engines! The Big Ships! We've did the lot! The greatest wee nation ever Goad put braith in. Sc-o-o-o-t-l-a-a-a-n-d!'

He subsides again, begins to mutter. The moment is past. After the mystic's ecstasy, the chafed knees, the petty aches, all the seedy little mundanities of everyday life.

'Somebody's fartit,' the ex-mystic snarls. 'That wis an English fart!'

It is his final sally. Instantly, spectacularly, he passes out. *Sic gloria transit.*

At the station his body is claimed by friends. They carry him up the Wembley Way like someone who has died before the citadel is stormed but who has earned the honour of getting there nevertheless. In the car park they cajole and slap and harangue him but he's beyond their help. They leave him behind a car and sell his ticket.

Meanwhile back at the park, the sun shines on a patch of heraldic green across which players move in complex armorial ciphers, expressing nationhood, whatever that is. Denis Law has discovered again that enthusiasm against which he hones his amazing reflexes. He is playing with a verve that suggests jackets for goalposts. Jim Baxter doesn't just beat opponents, he demeans them. There are some people with white shirts there as well. Playing nearly all of the game with ten men, the Scots massacre the English 2–1.

Later that same evening: the scene is London – all of it, it seems. Nearly every tube disgorges its statutory quota of wild faces and raucous Scots voices. Nearly every taxi at nearly every corner nearly runs down a Scotsman. London is a swirl of tartan scarves, a bob of tammies.

At a corner in Fleet Street a big man has a smaller man by the arm. 'Naw,' he is saying. 'Luk, son. Ye huvny really a bad team. Wan or two o' yese can play a bit. Yese jist huvny that extra somethin' we seem tae ha'e.' He is smiling in a kindly way.

In Blackfriars Underground Station a man at the head of a phalanx of nudging, grinning friends is stopping a well-dressed native to say, 'Excuse me, sur. But could ye direct us tae Soho?'

In Soho itself half-a-dozen betartaned figures volley out of a narrow doorway. The small card beside the doorway reads: 'Jane. Model. 3rd Floor.' 'Come oan, boays,' one of the men is gasping. 'Rin fur it!' Crippled with laughter, they make their escape as a fat woman appears in the doorway, hurling insults after them. The night absorbs the incident without explanation. Ah, sweet mystery of life.

On the train back up, a man leaning out of an open carriage-door is rescued by his mates as the train thunders towards Carlisle. Presumably, he had felt the rest of his life would be an anti-climax.

That was my first trip to Wembley. Ever since then, every second year except when I was living abroad, I've gone back – from what muddied motives I'm never sure. Maybe it's just that I think belonging to a country means acquainting yourself with all its manifestations. Certainly it is for me, and perhaps for most Scots who undertake it, a very private journey.

In my mind's ear I hear the girl who lives in the Tannoy-system saying: 'The train standing at Platform One is the Wembley Football Special. This train has an Inferiority Complex Car where light traumas will be served throughout the journey. This train goes by way of Paranoia, calling at Little Dependency, National Neurosis and Ultima Thule.'

Ambivalent, confused, struggling with my vast, invisible luggage, I'll be there.

Scotland–Argentina, 1978

Travelling overland to support the Scottish football team in Argentina is a bit like going to Wembley via Outer Mongolia. You miss having the point of your journey confirmed by tartan scarves fluttering from the windows of every second car. Instead, your passing is an odd inconsequence in landscapes where people can't quite locate you on their mental map. They say, 'Scotland? That is in England?' and 'You speak English quite well.' You wonder if you can arrive with your passion for the game intact.

Everywhere we have passed through seems a long way from the Horseshoe Bar in Glasgow, an old-fashioned pub off Renfield Street, where our group met to finalise plans. There are six of us: Gerry McDermott, a 25-year-old bus driver from Castlemilk in Glasgow; Charlie Gibbons, a 20-year-old labourer from Castlemilk; Alister Steele, a 21-year-old barman from Glasgow; Alasdair Buchan, a Scottish journalist living in London; myself, and Peter Stone, a professional photographer from Wraysbury, who must sometimes feel as outnumbered as an Englishman at Wembley.

The plans sounded simple in the comfort of the Horseshoe. We would all meet up in London on April 14 and take the Laker Skytrain to New York. From there we would go by bus and train through the States, Central America and South America to Córdoba in Argentina, where Scotland are scheduled to play their first matches in the World Cup in early June. Only once would we take a short flight, from San José in Costa Rica to Bogota, the Colombian capital, avoiding the problems of the Darien Gap in Panama.

That meeting in the Horseshoe was like the first scene of an old film plot, the one where the disparate group of people come together to fulfil a common purpose. We weren't planning to rob a bank or find the treasure of the Sierra Madre but we did follow the script to the extent that Charlie Gibbons and I managed to have the statutory quarrel.

Peace was restored but a nice amount of tension had been created. Apart from one travelling-bag, some of us started out, I think, with some cumbersome preconceptions. This was Superwembley, to be approached with a kind of fierce insouciance. It's a quality which is characterised for me by a fan I met on a Glasgow bus after one trip to an international match in London. When I asked where he had stayed on the Friday night, he said, 'Oh, we didn't *stay* anywhere. We just sat about fountains an' that.'

We arrived in New York roughly in that frame of mind. I managed to make this seem just a normal trip by losing my wallet in the taxi coming in from Kennedy Airport. Luckily, I never keep money in it. We checked in at the YMCA on West Thirty-Fourth Street and Charlie Gibbons said, 'Come on. We'll go out and see who's first to get mugged.'

We fell on the neighbourhood like locusts, seeking instant New York. We moved through a succession of bars where everybody's accent seemed to have been flown in that day from Ireland. The names of them should have given us a clue to what we would find – 'O'Reilly's', 'Killarney Rock'. We spoke to a spectacularly drunk Irishman who was trying to decide who was the best foot-baller ever and who was changing his mind every other minute with the arbitrariness of God. But one he favoured strongly was someone called Beckenbounder.

Suddenly, most of us were pleading jet-lag. It was one o'clock in the morning and complicated calculations took place about what was the real time and how long we had been out of bed. The rest retired but Charlie Gibbons and I are congenital sufferers from the Scottish fans' compulsion to hang onto every occasion in the hope of witnessing its miraculous transformation into an event.

We ended up in another bar in Jackson Heights. It was about four o'clock in the morning. 'Jet-lag,' Charlie Gibbons said. 'We gave it a walloping all right,' and went quietly to sleep.

Still, we had our revelation. On the elevated railway back into the city, a clean-shaven man with a cigarette behind each ear declared himself to Charlie. 'Not many people know,' he said discreetly, 'that I am Jesus. But I have touched you and now you will be in heaven with me.' Charlie Gibbons thanked him.

But that first sortie into New York came to be felt as an attempt to meet a new situation with an old tradition, rather like the Polish cavalry attacking tanks. Unlike London, the streets of New York offer the marauding Scotsman no facile sense of national identity through contrast. In New York contrasts are infinite. They tend to dissipate a sense of identity rather than precipitate one.

The sense of alienation we felt was paradoxically increased by going to a football match on the Sunday. New York Cosmos (complete with Beckenbounder) were playing Tulsa Roughnecks. The Giants' Stadium in New Jersey has superb facilities which reminded us that Hampden Park resembles nothing so much as a public lavatory for over 100,000 people.

But at the centre of the hot-dog counters and the excellent seating there is astroturf, the synthetic surface of which makes deep tackling a thing of the past. The way that manufactured grass rejects instead of complementing the impact of the players precludes ultimate athleticism and with it, to some extent, the passion of the spectators.

The organisers have tried to cope with this. They have, of course, the cheer-leaders, 12 ladies in skimpy costumes doing mysterious semaphoric things, using what appear to be powder-puffs with elephantiasis. Their skin glows like fairy-lights. As someone remarked, 'Imagine that in Glasgow. There would be a break-in in five minutes. They'd have to renew the women every week.'

There is also a television screen that tells you how you should react. 'Ouch,' it says for a foul. 'That was a no-no.' 'Did you see that?' it says. 'Good grief.' But I think my favourite thing it says is 'Charge' to the sound of the bugle I used to hear as a boy when the cavalry were coming.

There is, of course, a case for informing the crowd about a sport which is new to them. But that hardly justifies giving their reactions a lobotomy. The television screen even does a rhythmic handclapping sequence to which the crowd responds with 'Cosmos' like an internment camp of brainwashed detainees. I kept waiting for the screen to flash 'Keep breathing'.

Sitting among the computerised crowd, the six of us made up a desert island of our own. Someone muttered, 'Trades Description Act.' Without warning, Gerry McDermott shouted in a voice that rose into the bland sky like a flare, 'Come away, Tulsa!' But they didn't. Cosmos scored a few minutes from time from a Beckenbauer free-kick that bobbled mysteriously through the defensive wall. It looked as if Tulsa had been doing set-piece practice on how to let in goals. Even soccer was a different game here.

What New York taught us, the rest of America confirmed: our journey to Argentina lay through almost complete irrelevance to others. It was going to be a long way through which to carry our commitment without refuelling from outside sources.

The strain this put on our group was heightened by the next leg of the journey, by Greyhound bus to New Orleans for 33 hours solid. During most of that time, it seems to me, the big blond man opposite explained carefully to his black girlfriend, speaking in a gruff southern drawl, how he 'beat the shit out of' an impressive assortment of people – including, if I heard him right, his father.

The only other incident I recall from that sequence of weird dreams, shifting pains and stiff-legged walks to Coca-Cola machines happened at a lunch-counter. A Negro who was tall enough to be on stilts complained to the man at the cash-register that he had put a quarter in a vending machine without result. He wanted his money back. The man, white, fat and perspiring, explained very politely that the machine wasn't his responsibility. He called the Negro 'sir'. 'Sir' wasn't mollified. He said, 'There are guys around would blow your head off for 25 cents. And maybe I'm one of them.'

Neither of these casually gathered conversations was calculated to make us feel more at home. As if looking instinctively for an antidote, we went to play a game of football in New Orleans, having bought a ball like a talisman. As a salve to our fraying nerves, the game was as effective as a salt bandage. Charlie Gibbons and Alister Steele fell out over a tackle in which Charlie seemed to be standing in for a scythe. Our communal purposefulness degenerated into aimless bickering. Charlie disagreed with everybody.

Once when he vanished from the group, I found him in a fire-station, sitting in the cabin of a huge fire-engine, morosely studying the controls, with a rough-looking middle-aged man shouting at him, 'Hey, Mac, what the hell you doing?'

I think I know what Charlie was doing. He was looking for a Wembley substitute, an anecdote in embryo that would convince him he really was a Scottish fan en route to a game. 'I was going to ask them if I could go out to a fire with them,' he said. And, 'I still don't believe I'm going to Argentina.'

That sense of disbelief was affecting all of us. It found us after the next stage of our trip sitting in a bar in Laredo, a matter of minutes from the Mexican border and passing a Spanish dictionary among us. We were plucking at desultory phrases, rather as if David were to begin hunting for stones in the shadow of Goliath. We found a few. '*Lo siento mucho* – I am very sorry' was suggested for Charlie. With a face that butts like the prow of a ship into every problem and with his red hair, he sometimes comes into places in the manner of a longship bent on pillage. It was felt that in the land of machismo he might need to know how to apologise.

Central America was an endless Tica bus-run with lay-bys. Mexico City was the first. It is a stunningly grand centre with a scatter of abysmal squalor round its hems, like a mother who keeps herself in style at the expense of her children. Alasdair Buchan was handling the language well but we were finding other problems.

Food was one. The first thing we ate in Mexico was enchilada in a cheap café. A glance round the table suggested a convention of aloes-tasters, except for Gerry McDermott. 'Magic,' Gerry announced. The word was prophetic. Gerry was to eat everything from tacos filled with what appeared to be Kennomeat to unidentified dead objects. All were 'magic'. Gerry's philosophical adaptability extends to more than food. Cast away on a desert island, he would probably take delight in the absence of noisy neighbours. He went sightseeing in Mexico City dressed only in shorts made from cut-off jeans, a denim waistcoat and training-shoes. He attracted more attention than a historic building. The citizens seemed to find his whiteness as weird as ectoplasm. Gerry accepted their curiosity like visiting royalty, acknowledging the wolf-whistles casually.

His *sangfroid* was helpful coming into Guatemala. Our bus underwent four separate border checks. Twice soldiers came on dressed as arsenals. On the fourth occasion a young soldier with a face as flexible as a no entry sign was ripping open plastic bags belonging to a dismayed woman. A young man was being taken off the bus. But Gerry had noticed a fruit-seller at the side of the road near to the window at which Charlie Gibbons was sitting. It was somehow comforting amidst all the Guatemalan tensions to hear Gerry's archetypally Glaswegian voice calling, 'Charlie, Charlie. Gonny get us a pineapple?'

After the troubles at the border, Guatemala City seemed a friendly place, although Alasdair Buchan, Peter Stone and Alister Steele, who were sharing a room in the hotel, claimed that their luggage had been gone through while they were out. They suspected the police.

The rest of us were sceptical, mainly because our own luggage was boringly intact. It was a matter of pride. We liked to think that as aliens we were as undesirable as the next person.

There was no time to brood on it. El Salvador was next on an itinerary that was beginning to feel like a holiday booked through Kafka Tours – the more you travelled the less likely it seemed that you would ever arrive.

In any case, El Salvador is hardly a place where many people would want to arrive. Coming in on the bus towards the capital, San Salvador, we noticed the signs of Americanisation that run through Central America like an acne. In some places the name-signs of towns all have Pepsi in huge letters and the place-names in smaller lettering. It is as if everywhere is just a subsidiary of Pepsi.

San Salvador depressed us totally. We played cards in a café while it rained. We went for a walk and came into a square. Along one side of the square, under a colonnade, families were sleeping on the pavement. Charlie Gibbons said he felt as if he was walking through people's living-rooms. We were glad to leave, partly, I suspect, because we felt our presence there as frivolous.

Honduras was just a place we passed through in the bus. But it gave us one good experience. Waiting at the border, we took the ball out for a game and were joined by Hondurans of various ages and sizes. It was an Esperanto moment. Unable to talk to one another, we stood in a ring and communicated with the ball, showing such tricks as we had before we passed it on, like a competitive dance. One man said, 'Bravo.' Another said, '*Si señor*,' as if answering a question.

That day the bus took us through three countries, El Salvador, Honduras and Nicaragua as far as its capital. It was like getting the cultural bends. We knew the place we disembarked at was called Managua. Beyond that, all was numb. The strongest sense of identity we had was our luggage.

Next day that feeling of having no centre was eerily matched by the city we found ourselves in, as if our arrival had put it there. Managua is still recovering from the earthquake of 1973. Clumps of buildings are separated by large patches of overgrown desolation. It is a city which seems to defy you to walk anywhere purposefully or to find anything to do, except perhaps to sit in one of the makeshift cantinas.

Gerry and Charlie, the inexhaustible improvisers, found a partial solution. They organised lizard-hunts and rat-hunts among the ruins. They claim to have acquired their hunting skills 'up the Rezzy'. In the sapping humidity of early afternoon they brought Carmunnock Reservoir to Nicaragua.

A couple of elderly Managuans watched from the shade with perturbed curiosity as Gerry and Charlie ran around like headless chickens, shouting urgent advice to each other and trying to catch a lizard in a tee-shirt. Their lack of success could perhaps be attributed to tiredness. We all needed Costa Rica, the halfway stage where we had decided we would try to recuperate from our travel-shock on a beach.

We chose a place called Manuel Antonio. To get there, we were told to take a bus from San José to Quepos. We weren't told we would have to take it by storm. At the terminal we joined what we thought was a queue. It turned out to be an ambush. As soon as the bus backed in, the queue became a riot. People were clinging to the bus while it was still moving. The driver ignored them. A man was knocked down. Everybody ignored him. When the door of the bus was suitably thick with heaving bodies, a horn sounded teasingly 20 yards behind us. It was another bus for Quepos. We went for it. Only Alister Steele managed to get in the door. The rest of us threw our luggage in a window and climbed in after it.

Manuel Antonio was worth the hassle. It has several beautiful beaches set in a National Park. Having duly acquired our sunburn, we organised football matches on the beach involving several Swiss, an American, a Norwegian and a waiter called Jorge. Charlie and Gerry graduated to iguanas, with the same success rate as for lizards. Gerry wasn't worried about the questionable legality of hunting iguanas in a National Park. He has already successfully defended himself in a Glasgow court on a charge of shooting grouse out of season. Charlie still smiles when he remembers appearing as a witness and having to face Gerry, thumbs hooked in the lapels of his bus-driver's uniform, saying, 'Now, Mr Gibbons, tell the court in your own words . . .'

From Manuel Antonio we returned to San José to catch our flight to Bogotá. We were over the exhaustion but the sense of being an eccentric and embattled minority about to enter a vast continent still frayed our commitment a little.

Only Alister Steele, the quietest and most single-minded of the group, was still thinking of Argentina. But Gerry and Charlie admitted to me that for them the trip had become the thing and that it wouldn't matter too much if they didn't see the World Cup. From what we had heard of Bogotá, that seemed a possibility.

In the plane from San José, we were preparing ourselves. All through Central America we had heard travellers' tales about the Colombian capital that made New York sound like Toytown. But Gerry didn't seem too bothered. Sitting 20,000 feet above South America, he leaned forward and prodded Charlie, who had never flown before this trip.

'Charlie,' he said, nodding at the steward. 'Gonny ask that man to open a windae?'

Gerry's nonchalance was a nice antidote to the paranoia the journey was tending to develop. You begin to feel in your pocket constantly for the shape of your passport, you watch manically out of bus windows as luggage is being unloaded, you riffle through your travellers' cheques like checking a pulse.

Bogotá began as a robbers' encampment. It believes in tradition. 'To get through Colombia without losing anything, you must become paranoid about your money and your luggage,' we had been told in Costa Rica by a serious Norwegian girl with a Belfast accent. Yet for us Bogotá turned out to be one of the friendliest places we had visited. It is true that the friendliness had something heavy-lidded about it, a sort of take-a-drink-or-I'll-break-your-arm quality, which reminded Gerry of Glasgow.

We met it on the plane. Across the aisle from three of us there was a Bogotáno family – mother, son and daughter. They adopted us for the flight. The son told me his house was my house. The daughter asked if I was married. The mother shared with us a bottle of Napoleon brandy. She didn't drink, the son told us – only when she was flying, because she was terrified. We finished the brandy, the mother was drunk enough to open a door and go for a walk, they were all insisting that the three of us visit them. The worrying clauses were that we had to go before checking in to a hotel, so that we would have all our luggage, and that the three other members of the party couldn't come. Was the guest-limit arrived at in relation to the number of places at the table or the number of sons waiting in ambush? Reluctantly, we went to a hotel.

Subsequent evidence suggested it was perhaps not a bad decision. In the hotel we met a young, powerful Australian of 6 ft. 2 in. who told us that on the street he had noticed a small man who walked past him and then kept looking back. Suddenly, the man turned and ran full tilt, hitting the big man in the chest. While the Australian fought him off, hanging grimly on to his travelling bag, another small man came up behind and took his wallet. Then both ran off. We met a 68-year-old New York florist who had prevented his wife's bag being snatched by beating off the thief with a 7-Up bottle. 'I just happened to have it with me. I didn't come outta the Bronx to find out how to get mugged here.'

Our only crisis came dressed as camaraderie. On our first night in Bogotá, Charlie, Gerry and I found a kind of nightclub. We saw people knocking at a door and being admitted. We thought we might as well do the same. A huge, uniformed commissionaire let us in and locked the door behind us. We came down a long staircase into a wide bar. In an adjoining room, through an archway, there was a disco.

As we sat at a table drinking beer, which was all we could afford, we achieved the conspicuousness of the strange. We were fair-skinned and sunburnt and dressed in our own peculiar motley, which included tartan scarves for Charlie and Gerry and a tartan bunnet for me. We must have seemed like a gipsy encampment in the corner of the room. Men and women came out of the disco to stare at us and talk among themselves. A small, powerful man seemed to appoint himself spokesman for the natives. He came across and sat beside me.

'Americano?' he said. When I put him right, he became almost rapturous. He sighed, he shook his head, he spread his arms wide. 'Scotteesh,' he said. He savoured the joyousness of the word. 'We lov the Scotteesh.' I assumed he meant the people, not the dance. 'Geerls?' he said. 'You want geerls?' He raised his hand and snapped his fingers. The fat man who seemed to be the proprietor conferred with him briefly and three women appeared, two of them sitting beside Gerry and Charlie and the third sitting on the other side of me from the small man. He became Benjameen and I became Weelyam. He gave me his card. 'Weelyam,' he said. 'Tomorrow you come to my office. I show you emeralds.'

He held up a clenched fist to demonstrate the size of the emeralds he would show me. I began to wonder about Benjameen. He was talking to three people who looked as if they had fallen off the back of a dustbin-lorry and he appeared to be trying to clinch a deal in emeralds. Things became worse.

'*Aguardiente*,' he said. 'You have tasted *Aguardiente*?' My vestigial Spanish suggested to me 'water' and 'ardent' and I conflated them to 'fire-water'. I shook my head. Benjameen was already snapping his fingers again. He and the fat proprietor spoke and a large bottle and small glasses arrived at our table. Benjameen broke the seal on the bottle but didn't take the cork off. He placed the bottle in the middle of the table. Gerry reached towards the bottle.

'Gerry,' I said with a certain muted urgency. 'Don't take the cork off the bottle.'

'Why?'

'Because if you do, it's your bottle and we can't pay for it.'

Gerry nodded. A chilly silence descended on our table. The women were sitting very still. Benjameen read each of our faces carefully.

61

'Problem, Weelyam?' he said.

I asked him how much the bottle cost. It cost more than we had among us. I explained that we couldn't pay for it.

'I ask you to pay?'

'No, but . . .'

'You like to insult me?'

Oh, no, Benjameen. You're a lovely wee man, right enough. But this is all going funny. I'm not sure of the macho faces staring at us round the room, often mustachioed, and wearing ambiguous smiles that suggest the milk of human kindness could go sour any moment now. Especially, I don't like the long staircase and the locked door and the big man in front of it. And I don't like Charlie's hissed suggestion: 'Wullie, do ye want tae make a run for it?' Let's talk.

I talked to Benjameen. I told him of the unbreachable Scottish tradition, which I was myself interested to hear about, that it was shameful to take a drink from a man if you couldn't buy him one back. I told him that we had just arrived in Bogotá and had been too late to cash any travellers' cheques, which we had left at the hotel. I said that we would cash some cheques next day and come back here and we would all swim in *Aguardiente*. I spoke for several minutes.

When I stopped, Benjameen was staring at me. His stare went on for a while. Suddenly, he leaned across and embraced me.

'I like you, Weelyam,' he said. 'Tomorrow we come here. Enjoy. Then I take you to my office. Emeralds.'

I was glad Benjameen liked me. We contrived to leave soon, amid elaborate promises about the morrow. On the street, Gerry seemed to be taking them seriously. Charlie and I felt we should only keep our promises if we could get the SAS to accompany us.

The rest of our time in Bogotá gave us no hassle. But the city took a delayed-action revenge. Just inside Ecuador, Gerry found that the second last traveller's cheque in his wad was missing. It was worth $100 dollars. His reaction was linguistically baroque. Freely translated into the language of the television screen of the Giants' Stadium in New Jersey, Gerry said, 'Ouch. Good grief. This is a no-no.'

His anger was understandable. He, Charlie Gibbons and Alister Steele worked from last October to gather the money for Argentina. Having amassed £800 each, they translated it into exactly $1,480.42 before leaving London. All have given up their jobs, although Charlie and Gerry have promises of re-employment. Alister accepts that he will have to find something else when he goes back.

Alister has emerged as the Gulbenkian of the group, with more than $700 left. He has the capacity to travel vast distances as if through a tunnel, uninfluenced by anything but his determination to arrive. Charlie and Gerry are more seduceable. Their sense of purpose is so lightly built, it could trip over a daisy. It is a source of wonder even to themselves that they still have $650 left. In their worst moments they have imagined watching the World Cup on television in La Paz. In their best moments, which are at least 23 hours of every day, they have always known they will get there.

Both feelings had their turn in Quito, the capital of Ecuador. It is a beautiful city where the buildings grow up the sides of mountains. Gerry's cheque was refunded and he and Charlie, after winning modestly the first night at the casino, lost heavily the second. That second night was like a barometer for the rest of the journey.

We fled the scene by bus, travelling 13 hours to Huaquillas. Standing a hundred yards from the Peruvian border, we found that Charlie's hand-luggage had been stolen, containing wallet, passport, medical certificates and air-ticket from Argentina back to London.

He, Gerry and I returned to the British Embassy. The misery of having to do the same boring overnight journey three times was mitigated by the speed with which the Embassy in Quito dealt with Charlie's problem and by the marvellous hospitality of George Rae, Assistant to the Defence Minister, and his wife Margaret. We were given the meal of our dreams. Fish-and-chips starvation had set in as early as San Salvador, where we had talked for a long time about places in Scotland to get a good fish-supper. This had been the first injection of the real thing since we set out.

We came back to Huaquillas without rancour. Anyone who has seen Huaquillas would find it hard to blame someone for stealing there. It is poverty made into a town, a penal settlement without barbed wire. Ramshackle houses float on a sea of dust where dead dogs lie at the side of the road and pigs snuffle, eating anything that doesn't move. In the café we went to, they take your order, then go out and buy it and cook it on the premises.

We crossed the border into Peru, went to Tumbes and caught a bus for Lima. It was supposed to be an 18-hour journey. It was dark when we left and the night was the pleasant part.

Daylight showed us the coastal desert with the cousins of Huaquillas along the way. In one of them, Huarmey, the bus was stopped. The road was blocked by a barricade of rubble. Many people stood around, staring at us. The driver tried to take a detour and the bus was stoned. We turned back from Huarmey and drove some distance along the road to Tumbes.

The people were protesting against a 60 per cent rise in fares brought about by the increased price of petrol. We were on their side. After a long delay, during which we managed to beat a team of Peruvians 3–1 (may it prove an omen), a truck-load of soldiers with tear-gas guns arrived and we followed them back to Huarmey.

It wasn't a pleasant experience. All the men were taken out of the buses to clear the road while the people of the town lined up silently on either side to watch. Unnecessarily, it seemed to us, a soldier fired a tear-gas canister into a section of the crowd. I never want to be on the safe side of one of those things again.

The road was cleared. After a brief, half-hearted ambush by some children, we drove on to Lima. There, I think, the haunting sense of how irrelevant we were to the places we passed through finally expressed itself, like rejection symptoms. We went into a downer.

Mine took a physical form. Lima being in a state of crisis, I followed suit. I spent our two days there in extreme and inexplicable pain. I have experienced migraine for most of my life. This was just as sore and it was continuous. The pain was somewhere inside and, I thought, towards my back. Gerry, presumably using the bus-driver's handbook of medical studies, diagnosed a pulled muscle as a result of our heroic victory against the Peruvian team. I lay face down on my bed and he gave my back a pummelling, of which I thought I might very soon die. Gerry called it 'massage'. If Gerry is a masseur, Jack the Ripper was a surgeon. He became so involved in what he was doing that I could only bring my agony to an end by saying that, if he didn't stop, I would have to kill him.

I summoned professional help. A suave doctor visited me in my hotel room, gave me a cursory examination and suggested strained muscles. I wondered if he drove buses between patients. He gave me two pain-killers, one which he administered and one which a nurse would give later, and a bill for $40.

I put the nurse's visit off twice, hoping to keep the second injection until the pain became unbearable. When I finally sent for her, her professional pride was deeply hurt at being kept waiting. She was roughly the size of two Valkyries. When I asked her where the injection would take place, she slammed her buttocks angrily. I prepared. The needle went in like a bayonet and then she proceeded to knead the wounded part like a recalcitrant doughball for what felt like three days. Finished, she asked briskly when I wanted the next injection. I said I was going away, very far away.

Meanwhile, Charlie and Gerry had been arrested. Having gone to a basement nightclub and bought drinks for several ladies who had graced their table, they discovered that the woman who ran the place was loading the table with empty bottles from mysterious sources. Since the bill was arrived at by the simple device of a bottle-count, they knew they were being conned. They calculated how much they owed and offered to pay. The owner claimed the bill was three times their offer. Some unseemly scuffling ensued. With the aid of an empty beer bottle in either hand, Gerry and Charlie won their way to the stairs up to the street, only to be met by the police coming down.

The arresting officer was a jovial man. During that night in jail, he suggested to Charlie that in Lima castration was the punishment for non-payment of bills. Everybody joined in the joke. What wasn't so funny was the way the jailers treated a homosexual who had been arrested. Apparently, they made him sweep the floor and tidy up, encouraging him with slaps and kicks. It was typical of Charlie and Gerry that they should emerge from a bad experience not dismayed but excited, having become overnight students of the Peruvian penal system. Late in the morning, the owner of the nightclub appeared and settled for the amount the prisoners had originally suggested.

But the delay had cost us the bus to Arequipa. It didn't look as if there would be another. A general strike was looming in Peru. In the travel agency in the basement of the Lima Sheraton, a very efficient lady told us, 'Arequipa's burning!' She warned us that if we wanted out, we had tonight and possibly tomorrow morning. After carefully checking the possibilities of internal flights and charter planes, she advised us to take a Lufthansa flight that evening to La Paz, the Bolivian capital. We did.

In La Paz another doctor told me I had tonsillitis and gave me further medication. But the condition showed little sign of improving until an English doctor and his wife checked into our hotel. Professor A. Guz of Charing Cross Hospital – may he live forever – put his hands on my ribs, asked me to breathe deeply and said, 'Hm. Pneumonia. Right lung.' He gave me a week's supply of antibiotics and painkillers and said I was okay to travel on. National Health Service, 'tis of thee I sing.

La Paz was our last stop before Argentina. It is the highest capital in the world and it looks like it. Every other street has ambitions to be a mountain. The hardness of the life is indicated by the fact that even breathing doesn't come easy. With my pulmonary problem, I spent much of the time chasing individual breaths like butterflies.

The Victorian train taking us towards Córdoba travelled for 48 hours through beautiful country, across the Bolivian Altiplano. We did a lot of retrospective thinking. If we have passed this test of Scottish fanhood, it's because we reached Argentina with our passion for football tempered by what we have seen. We will perhaps be better supporters because the distance we have come has put the game into proper perspective. Maybe every fan should make this kind of journey.

I've often thought of football supporting as a form of working-class tourism. In our own case, some of us aren't sure whether the journey was to see the football or the football was just a pretext for the journey.

We have so many negatives of experience still to be developed. Uncertainty is mainly what we feel, even about how much football matters. At the moment only one thing is sure.

We came to Córdoba.

★

Travelling hopefully from Scotland to Argentina isn't half as good as arriving. Those of us who have made the journey overland, the Panzer division of Ally's Tartan Army, have found ourselves disarmed and captured instantly by the irresistible generosity of the Argentine people. Advice, lifts, telephone numbers, meals and lodgings are thrown at us like confetti at a wedding. Round every corner, you bump into Santa Claus. Everybody who decided to play the long odds of trying to make it on the cheap to Córdoba finds that he has won the pools.

Some of the permutations used have been pretty bizarre. They include an interesting system devised by two original thinkers from Tarbert, Ewan Robertson and Jim Blair. Setting out last November, they came to Córdoba via Scandinavia, New York and Miami. They cycled from Bogotá almost to Lima, ruining three wheels on the way.

Not all the punters are Scottish. The recipients of the Argentine blank cheque include an Englishman and an Irishman from Vancouver, two Geordies from Australia, and an 18-year-old from Birmingham. And not all the punters are men. Annie Johnston is here with her husband, Brian, whom she married in Kirkwall on 21 April. The omens for their marriage are propitious. It seems a sensible arrangement to bring your wife on the honeymoon.

As varied as the journeys are the people who have made them. Jim Fisher from Cardonald in Glasgow, a teacher of handicapped children who was side-tracked from looking for work in America, is mature and thoughtful and gives the impression that he got his last surprise when the midwife slapped him. He has found the whole trip comparatively easy. But then he seems a fair representative of that particular type of Scotsman who might raise one eyebrow at an earthquake, presumably keeping the other one for when God introduces himself.

The Heinz factor that unifies all these varieties is simply what happens when you arrive. You are swamped with hospitality. No matter where you come from or how you got here. If you are supporting Scotland, you are in. Here a tartan bunnet is better than a Barclay card.

The ultimate expression of this occurred when the Scottish team arrived. A bus-load of supporters were allowed to join the cavalcade into Alta Gracia, 30 kilometres from Córdoba and where the Scottish team are quartered in the Sierras Hotel. Thousands of people lined the streets, cheering and reaching up to the windows of our bus to shake hands and ask for autographs. Bemused supporters scribbled their names on bits of paper and found them received like precious gifts. For well over an hour, everybody was a star. The equality of players and supporters extended into the hotel. While Ally MacLeod read out room numbers, people with tartan tammies and lion rampants round their shoulders listened as if waiting for their own names to be called.

Later, when we spilled out into the streets, the dream sequence went on unbroken. In a bar a crowd of people crushed round our table, the back rows standing on chairs to watch the miraculous way in which Scotsmen raise glasses of beer to their lips. Names were asked, addresses given, gifts presented.

Dave Ednie, tall and handsome in Highland regalia, with the kind of blue eyes that look as if they could stand in for laser beams, was more besieged than most. He expressed it for everybody.

'A fitter fae Edinburgh. You spend all year up to your armpits in grease – and then this,' he said.

Back in Córdoba, we have continued up to our armpits in friendliness. The Scottish contingent has its headquarters at 136 Dean Furnes, a restaurant near Plaza San Martin where cut-price meals and bottles of beer are dispensed. A man called Miguel E. Skrzpek, who makes an anthill look lethargic, arranges special concessions for Scotsmen.

More are arriving every day. They will discover that in the fans' World Cup, the Scots appear to be well in the lead. The only niggling worry is that some of our fans may possess, like some of our teams in the past, that Scottish talent for snatching defeat from the jaws of victory. Already a couple of abuses of hospitality have occurred, the sort of thing that in Glasgow would have qualified the perpetrators for minor plastic surgery.

If such instances remain as trivial and isolated as they have done, then the World Cup will have proven itself to be truly a way to bring people happily together. If not, then it is impossible to avoid the thought that people as capable of such spontaneous warmth and overwhelming affection as the Argentines might also command other kinds of spontaneity.

The journey, it begins to seem, might have been scripted by Cervantes. Those of us who have travelled from New York to Córdoba using anything to get here from Greyhound buses to a Victorian train across the Bolivian Altiplano, like Don Quixote changing crazy horses, feel that we have been hurrying merely to confront our own illusions. Our destination finds bleak reality behind them.

Wakening up to face facts has brought some fierce reactions. In our own small group of six hopeful travellers, the most severely affected has been Alister Steele, who has from the start approached the trip as if each new country were no more fascinating than a stepping-stone, the only purpose of which was to lead to the next one. All he wanted was to arrive. The defeat of Scotland by Peru taught him harshly where it was he had come to. He left the stadium in tears and gave away his ticket for the game against Iran, as well as every tartan accoutrement anyone would take. Charlie Gibbons and Gerry McDermott were more cautious. They waited until Scotland had drawn with Iran before deciding to join Alister in leaving for home as soon as possible.

At Córdoba on Wednesday when Scotland drew with Iran the most intense confrontation of the day happened after the game when some Scottish fans got as near as they could to the exit-tunnel and hurled abuse at their own team. It was a moment both futile and ugly, like a schizophrenic having a quarrel with himself. Men who had travelled thousands of miles turned against their own reason for coming and shouted obscenities at it. Between the baffled faces of the players and the baffled rage of their supporters a Lion Rampant fell to the ground like something too heavy for either to hold.

The hurt goes deeper than a one-all draw with Iran. That tedious game where everybody seemed to be moving through three feet of water has merely obliged the fans to acknowledge what they have reluctantly suspected since Saturday. If Peru presented us with the corpse of Scottish football, Iran has signed the death certificate. As far as many of the supporters are concerned, the cause of death was cardiac failure. Time and again people have told me here that defeat is all right ('we've had a lot of practice') but not defeat without honourable commitment and effort. The suggestion is always to the effect that the amount of heart shown by the Scottish team in both games wouldn't fill a contact lens. That charge is all the more severe when set against the commitment shown by the Scottish supporters in just being there. Some have put themselves in hock for months ahead. Others, like Robbie Sterry, a 19-year-old from Perth who has less than $50 left, will find it a hard way home through the gloom.

The pain they feel is a bit like that of unrequited love. One supporter, a huge young man from Aberdeen called Raymond, a kind of one-man supporters' club, epitomised it to me. At the beginning of the game against Iran he was waving his Saltire and leading a section of the crowd in singing. Fifteen minutes before half-time I found him crying in his beer behind the stand. In the second-half he was back to full voice, while the torpor of the match made no reply.

Such demented hunting for a response to brute events has been shared to some extent by all of us. After Wednesday's match, the Sorocabana, a bar in the Plaza San Martin, which is now a temporary Scottish colony, became a kind of trauma-ward for Scottish psyches. Normally undemonstrative men embraced, as if trying to be a bandage for each other's pain. Dead-eyed conversation would erupt gradually into *Flower of Scotland* and *We'll Support You Evermore*. Frequently after the songs they would subside again, like people recovering from demoniac possession. Having just finished singing, one man said to me, 'Who needs to support that load of rubbish?'

Charlie Gibbons gave a German supporter his ticket for the game against Holland at Mendoza and danced among the tables with Louise. Willie from Kirkcaldy thought we should pay more attention to politics. Frederick William Turner, 'Topsy' for short, a coloured Scotsman from Dumfries, refused to mitigate his exuberance for any result. The Argentinians helped, as they sang along with us. One even reminded me of their own débâcle in 1966.

The statistic of seven women to every man in Córdoba was another source of soothing. Since the Scots arrived, beautiful girls have turned up in bars asking questions like, 'You know where is Robert? He has the red hair.' Wednesday night was no exception. I'm still haunted by the bizarre image of a handsome, kilted Scotsman explaining with great linguistic difficulty the exact nature of the Scottish team's failure to a stunning blonde, while her eyes ate him whole.

But while the camaraderie of the supporters was real, the pain of their alienation from the team they came to support remained extreme. They are left with a deep affection for the spontaneous generosity and kindness of the Argentine people and a sense that nevertheless they have been cheated of their true purpose in coming here.

It is mathematically possible that Scotland may still qualify. Even if we do, the feeling will remain that a betrayal has taken place. The sense of betrayal will not lie in the failure itself but in the spectacular inadequacy of our attempts to avoid it. On Wednesday most of the blame was being heaped on the man some of them have rechristened, in that gallows humour honed on constant failure, Ally McClown. 'You promised everything, you gave us nothing,' somebody shouted.

It is perhaps a particularly Scottish trait, assumptive optimism. It is a belief among many fans that it has led to the arrogance of inadequate preparation. It has left us with the question that was being chanted sardonically in the Sorocabana on Wednesday night: 'Oh, why are we so bad?'

It seems possible that the answer to the endlessly arid rotation of euphoria and despair in the Scottish support lies not in changing the team but in changing the fans. For years the terracings of grounds where Scotland have played have been covered by Scottish magi who seem to need nothing less than to see their lives given meaning on a football pitch. This time our stable in Córdoba has revealed to us nothing but a not unfamiliar pile of manure.

Yet like someone whose arm has been long since amputated we insist on continuing to feel the pain. Last week in Córdoba a Scottish fan, so wild in his Highland attire he made Harry Lauder look like an Englishman, told me at great length how the Scottish team had robbed him of his identity and made him a laughing-stock in the town. It would have been facile to suggest a pin-stripe suit. His pain was real. It is its reality which is depressing. As someone who in Córdoba has shared in that experience to a degree unprecedented for me, perhaps because it took me six weeks to get here, I find the intensity of my own initial reactions to the performance of a football team disconcertingly extreme.

Passion, of course, is an essential part of the game. Like theatre, the excitement of football begins in the preparedness of spectators to give themselves up to the temporary importance of what is happening. Like theatre, football allows the cathartic expression of strong feelings in a safe and stylised context.

What worries me about the Scottish supporters' relationship to the game is our tendency to want to storm the stage, the apparent willingness of so many of us to make our lives just an adjunct of our chosen form of theatre. Like inhabitants of some weird psychological outback, we succumb to a naïvely total identification with the performance that is roughly equivalent to wanting to shoot the actor who plays Richard the Third. If the World Cup is the West End of football, the Scottish game is a crude and ineffectual form of group therapy in which players and fans desperately improvise towards some mutually acceptable sense of themselves. Instead of being a natural extension of our lives, an expression of ourselves, it remains the nexus of a stubborn national neurosis.

One possible cure might have been success. Winning a World Cup could presumably allow us to admit that it is only a game and that after all the Scottish Messiah isn't going to appear wearing a 9 on his jersey. But the Argentine experience should remind us that if we're going to wait that long, we could all be doolally enough, before it happens, to make playing headers with a concrete ball the national sport.

Failure looks like the only teacher who will turn up regularly. In the absence of very much else, maybe we can learn from our mistakes. For years now we have been hitching a wagon loaded with the bizarre furniture of Scottishness to a team of ants in the hope of going somewhere. Every time they die in harness, we renew them. Now it's surely time to accept irrevocably the alternative conclusion that we're asking football to do more for us than the nature of the thing allows.

There are already isolated signs that some Scots are newly anxious to release the game from its current megalomaniac status and let it revert to being a pleasant part of our lives. Many times in the past couple of weeks people have suggested to me that they will never support Scotland in the same way again. These include supporters who have travelled overland, some who took a package-deal for the duration of the games, some who did the same for the first fortnight, and others – the kind of punters that might bet on a dead horse – who didn't arrive until after Scotland's first three games.

I'm not suggesting they're going to take up politics. But all of them gave the very strong impression that it would be a long time before they would invest a few games of football with the same kind of exaggerated importance again. I think for such an evaluation to become more general would be healthy both for the team and the supporters.

In my own case, the forcible bursting of my oxygen-tent of preoccupation with Scotland's chances here has, apart from a brief period of strangulated adjustment, left me glad to inhabit a wider context again. With your own team out of the reckoning, it's at least easier to take in the wider connotations of what is happening here, perhaps encapsulated most effectively and worryingly in the recent scene where an Argentine crowd had to be prevented by the police from attacking the Mad Mothers of the Plaza de Mayo, that group of people who demonstrate regularly in Buenos Aires against the unexplained disappearance of relatives. The fact that the motivation of those who objected to the demonstrators was that a bad impression was being given of Argentina, may indicate the extent to which this World Cup has been conceived as an exercise in press relations.

Such realisations cannot detract from the overwhelming warmth of the Argentine people in the streets nor, glimpsed as they are in the passing, can they be more at the moment than misgivings. But at least to be aware of them, to be conscious that not all the shadows over the games come from the floodlights, has to be healthy.

Of course, one lucid interval doesn't make a cure. It may be that by the time Wembley comes round we will all have suffered a complete relapse. Certainly, I will want to be there as well as, God and the Clydesdale Bank willing, in Spain in 1982. After all, football remains simply the best ball-game in the world.

But apart from changes in the team-formation, I wouldn't mind seeing some significant tactical rethinking among the Scottish fans, so that if things go wrong – which in the context of Scottish football is almost a synonym for 'according to plan' – they have a stronger sense of identity to call on than can be entirely contained in a dark blue jersey. Even supporters in a crisis need to be able to field substitutes.

Buenos Aires, a couple of days after the 1978 World Cup final. I am sitting in a café, staring out at the city of Jorge Luis Borges. The way I feel, I might as well be one of his creations – say, Funes the Memorious – caught in that strange place where the present endlessly repeats the past and wonders where the future is. I am on coffee, symbolic end to a wild experiential spree. Where have I been? What has happened? What does it mean?

Yesterday I noticed beggars on the streets. After several weeks in Argentina, those were the first beggars I have seen. I had been told that the military régime had swept the cities clean of the destitute before the tourists came. I believe it now. Those down-and-outs, emerging like embarrassing relatives from back rooms, seem almost apologetic at finding some visitors still in residence. The sight of them has been like acid applied to an etcher's plate. The irrelevances burn off.

Scotland failed again. Holland, the best team in the competition, lost the final. So what? My football supporter's gloom comes into perspective. Never mind the results, feel the experience.

Scotland 1–Peru 3. But what about that night on the darkened beach at Manuel Antonio with the American Peace Corps workers – the beer, the singing and the laughter? Or that time in the Mexico City nightclub when we had the Tequila Sunrises that almost became sunsets, because they presented us with a bill that was a work of towering fiction, Tolstoy in figures, and there was no way we could pay and we left the real amount in payment and had to slip out one by one and I drew the short straw, leaving last with my tartan bunnet in my pocket, cunningly disguised as a Mexican, and, once we were all together, we had it away on our toes?

Scotland 1–Iran 1. But, if I hadn't come all this way to endure the game, I would have missed that night in Queen's, the dawn walk with Charlie Gibbons through Greenwich Village, the exciting threateningness of San Antonio in the early hours of the morning when three of us had insisted on walking to see the Alamo before the bus left. I wouldn't have met up with Toni Ossenstetter, the marvellous German enjoyer. And, therefore, I would have missed his heroic moment at the Honduran border. The woman behind the stall had only bottles of beer and a huge bowl of eggs. 'Two eks,' Toni said. 'A beer. *Cerveza. Ovas. Dos.*' The woman's opaque eyes flickered. She filled out a glass of beer and expertly cracked two eggs into it, one in each hand. While Toni remonstrated, she gave him his change and waved him away. Toni had made a mistake. It wasn't the eggs that were hard-boiled, it was the woman. But he turned towards our laughter and toasted the vagaries of life.

Scotland 3–Holland 2. All right, our one victory had been too little too late. But I would remember Robbie Sterry, the 19-year-old from Perth who had travelled alone to Argentina ('Mugged twice, right enough. But I also spent a week oan a millionaire's yacht in Panama'). I had said goodbye to him on a street in Córdoba. He was standing with an attractive girl who seemed to have been surgically grafted on to his arm. 'Ah think Ah'll stey,' he was saying. 'Her father says he can get me a joab on his ranch.'

Whichever way you look at it, the experience has been interesting. Strange images well to the surface from the past couple of months.

I remember a café-bar in Alta Gracia. It is the night after the arrival of the Scottish squad. A group of us are sitting at a table. Some women are seated at an adjoining table. We are chatting, the banality of our conversation spiced by the need for difficult, simultaneous translation. Some of the Scottish players come in. They exude that aura of honed healthiness that athletes often have, like the one in the *quattrocento* painting you notice first.

Four of them sit at a table next to us. There is some banter. One of the players suggests to the women that they are talking to the wrong people: 'They're just supporters. We're the players.'

When I go to the toilet, the same player follows me in. He asks me if I've had it off with the woman who is sitting nearest me. I say no and, if I had, does he think I would tell him. He shakes his head and shrugs, as if he regrets bothering with someone so crass, who doesn't understand the finer points of male etiquette. I think the omens are perhaps not good for the hopes of the nation, if this is the kind of spirit that is carrying them.

It gets worse. When the players at the next table leave, there is a tear in their price-stub, which means the bill is paid. But the bill has not been paid. We discover this when the proprietrix appears to have launched into opera – Puccini, I think. When one of the women at the nearby table calms her down, I ask how she managed to do it. She explains that she has said that I will pay.

The bill isn't much but I'm not sure I can afford the suppressed anger that will come from subsidising people who could probably lose my whole budget for the trip from a hip-pocket and hardly notice it was gone. And they're the ones I've travelled 7,000 miles to see. I ask to use the phone and contact the hotel where the team is staying. I explain what has happened, to the player who comes to the phone. This could be very embarrassing, I suggest. I'm prepared to pay but I would like the money back tonight. It is agreed.

After I have paid, Charlie walks with me through the darkness to the hotel. We walk into a scene from John Le Carré's wastepaper basket. Armed guards are patrolling outside the building. They are not happy to see us. We are all still arguing in monosyllables and sign-language when a player emerges from the darkness and jumps the small perimeter wall. He isn't one of those who were at the table in the bar.

It is a refreshing and reassuring exchange. He squares things with the guards. He repays me and we talk a bit. He offers tickets but we have all the tickets we need. He is intelligent and gracious and understanding. Maybe we have a chance after all. Charlie and I walk back to the bar with some renewed faith.

But perhaps that's the night when I finally decide that you shouldn't invest too much serious emotion in supporting football. There had already been a scandalous picture in the Argentine press of a Dutch player, I think, in bed with a woman. Word was the photograph had been posed by models and then an insert of the player's head had been grafted on. If you can walk into a publicity minefield like that and, on your first night out, behave as carelessly as someone at the next table had done, there have to be questions about how seriously you're going about your business on the park.

But I'm philosophical about it now, in my Buenos Aires café. Another image has displaced the bright bar in Alta Gracia. We are on the train across the Altiplano. It is dark, in the early hours of a cold, high morning. Most people are sleeping or pretending to sleep. I am chewing some of the coca leaves I bought in a street market in La Paz. They are supposed to keep out the chill, I have been told. Somebody must have been kidding me on or else I've bought a midget lettuce.

We are passing through nowhere in particular as far as I can see but every so often the train will stop and someone will get off and be absorbed by the vastness of the night. The train stops again. A small, solid Indian woman further up the carriage stands up. She seems to have all of her possessions in a large, knotted sheet. I look out the window. As far as the light reaches, there is only flatness and, beyond that, blackness. I wonder how she knows this is where she gets off. She has been patiently feeding her travelling-sheet through the small window beside her. It finally falls like an enormous jellyfish on the ground outside. The train moves off.

The woman begins immediately to scream and weep. I get up and move towards her. But there is not much point in that. I can't communicate with her and she can't even see me, her eyes closed in screaming desolation. The guard arrives to see what the trouble is. She jabbers at him through her tears and I make what I hope are fluent gesticulations. He waves both of us off impatiently and goes away. The woman ignores me and sits down, rocking and weeping inconsolably. I come back to my seat and sit down. The woman weeps on relentlessly.

I can't get my head away from what has happened. Why the hell didn't she just carry the sheet out with her? She presumably carried it in. She must have thought she was being clever, saving herself the trouble of struggling with it. Well, she wasn't having much trouble carrying it now. By the time she gets back there, if she ever does, her stuff will probably be divided out among the natives. How will she get back, by the way? There's probably a train every three days or something. Will she have the money? My useless sympathy and her tears worry at each other until I take the easy way out. I fall asleep. By the time I waken, she is gone – except that she stays fixed in my memory, rocking and weeping, rocking and weeping.

Why does that image haunt me so much, Jorge, even here in your city? Maybe because it is the essential emblem of our journey, a cipher of all the similar moments we have passed through in our preoccupation to get to a few football matches. That moment on the train is echoed endlessly in my memory. I am teeming with images of the varieties of living which I can never reconcile with one another: the big, blond bear of a man on the bus from New York to New Orleans, who was giving his beautiful black girlfriend orgasms of delight by describing in detail the number of people – including his father – he had 'beat the shit out of'; Benjameen of the emeralds in Bogotá; an overnight stay in the Hurlingham Club outside Buenos Aires, where I found an Englishness more extreme than I have experienced in the Athenaeum or the Garrick Club; the whistling homosexuals under the lamplight in San Antonio; the dark, impenetrable eyes of the sad man at the cantina in Managua; the casualness of dying in Guatemala City; the walk alone at night in New York, from Times Square to Costello's, not a stroll I recommend doing twice; dark faces watching me from doorways when I go out at night to buy cigarettes in San Salvador.

The woman in the train on the Bolivian Altiplano – her image is the hole worn by actuality in the purpose for the journey in which I had dressed. Through it, countless other images are reaching me. My preoccupations have caught a chill from reality. I am fevered with remembrance. Willie the Memorious, right enough. I need one all-enveloping sense of things in which to wrap myself.

The kindness of the people, that is it. More than by anything else, this journey has been unified by the kindness of the people we have met: from the busy barman in Queen's who insisted on writing down for Charlie and me a list of the places it was safe for us to go in his domain, to the man in the restaurant in Córdoba we had thought must be a waiter. He checked that our carafe of wine was empty and then it transpired he wasn't just clearing it away, he was wanting to replenish it for us out of his own pocket because we were visitors to his country.

Throughout the whole trip I have never learned how not to be overwhelmed by the effortless generosity of strangers. I met it in a lot of places – America not least – but maybe all of those other people will forgive me if I single out the Argentines. They taught me to love Latin Americans. Just to say hello to some of those people is like turning on the sun.

Their warmth had a particular focus for me. I was more or less adopted by a family in Córdoba, maybe because I had lost so much weight with my illness. I had become worryingly thin. My brother, Hughie, who was there to cover events for the *Observer*, expressed his concern not too gently, as brothers will. When he saw a strange woman come up to talk to me in a bar, he said when she had gone – ever fraternally supportive – 'Well, that's one necrophiliac we know about in Córdoba, anyway.'

The family insisted on feeding me steaks. They had an uncle – who was a specialist – give me every type of medical examination. He told me I was all right but that I had gone through dry pleurisy on the journey and that I should stop smoking. They found me an apartment in which to stay in

Buenos Aires during the final stages of the World Cup. They even forgave me for supporting Holland in the final.

So why should I worry about a few football results? We lost but we won. Time to go home. I've got all the presents. But my daughter always bothers me in this area. Siobhán seems to think my taste in presents is abominable, and she's probably right. I'll bet she hates what I've got for her. I'll buy her one more thing, that's what I'll do. When your aim's not too good, you'd better use a scatter-gun. But remember that time in New Orleans when that big man on Bourbon Street tried to invite us into the transvestite show?

A man passes me in the café and smiles and I nod. Yes. Definitely, the kindness. Argentina – not the régime, just the ordinary people – *te amo del uno al nueve. Sin cero.*

I finish my coffee. Okay, Jorge. I'm glad I came to your place. It has been enough. I remember vivid, raucous days and sweet, soft nights. Who needs to have won at the football?

Scotland–Spain, 1982

Last Tuesday, Scotland's football supporters, the Tartan Magi, came to Malaga. It was four years since I had seen them straggle away from stadiums in Argentina like a national identity crisis. A letter I received from a supporter I'd made friends with in Córdoba symbolised for me how long the way back must have been for many of them. It was sent five months after the last World Cup ended. It was postmarked Guatemala.

That fan eventually made it home but the way back from the disillusionment of the Argentine experience is still an uncompleted journey for the Scottish supporter in general. We lost more than the game with Peru and our best-ever chance on paper of qualifying for the final stages. We lost what we had thought was our right to beat the best. A country whose team can only draw with Iran may have to learn to live with diminished dreams. I wondered if we could.

There was something else I wasn't sure we had lost but found myself hoping we had – our exaggerated sense of the importance of football. After our first two games in Córdoba, some of the bars looked like wards for the shell-shocked. Several supporters I knew headed home after the second match. Surrounded by unrepeatable possibilities of experience, they felt that only the football mattered. Two of them in particular were desperate to get home in time for the Tarbert Fair.

Those two imbalances, an unrealistic assessment of Scotland's potential as a footballing country and a preoccupation with football that parochialises experience, were what I hoped the last four years had gone some way towards setting right. So La Roselada stadium in Malaga seemed an important enough place to be last Tuesday night.

The omens I had gathered before the game were about as easy to decipher as tea-leaves. There were stories of the sort familiar from Argentina of unusual modes of travel, like busking in a van or travelling in a double-decker bus converted to provide sleeping accommodation upstairs. What was new was that a significant number of travellers seemed to have brought the hopefully civilising influence of women along with them.

There was the not-unfamiliar tendency to outbreaks of irrationality, a mild kind of verbal rabies, as when one supporter told me in the Melia Hotel, Torremolinos, that, having watched Brazil play Russia, he had noticed that both teams were rubbish. But counter-pointing that were quite a few supporters suggesting that for Scotland to qualify from a hard section would be a major achievement.

Looking round the stadium on the night, I found myself believing tentatively that a cure for our peculiar elephantiasis of the football match was perhaps possible. Travel agents had suggested that between 7,000 and 10,000 Scots would be there, about half of them as families, a situation which implied that some Scots were attempting the novel feat for us of combining football with life. They seemed to be more numerous than 10,000 but then they always do.

They were pleasantly vociferous and their banners carried hints of life after football: sending greetings to women and naming pubs that were presumably the starting-points for their journeys. One which I wasn't sure I could decipher, because it kept furling inconsiderately, seemed to say, 'Ally's Dream – Stein's Machine'. I hope it said that, because that implies the replacement of vague aspirations by practical methods, a change of attitude Scotland could benefit from in areas other than football.

And then there was the game against New Zealand, a familiarly Scottish event and yet somehow different from the past. When we were 3–0 up at half-time, I had the wild idea that for the first time in my experience we were going to score the number of goals commensurate with our superiority in a game. But that, of course, isn't the way we play. Instead, we gave away two goals. I recognised a moment as familiar as my own face in the mirror. That was the real Scottish style, as native to my country as kamikaze is to Japan.

While we were struggling to keep the score at 3–2, I was thinking, for Malaga read Córdoba. But that wasn't true. We scored two more. It seemed to me we had come to a different place. It wasn't the zenith of footballing prowess but it was a determined and difficult realisation of some part of our potential under stress. It was the sort of achievement I felt our fans should learn to appreciate. They did.

In the bars around the stadium afterwards, there was much talk of Gordon Strachan, who at times had played like a Michelangelo being helped by ten men who paint by numbers. There was acknowledgment of the problems the Scots had faced and a qualified respect for the way they had overcome their own self-destructive tendencies. There was also a relaxed enjoyment of being in Spain.

As a group of us walked the centre of Malaga for more than an hour in the early morning, looking for a taxi, I had some recurring thoughts. Whatever the results for us by the end of this World Cup, perhaps Jock Stein will have helped the supporters towards more realistic expectations from the great game. Perhaps the supporters will have come a little closer to accepting their journeys abroad for what they are, a working-class version of the Grand Tour, a way to see a little more of life. Perhaps together, manager and supporters will have helped to bring that wildly vaunting side of the Scottish character more into line with the dourly practical side.

Scotland–Italy, 1990?

Earlier this week, I felt something like a surge of the old involvement. Andy Roxburgh, Scottish football manager, had announced his squad against Norway for the World Cup Finals in Italy in 1990. But it was a ghostly feeling.

What I experienced was adrenalin remembered rather than adrenalin actually felt. I couldn't use the excuse for my low-key response which I have sometimes used lately – that some of the names were about as exciting as a laundry-list. Any current squad which contains the names of Ally McCoist and Kevin Gallacher promises excitement. It couldn't be that.

Perhaps it's just that I am not the Scottish supporter I once was, I thought. Otherwise, why were my thoughts this week all about old campaigns that seemed as distant as the Napoleonic Wars? The Massacre of Wembley (1967). The Retreat from Córdoba (1978). Brooding on the sometimes painful past I have shared with the Scottish football team, I decided that the reasons for my less than enthusiastic reception of the news of their next endeavours were both public and personal.

I'll come to the public reasons later. For we old campaigners love to dwell on the personal ones, to tell about the times when we received the wound that marked the end of our most active phase of combat, made us not quite the force we had been. I can remember when, after numerous flesh-wounds of frustration and disbelief and disappointment, I finally copped the big one.

It was a hot summer evening in Seville. There were six of us sitting at a pavement table at a bar. We were all talking with a kind of passionate bleakness. Two were wearing kilts and the rest of us had a splash of tartan somewhere, like men not fully demobilised from some Highland regiment.

We were talking about football. At the stadium, ten minutes away, Brazil had just beaten Scotland 4–1 in the 1982 World Cup. I remember trying to establish, with a certain venomous determination, how there was nothing to discuss, how for me something had been experienced, that was all. You might as well start to criticise a sunset.

What I meant wasn't that Brazil were bound to beat us, for football is more a game of chance than most people who follow it admit, and strange things happen in a match. What I meant was that such events merely take place and can't be asked to carry the weight of significance some Scots have put on them.

Around us in the hot Spanish evening there was laughter that seemed to have a foreign rhythm, like castanets. There was much animated conversation and extrovert gesture. I felt we were inhabiting a different evening, huddled round our table as if it were a camp fire, exchanging opaque preoccupations, nursing the iron rations of our drinks, somehow psychically on the run. From where to where? We had found the bar down a side street and there weren't many Scots here besides ourselves.

But I thought of the other remnants of our retreating army holed up briefly in various places around Seville, lions that were supposed to be rampant drooping from their shoulders on dusty flags, fair vulnerable faces raw with Spanish sunburn. We would be drinking not beer but *cerveza*, surrounded by the mysterious beauty of Seville, which most of us would never see, for we were leaving in the darkness. And we would be debating whether the mid-field should be changed or if Big Jock Stein was really the man for the job. We would be practising that strange cosmopolitan parochialism that comes for Scots with the passport.

I was the only one there to have attended two World Cups. I don't think I pulled rank but I couldn't help seeing in a couple of the hurt faces beside me a bafflement that looked like a direct descendant of my own past experience. This doesn't mean that I was no longer hurt. The best ball-game in the world is about passion, not serious passion, just an innocent mayfly form of it. If you don't care what happens at the game, you shouldn't go.

I cared all right. But I thought the bafflement I saw was about more than losing a football match. I thought it was about other kinds of defeat. The hurt seemed disproportionate to the wound. It was as if you should jocularly click Achilles' heels and find him dying on you. I wondered what kind of genetic malformation was in some Scots that our nationhood was located where our sport should be.

And I remembered Argentina. That was the time in the summer of 1978 when Scotland went to contest the World Cup in Córdoba. At least, in Europe it was summer. In South America it was coming on to winter and as for the Scots, well, they arranged to bring their own clouds with them. The whole expedition was a small and singularly daft disaster, something which would later occur to me as being a B-picture remake of the Darien Scheme.

It had begun, like a lemmings' rush, in a great and energetic euphoria. The nation seemed mobilised in rabid support of its team. Numerous artifacts relating to the World Cup were on sale. There was a boom in saltire and lion rampant flags. It was a fly man's market. Wild schemes were hatched by desperate men in pubs about how to make the 7,000-mile trip to Argentina on almost no money.

Having already set out on one of those trips, I was fortunate enough not to be one of the thousands who paid admission money for the privilege of standing on the terracings of Hampden Park to cheer farewell to the Scottish team. Nor was I, therefore, one of those who lined the route to Prestwick Airport, waving and cheering.

That was how it started. It ended in a black orgy of recriminations. The team-manager was a dumpling. The players were useless. Scotland was rubbish. Stories were relayed to those of us who were still in Argentina after Scotland's failure to qualify for the final stages of the cup. They conveyed images of a nation exaggeratedly bereft, of men who sat in their living-rooms decked out in tartan tammies and scarves, throwing empty beer cans at television sets (at least we hoped they were empty or the nation had really gone doolally), of children tearfully ripping World Cup wall-charts from their bedroom walls and too depressed to go to school.

Even allowing for the way rumours inflate with distance, the Scottish reaction did seem too big for its roots. It reminded me of a cousin of mine who at the age of four was found pursuing a girl of the same age with a small axe. Questioned about his behaviour, he explained that she had hit him with a stalk of grass. It had been, it must be admitted, a big thick stalk of grass. Similarly, the sequence of events that had preceded the grief of Scotland looked too small to cause so much trouble but maybe, given the right unhealthy conditions, one tsetse-fly could cause an epidemic.

The sequence of events in question was a simple one. Scotland had lost 3–1 to Peru, drawn one-each with Iran, and beaten Holland 3–2. Those results, which must look to the uninitiated as meaningless as runes, decipher – given the requisite knowledge – into a small, sad epitaph on the Scottish sporting psyche, a minor classic of found poetry.

Peru in 1978 were a team that could be very easily beaten. Iran knew about football the way a two-year-old can be expected to comprehend the human condition, whereas Scotland is claimed by many Scots to have invented the game. Holland were simply the best team in the competition, unlucky to lose in the final against the host nation.

You see what we did? Where it was easy, we failed. When it looked impossible and no longer mattered (since we weren't going to qualify anyway), we won. Ah, those results in Argentina, a kind of Lowland pibroch. We were celebrating something sad about ourselves with them, perhaps the Scottish talent for self-destruction, for never quite believing in a cause until it's lost.

Writing from Argentina before we had kicked a ball, and when things looked bright, I expressed my fears about our ability to snatch defeat from the jaws of victory. We had done it again.

I couldn't help feeling the recriminations were a smoke-screen generated to make us miss the essential point. I could see some validity in the objections against the manager and the team, it was true. Ally McLeod had gone inadequately prepared. The first time he had seen Peru play was when they were beating us. That was probably a bit late for the subtle deployment of tactics. On the field, some of the players gave the impression they should have been wearing kiss-me-quick hats and flip-flops. They seemed to imagine they had booked up with SFA Holidays Ltd, and been misdirected on to a football pitch.

So I could share the Scottish dismay at the lack of preparation and the irresponsibility of some of the players. But the intensity of the reaction still overflowed the facts. The vehemence against manager and players seemed to me a way of hiding from the most obvious facet of the Argentine fiasco: not the depth of disappointment that followed but the height of expectation that preceded it.

The irrationality of the original demand was concealed behind ostensibly rational excuses. It was as if, after the ant had failed to pull the wagon, we should examine it carefully, nod sagely, and explain that one of its legs was broken.

I was thinking of this at a pavement table in a bar on a hot, dark evening in Seville, not necessarily coherently, probably as a succession of badly edited scenes in that Scottish home movie I had been running in my head for so long.

I was aware that Spain 1982 was my Russian campaign. I was the veteran who had gone through one self-imposed winter of the spirit too many. This was it for me. I would still support the team, of course. (What else could I do? I'd have to take out Martian citizenship to do otherwise.) But I was deserting from that army of displaced passion that was Scottish football supporters. I thought they were fighting on the wrong front. In the absence of Eliot's 'objective correlative' for their feelings about their country, they attached those feelings impossibly to football.

I didn't go to the World Cup finals in Mexico in 1986. I would like to be able to say that was the calm, rational decision of a man who had taken the cure. But the truth is I didn't have the money.

If Andy Roxburgh and his players qualify for the finals in Italy in 1990, if I'm still around, if I'm not in hiding in the hills from an overdraft, I would like to go and watch. But I wouldn't go on the same terms as I went to Argentina and to Spain. Even if I were tempted to have a relapse and start attributing too much importance to football again, the present circumstances in Scotland would effect a speedy cure. These are the public reasons I mentioned earlier.

I believe that the Scottish national team no longer has the significance for us it once had. I believe the time is over when Hampden Park, and even

81

Wembley every second year, could stand in for a Scottish Assembly – a pre-political form of one, it is true, a jostling, incoherent claim to the difference of Scottishness. The Scottish football team can no longer give us a makeshift surrogate national identity.

There are two main reasons for this, I think. The first is that there has been a change in the conditions which for so long helped football to be one means of reminding the Scots of who they were. The muddied reservoir of residual Scottishness that collected intermittently in the bowl of Hampden was fed from a lot of tributary sources: a distinctive culture, a distinctive political history, a distinctive sense of social equality.

Those sources have in the past nine years been dammed and diverted into an imitation of Englishness. Any football crowd that from now on gathers to support the Scottish team is likely to be an increasingly disparate group of people, a discordance of voices, a dilution of Scottishness.

The second reason is that the game itself has begun to experience that process of dilution. Football is being denationalised in Scotland. The old dominant principle of the home-bred player as club-patriot is challenged by the new principle of the player from outside Scotland as mercenary. It is an understandable development but one effect will be to transform the significance of the game in Scotland. If the trend continues, the most effective teams will function like multinational corporations. What their fans will be identifying with is less something Scottish than something successful.

And yet another insubstantial prop of the disintegrating Scottish identity will have gone. From this distance, the pain of those Scottish supporters in Argentina seems maybe not so exaggerated. Perhaps they sensed that time was running out for football, as for other distinctive aspects of Scottishness. The following year would see the 'yes' of the referendum rejected because the decibel-rating wasn't high enough and the election of a government savagely inimical to the populist traditions of Scottish life. Thinking of that, I recall two moments from that pivotal time in Argentina.

At the end of the match against Iran, I watched an enraged group of supporters surround the team bus. The fans were kicking and spitting and swearing and heaving, as if they wanted to overturn the bus with the team in it. It was a painful performance to witness.

Of course, other supporters can react violently to failure. Some Italians, for example, retain certain instincts of the amphitheatre towards their team. But the Scottish supporters' condemnation of their team was different, rather pathetic. It had a helpless, self-lacerating quality to it, like one of those tantrums children know are hurting themselves but which they can't see how to stop. It was less a response than the search for one, less an answer than a question.

I think one man I heard at half-time during the same match came fairly close to articulating that question. He was a huge young man from Aberdeen. During the first half he had been standing up waving a Saltire and haranguing the Scots around him: 'Come on, boys. Sing. Sing. We've goat tae lift them.' The way the team were playing, it would have needed several gib-cranes to lift them.

At half-time I went out to one of the stalls behind the terracings. I noticed a small concerned knot of Argentines in their blue official attendants' uniforms. They were surrounding the big man with the flag, which was now furled. He was weeping very noisily into his carton of beer. As I approached, one of the Argentines turned towards me.

'What is problem?' she asked.

It was a beautifully innocent question. Perhaps if we'd all had a few spare years we could have gone into it. As it was, the big man looked up at me through his tears and, in the intensity of his small moment of passion, found a not unmoving interim answer. Touching my arm, he said, 'We'll never do anythin' richt, will we?'

Now, ten years later, my answer to his question would be: not unless we hurry. For if we don't do whatever we're going to do soon, there will be no 'we' to do it. Scottishness will be no more than a quaint province of Englishness. I think we are engaged in a war of attrition with forces that seek to erode our identity. We won't win that war with a few skirmishes on a football field.

Dreaming Las Vegas

THE CHICKEN WAS PERHAPS A PORTENT. IN ANCIENT ROME the soothsayers used to cut open birds to read the omens in the entrails. They would have had trouble with this one, especially if all they had had to work with were a plastic knife and fork. This chicken had an effective security system. You could go all round about it but you couldn't break in. I looked along the row I was sitting in. Our puzzled concentration suggested a group of examinees undergoing a bizarre intelligence test: how to open a chicken. Nobody was getting a pass mark. Or perhaps it was one of those clever, double-edged tests where what you think is failing is really passing. Perhaps the measure of your intelligence was your inability to get into the chicken. After all, if it was that difficult to cut, who wanted to eat it? I turned to my son, Liam, who was in the window seat.

'They've given me the window-display by mistake,' I said. 'This chicken's made of plastic.'

Would the town we were flying towards prove any more authentic?

'This your first trip to Vegas?' the man on my other side said. It was. He was a Vancouverite and a Las Vegas devotee. He started to outline some of the pleasures we had ahead. He was one of a group of six friends on the chartered flight from Vancouver. His wife, a woman of nervous but determined self-assurance, sat across the aisle from him. I liked the man but his enthusiasm for the town was making him sound like a tour-operator and I didn't want my sense of the place to be predetermined. I kept changing the subject during the flight, with Liam's help, until the procedures for descent began to happen.

'Look at them lights,' the man said. 'That's Las Vegas.' They were impressive, all right – a great meadow of luminosity in the darkness with regular avenues of lights running through it. Of course, all cities you come into from the air and in the dark are made of lights. But somehow Las Vegas seems more essentially constructed out of brightness than any other place I know, an image so dazzling that it's difficult to see what substance is behind it. The taxi from the airport took us through what appeared to me one of the great architectural curiosities of our time – a city built of neon. Caesar's Palace. The Sands Hotel. The Golden Nugget. Those are places? They look more like advertisements.

The first shock of the strange I experience in Las Vegas is its suddenness. I do not mean the suddenness of its impact. I mean the sense that it has only just happened, grew here tonight like some weird desert mushroom. Most cities you come into for the first time feel complicated. They make difficult, tortuous statements you realise you may never understand. You wonder what their past was. Las Vegas doesn't bother with the complexity of a statement. It's just a word: money. It has no past. Yesterday? What's that? There's only now.

Our hotel confirms that sense of the moment with no discernible antecedents, as hotels tend to. It is long corridors where pale strangers pass one another in the dead light. Our double room has a stale, antiseptic smell. Nobody in particular has left and nobody in particular takes their place.

In Las Vegas they like places to have themes, as if they were fancy-dress parties, which in a way they are. Where you have no history, borrow some. Our hotel is the Imperial Palace – mandarin motifs and lattice woodwork. You might as well be in China. Sure. This place is as Chinese as spaghetti.

We dump our bags and – eager plungers into experience that we are – go down to the gaming-room. And that's it, really. In some basic psychological sense, we never get out. We may move around to different places but they might as well be the same one.

Something happened to us that first night in the place. I'm still uncertain what it was or how to analyse it exactly. Maybe you could call it the Las Vegas effect. It has something to do with time, for sure, and how it doesn't seriously seem to be there. How can you have time without any continuity? It has something to do with identity and how it's hard to have any that isn't subservient to a slot-machine or the turn of a card. Las Vegas, it seems to me, is where you can go to be nobody for a time. It shimmers like a mirror of narcissistic pleasure but the more you stare into it the less anybody looks out. You become a function of the place.

Somebody told me they oxygenate the atmosphere in those hotels to keep you awake for the gambling. I don't know if they do but something happens there to make you go on, compelled as a somnambulist, to repeat the same rituals beyond any serious exercise of will that you have performed. When you're not gambling, you're watching other people gamble.

I remember once in a casino surfacing from my stupefied automatism and looking around me. The moment was like the feeling I used to have occasionally as a boy when the strangeness of the ordinary would assail me. This is like some religion, I thought. All around were rows of people sitting devotionally in front of their slot machines and spinning them like prayer-wheels. God of chance, give me the accident I need and I will take it as personal sign.

Another time, I suddenly thought, these people are supposed to be on holiday. But they don't look as if what they're doing is having pleasure. They look like workers, workers in money. They sweat. They are compelled. Their time is not really their own. Their hands stink of verdigris. They can't see the emptiness of what they're doing for the need to keep doing it. If they had them doing this in a factory, they would go on strike.

But nobody does, not us either. After all, the workers have good conditions. The food is amazingly cheap and swiftly available at any time. You can even have edible chicken. While you're doing your stint of hard graft, pretty girls, dressed in ways that do not tax the imagination, will come up to you in the casino from time to time and serve you a drink that costs no more than the tip. Who needs shop stewards? You take a break whenever and as often as you decide.

But the break isn't really a break. For what can you do with it? In a place that exists for gambling, you are liable, like a neurotic workaholic, to wonder what's happening at the casino. You'd better get back to it. I bet somebody's winning at that table right now. Maybe that machine that almost paid big is ready to disgorge the jackpot.

At the end of a shift, Liam and I used to lie on our beds and stare at the ceiling, like people convalescing after an operation for removal of the will. I suppose we felt much the way labourers must feel who are too exhausted to enjoy or make positive use of their rest time. We kept making desultory plans to do other things we never quite got round to. We threatened more than once to go and see a show.

One idea in particular became a kind of obsession with me during those listless but sometimes lucid intervals when we lay wondering what the hell we were doing here. It was like the escape plan a prisoner may devise. It may never happen but he needs it to help him through the day. 'There must be real people living here,' I intoned into the stillness. 'In Las Vegas, I mean.' I meant people who go to their work and try to bring up a family and have meals where everybody argues about how everybody else is cramping their fulfilment. Where were they? My plan was for us to get in a taxi and ask the driver to take us to reality. It might not have worked. But I still sometimes wish we'd tried it.

What we did do was walk sometimes and go into other places. Las Vegas during the day: the heat outside will drive you into any place and every place will drive you into the heat outside; a desert within a desert, the human within the natural. Sometimes the town seemed to me merely an intensification of the emptiness of Nevada around it, the way the mirage of an oasis might make you thirstier. Caesar's Palace, for example. Into all of that mock grandeur you are fed inescapably on a conveyor belt while the fruity American voice of Caesar on the endlessly repetitive tape says, 'Welcome to my palace', and tells you about his slot machines. The historical disjunction is total and you realise this couldn't be anywhere. You feel embarrassed for Caesar, both Caesars. The American capacity for cultural kitsch is amazing. It is as if an art thief should break into the Louvre and steal the frame of the Mona Lisa.

Back in the room, I notice an increasing tendency in us to swap anecdotes and memories and maybe even the odd quotation from a loved writer. We are squeezing every drop of cultural sustenance we can from whatever is to hand to moisten our parched sensibilities. Back at the saltmines of the spirit, the toil of pleasure goes on, and on and on.

We are eventually airlifted out. The same group of Vancouverites are around us on the flight back. But this time the husband is sitting across the aisle from us and the woman is beside me. It doesn't take me long to regret the new arrangement. She asks me how I did at the gambling.

'I lost,' I say.

She isn't quite sure she has heard right. She asks me again, I repeat the shameful fact. She is embarrassed by me. I suspect it is the openness of my admission that has offended her. It carries no qualifying clauses with it about how I literally come within an ace of making it rich or how I'll beat Las Vegas next time. How can a man just sit there and admit he has been a failure? It's not what you do in her scheme of values. I lack class. I might as well have farted. I swear she visibly recoiled from me.

You've got to be more swept up, accentuate the positive. She does.

'*Well, we won.* All of us. Everybody won.'

Maybe you did, I think. But she reminds me of other returning holiday-makers I have known. I have been on holiday with people who would sit round a café-table on the last night abroad and synchronise their stories about how wonderful it had all been. They were like a committee preparing a press statement. The food hadn't really been so bad and that waiter had been so funny and the jellyfish stings had been nothing, when you think of it. Given the commonness of our desire to have the admiration of others and to protect ourselves from their feelings of superiority, we'll often say anything except we bought a piece of shit. This woman could have been chairperson to one of those committees.

She named in particular the three men in their group, repeating after each name the same word. 'Won.' 'Won.' 'Won.' It was a word she liked. I think perhaps she was trying to tell me something about the inadequacy of my manhood. Losing at Las Vegas equals castrato. She seemed uncomfortable at finding herself having to sit beside me, presumably in case failure was contagious. When will North Americans realise, I reflected in my philosophical, old world way, that you learn nothing from success? Failure is the great teacher. Therefore, I should have learned vast amounts. She was looking at – or trying to avoid looking at (beware the evil eye of destitution) – someone who had graduated *summa cum laude* from the University of Las Vegas, Faculty of Blackjack and One-armed Bandits.

We spoke stiltedly and intermittently until the chicken came. I thought I recognised it. Excuse me, didn't we meet on the flight down? I had a vision of this chicken as being legendary in the folklore of fowl, their version of the Flying Dutchman, doomed to fly forever from Vancouver to Las Vegas, from Las Vegas to Vancouver, trapped in its immortal inedibility. I looked again along the row I was sitting in – six people hesitantly miming a meal: a group exercise in the Chartered Flight School of Method Acting. I was relieved to see that my neighbour, votary of the bitch-goddess Success, was being miserably incompetent in finding a way into her chicken. But she managed to turn her failure into mine.

'You should be enjoyin' this,' she said. 'You're a loser.'

I discontinued the conversation for fear of brain-damage. I concentrated instead on recapitulating what it was I had learned.

Las Vegas, I had to admit it, is a triumph. People fly in there in countless numbers and then fly out again, telling everybody how wonderful it has been. As the woman on the plane might have said, you can't knock success. But you can wonder about the terms of that success and what it means about the way we live. I do.

For what has happened here? A group of gangsters got together and fabricated a city in the desert as a factory for making money. It would not have to grow. It would just be there. It would have no natural roots in human development. It would be life reinvented through the mechanical womb of finance. It would be a monument to sterility, since it produces nothing but money.

Ah, but you're wrong. Surely it does produce something: pleasure. Not really, since the pleasure does not merely exist as an experience, but must convert instantly into money, money lost or money gained. Whichever way you play it, Las Vegas wins, for its purpose is to turn everything into the pursuit of money. It is Capitalism triumphant. Here the workers will pay for the privilege of making your money. Harness their greed and it will serve your greed. Here labour is offered to the labourers as leisure, a pastime they have chosen.

It is a brilliant concept. Its efficacy troubles me, because I think it can lead to the perception of our lives as an exclusively economic phenomenon. That is an assumption that seems to be becoming more and more pervasive these days. When I eventually returned to Scotland from Vancouver (in August 1987), after about a year abroad, I wondered how far from Las Vegas I had travelled.

It wasn't that the people of Scotland had altered. But I noticed, with the perspective of prolonged absence, how much the terms of their lives were being changed. After all, they had by that time served eight years without remission for a crime they hadn't committed – the voting in of alien values they didn't believe in. Aspects of their society that should have had nothing to do with material values (like health and university education) were being determined by purely financial considerations. Scotland was becoming a plutocracy.

Las Vegas comes back to me from time to time, like a bad dream, some version of which we may all be living in one day, if the present Gadarene rush into materialism isn't diverted. It is the right-wing policies of our time apotheosised in a town. Monetarist governments should go there to do fieldwork in how it's done: offer the hallucination of wealth for all and get back the reality of money for a few. In return for the illusion of money you almost certainly will never have, it takes some of the money that you do have, as well as time and energy. It offers you pointlessness as fun – that is a seductive offer in times that are short of moral purpose. Turn your aimlessness into a pastime.

And it works. It works so well that I can imagine many of those who enjoy the place dismissing my sense of it as an over-reaction that misses the point. They would see my bad dream of it as originating in my dyspepsia with the times. And maybe they would be right. Las Vegas is about gambling, and gambling can be enjoyable. End of story. Nobody forced you to go there. Nobody held a gun to your head. But there are subtle modes of coercion, subtle modes of violence.

For me, trying to programme people into developing the basest aspects of their nature is an act of violence against them. On these terms, it seems to me, the city could be seen as a 24-hour-a-day larceny done on the human spirit. I don't think its smiling face should fool you. Someone who smiles doesn't always mean you well. I don't think you should be misled by its ersatz exoticism. Las Vegas is by Disneyland out of the Mafia – a jacket of fantasy with the bulge of a real gun in it.

Smoke Signals

TAXI DRIVERS ARE THE SOCIAL PARAMEDICS OF OUR TIME. No wonder their vehicles are called black ambulances in Glasgow. They drive around cities, giving succour to anyone who can afford the fare (and sometimes to those who can't, as several drivers have told me). Their cabs are always septic with the bacteria of other people's minds. They are among the first to catch the changes on the streets, the way people are wearing their lives these days.

This one would be in his 50s. I get in the cab and give him my destination. I'm going to have a meal with friends. He seems a mildly disgruntled man, but not in an obtrusive way. It is as if he is having some kind of argument with himself.

It isn't a long trip but, as often happens when I sit in a car or just about anywhere else for that matter, I feel a desire for a cigarette. But these are guilt-making times for nicotine addicts and some taxi drivers these days seem to see their cabs as small mobile extensions built on to their homes. They tend to regard you less as a customer than a guest they just happen to be charging. And he looks oppressed enough by unwanted experience already.

'D'ye mind if Ah smoke?' I ask.

His response is surprisingly vehement.

'Mind if ye smoke? You wire in. Ye're more than welcome.'

He takes out his own cigarettes and we both light up and our cigarette smoke mingles like the incense of a persecuted sect. We compare notes on these times that are so intolerant of human weakness, and he tells me a story he has obviously been needing to tell someone.

It seems his son and daughter-in-law were up from England staying for a week or two. Getting up late one morning, the driver noticed that his wife was looking worried and that there was 'an atmosphere in the house'.

'What's everybody so happy about around here?' the driver asked.

The son said that he had been explaining something to his mother, something which he and his wife had been discussing before they came up.

'It's something I want to talk to you about, dad. See when you and mum come down to us that fortnight in the summer?'

90

'Aye, Ah'm lookin' forward to that.'

'Well, Ah cannae have you smoking in my house. It'll be damaging my wife's health and my health.'

The driver asks me what I make of that. Skilled in the pitfalls of contemporary ethics, I prevaricate, like a shady lawyer trying to determine the strength of a case. Do his son and daughter-in-law, I wonder, have any children?

'No weans.'

I'm still hesitant to play Solomon in a stranger's family life. What, I flannel, was the driver's reaction?

'No problem,' the driver says. 'Ah told him his health would be fine and his wife's health would be fine. Because Ah wouldn't bloody well be there.'

The son and daughter-in-law have departed with no concessions made. The family is now divided. Every day since then the driver's wife, who shares his sense of outrage, has had 'a wee greet to herself'. The driver talks about how much of their lives they have devoted to their only child, the number of times they bailed him out when he was in trouble, the time six of his friends, after a stag night, stayed over at their house without an objection being raised.

'That's different,' his son had said.

When the cab has reached my destination, the driver talks on, takes fare and tip and talks on. He has a bitter bafflement he needs to unravel a little farther. He seems to feel himself besieged by strangeness and is mentally digging himself in, reinforcing his own principles.

At the dinner party I relate the driver's story as a kind of Gallup poll of contemporary attitudes. There is some sympathy with the driver but no agreement. In a room bristling with good health I am left alone to champion, through the coughs, my unhealthy taxi driver.

It may to some extent be a generational thing, of course. I am nearer in age to the driver than I am to anyone else present. Everybody else in the room is quite a bit younger than I am. (They usually are these days. Where are all these young people coming from, anyway? They didn't use to be there.) But it cannot be just that. If we aren't more than our conditioning, we may as well just take root and grow like flowers.

I see it as minor clash of moral values. The new idealism versus the old. The son realises that smoking damages your health, even secondary smoking, and therefore no one is allowed to smoke in his house. The father believes that there is an implicit contract between people, a contract of mutual accommodation. For one, entering his house is accepting his terms. For the other, entering his house is to share his terms, as he will share yours. One is a logical declaration of independence; one is an emotional insistence on inter-dependence. One deconstructs behaviour according to present knowledge; one constructs it according to past experience.

I can see the sense of what the son is saying. Why, then, do I agree with the father? It isn't because I think I can justify smoking. I have no defence to make of my own silliness in consuming so many cigarettes, except perhaps to say that I have always felt the point of life is to find out how to live as fully as possible, not how to avoid dying, a quest that seems in the end to be fairly futile.

I think I agree with the father simply because I find what the son achieves by his gesture disproportionate to what he loses. On the basis of very indefinite medical evidence on secondary smoking, the son has been prepared to take up a position that has altered dramatically the relationships of his personal life and those of his mother and father. In search of the hypothetical, he has damaged the real. In search of an unverifiable physical health, he has been cavalier with his emotional health and that of others – 'damaging my wife's health and my health'. What about the toxin of indifference he has introduced into two of the crucial relationships of his life? What about the reek of self-absorption he is blowing in his parents' faces? There is a point at which even the pursuit of health can become unhealthy.

It could, of course, be argued reasonably that all the father has to do is stop smoking, which would be to his own good, or at least stop smoking in his son's house. What's so bad about that? But I can understand the father's recalcitrance.

He wouldn't be entering a stranger's house. He refuses to pass a test in order to visit his son. He is asking to come in as himself, warts and all, even if there is an unconfirmed suspicion that the warts might be contagious. He wants tolerance from his son, as he has shown it to him.

In that intolerance, it seems to me, lies the difference between the new idealism and the old. The new idealism is intolerant and self-righteous; the old is tolerant and self-questioning. One is narrow and prescriptive; the other is broad and accommodating. The pursuit of health to the point of hypochondria is one of the most revealing aspects of the new idealism. In the narrowness of that pursuit so much else is relegated to insignificance. It is the personal equivalent of the conservatism that reduces social health to economics.

The yuppies of the body reduce life to personal economics. If it's not definitely contributing to your personal welfare, it's no good. If it's not materially productive, abandon it. What's good for you is the good.

The age of the socially deformed Adonis is upon us.

Beyond the Pint of No Return

IT'S JUST AFTER 11.30 ON A DULL WEEKDAY MORNING. MICK Murphy, alias Beef, alias several other people he claims to be, stands at the bar contemplating the remaining two-thirds of his pint of McEwan's. Already pushing 70, Mick has good reason to regret the way age arranges its remorseless ambushes. His gammy leg is giving him severe trouble and he's due in Kilmarnock Infirmary at noon. The possibility of amputation makes it seem like High Noon. What remains for a man in the bleakness of such moments? Mick finds it. He glances at the clock and says to the manager, 'Joe, keep yer eye on that pint. Ah'm goin' up tae get ma leg aff.'

Mick hobbles out under a private rainbow of style that makes Gary Cooper look like a wee boy. The day has brightened.

Mick has since died a two-legged death, but the extravagance of his spirit survives to haunt the pub where he used to hang the other customers over a cliff-edge of fantasy and leave them passing laughter like a rope in case they fell. He was Baron Munchausen in a bunnet. He had been the author of the Bond books but passed them on to Ian Fleming. He was the designer of the *Queen Mary* but some idiot changed the plans. He was one of the men responsible for cutting down the trees in the Sahara and making it a desert. He regretted the last accomplishment but it had been during the war and it was cold.

Mick's artistry was his own, but, to flourish, it depended on the pub he went to, an insignificant place in a side street in Kilmarnock, a remnant of an old tradition in a changing world. It's the resort of people with the true grain of character still showing through them in a time of plastic personalities.

It doesn't look much. It has been by-passed by the recent juggernaut of bad taste that has hit so many pubs and moved on, to call the resultant dire accidents renovation. There are no mosaics of bullfighters, no archaic murals with the paint still wet. There is a narrow bar, hardly big enough to stagger in, a gantry as unelaborate as a water-hole. The most significant furnishings are people.

Since they are real people, you must wait for them to happen. They're not performers. You don't go in and expect to be entertained. A stranger might go in several times and just be bored. But if you are patient and apply a few judicious tinctures through the mouth to clear the eyes, you may be present at one of those Open Sesame moments that show the riches often buried in the banal.

Late Saturday afternoon, for example, you may see the man who talks to the water-bottle. If you are in the bar, position yourself slightly to the right of the doorway through to the lounge. And wait. He should appear at the bar in the lounge, perhaps just after four, perhaps later. He's a man full of urgent messages, most of them incomprehensible. Apart from his weekly sessions with the water-bottle, like a convention of tick-tack men, he's fine. In fact, even during these sessions he's fine.

Or you may catch Danny making a telephone call. At such times conversation becomes difficult. Danny, a nice man from the Aran Islands, uses the phone as if it were God's hearing-aid. He's the only man who could make a transatlantic call without a telephone.

Or you might meet Jimmy, beyond the pint of no return, when his Belfast accent has regressed, or perhaps progressed, to its original intensity. Or you might find yourself, late in the evening, sandwiched between Jimmy and Danny, enjoying happy incomprehensibility in stereo. Or you might experience, like me, a strange hour within which an electrician tells you he hopes to write the life of Cervantes and a brickie quotes from the updated Scottish version of *Candide* that he is writing.

The effect of such small perceptions should be to remove the cataracts of presumption from your eyes and let you see where you really are, in a room where examples of the benign eccentricity of many people have gathered over the years into an unofficial history of ordinary lives. That history has its small moments and its larger ones.

There was, for example, the time a large and burly stranger arrived to stand at the bar. Having dipped briefly into his pint, he turned to the man nearest to him and said, 'I had terrible trouble with that Ann Boleyn.' As he clarified the nature of the trouble, the other people in the pub slowly began to realise who he was, a reincarnation of Henry VIII from Cumnock. He came back a few times after that and his performances are still talked about. There are even heretical customers who claim he was better than Beef Murphy.

Nonsense, of course. But then the reputation of any great artist is likely to suffer a decline in the years immediately after his death. Do they forget Beef's endless inventiveness, his somersaulting speed of mind? What about the time he was alone in the pub with Mabel and the violent man? What about the Australian pitch-and-toss school? The time he was torpedoed? The time of the paper shortage? The time . . .

94

Anyway, Mabel behind the bar agrees with me. I'm glad Mabel agrees with me because, although she is a woman of great warmth and kindness, she is also the woman who, when two customers were threatening to get nasty with each other, offered to step outside and fight them both.

I could go on but if you don't get the picture by now, you never will, at least not from me. The picture is that this is how a pub can sometimes be, not a plastic factory for liquefying money but a place where people can prospect casual conversation for mutual nuggets of unexpected gold, explore small dreams, admit who they are or pretend to be who they're not and know it won't be used against them.

So how do you get there? I've been deliberately withholding because I don't want tourist buses turning up and buying postcards of the gantry. But, not being greedy, I don't mind giving some directions. You get off from pomposity at the very first stop.

You'd better hurry. They've installed a 'Space Invaders'. If you make it in time, let me give you one small house rule. Don't be cheeky to Mabel.

Darkness on the Edge of Town

THERE IS AN OLD GAME BEING RESURRECTED ON THE streets these days. It is called 'moshie'.

To play, all you need are some tenpence pieces and a small hole gouged in the pavement. The obvious place to gouge the hole is where four flagstones meet. By chipping away the corners carefully, you can make a fairly neat circle just big enough to admit a tenpence coin. The players stand on a mark and go for the hole in the ground. There are subtleties involved, such as striking the coins of other players but, since I'm not writing a rule-book, I'll leave it there.

It isn't hard to see that moshie has an ancestor – pitch-and-toss. The family resemblances are obvious. Both are games devised for hard days, when time is long and money short. Both games require for the playing of them only an open space and some loose change. Both games result in money gained by some at the expense of others.

But there are, between father and son, instructive differences which may help to some extent to illustrate the gap in social conditioning between our time and, say, the 1930s.

Pitch-and-toss happened in a place apart. It might be behind a pit-bing. (Miners were usually great gamblers. Presumably it came with the territory – the job itself was a big enough gamble.) It might be in a prearranged field or other open space at the edge of town or village. It might even be in a secluded part of a public park, with the cop-watch suitably positioned. Moshie happens on the pavement – preferably in a quiet part of a housing scheme (in front of boarded-up shops, for example).

Pitch-and-toss schools often involved the presence of very large numbers of men, as many as might have attended a not very important junior football match. In the Ayrshire of my youth, stories used to circulate of legendary pitch-and-toss schools, where the attendance figures varied elastically in the telling, perhaps according to the veracity or inebriation of the reporters. I have myself seen the traditional hard-case, wielding the big buckled belt which he swung with muscular panache around his head so that he could keep intact the charmed circle within which the penny-tossers, with an almost mystical concentration, sought the magical 'head-two'. Men of all ages attended. Moshie commonly involves a handful of people. They are likely to be more boys than men. No intimidating mob controller is required. Usually, they'd be hard pushed to constitute a crowd in a phone-box.

Pitch-and-toss could mean real winnings. The two pennies at the centre of it all were just the cipher for the side-bets. If those two coins were made to marry happily in mid-air, they could multiply into serious amounts of money. Moshie offers inevitably much more modest returns. The money directly involved in the game is the money you win.

Pitch-and-toss was sudden death. Once the pitch had been made and the penny nearest the centre of the cross drawn in the clay had been decided, it was all down to the toss of the coins. A new game would begin. A single game of moshie will take longer.

The scattered descendants of those crowds at the pitch-and-toss live in a significantly different community. It is a less cohesive one. They do not congregate in a specially chosen place. They make such a place of somewhere they happen to be. Moshie players are just a few casual friends. They have no hope of seriously improving their finances, because there isn't enough money among them to make that happen. It is good for the game to last as long as possible, since it is essentially just a way of trying to pass the time without the sense of involvement with others atrophying completely, through loneliness and boredom.

I first found out about moshie when I was presenting and narrating a television programme with Peter Legge of BBC Scotland. The programme is not about moshie, but there are some incidental images of young men playing the game in Easterhouse in Glasgow. Those images haunt me more, I think, than anything else we have put in the programme. They articulate visually the background against which the three interviewees are speaking.

The interviewees are themselves articulate enough, in their different ways. The idea was to let people who are unemployed speak of their circumstances, to give a platform to voices not often heard. The commentary was meant to put their various senses of themselves in a wider social context, to let them be seen in a coherent framework.

The making of the programme affected me more than any other I have done. Television is always invasive. Van-loads of technicians and equipment arrive at someone's house. Lights are set up all over the living-room. Furniture is shifted. A mirror that is causing a glare in the camera is taken down and replaced with a picture removed from another part of the house. A sound man, a lighting man, a camera man, maybe an assistant camera man, a production assistant, the director and the interviewer all surround the victim. And now, the manual might say, let's have a natural conversation.

The invasion seems all the more brutal when the conversation is about the personal life of the interviewee. One, George, was an ex-miner from Danderhall, a thoughtful man who had accepted redundancy. One was Lynda, a single parent with two children living in Glasgow (in Castlemilk), a woman of great strength of purpose. The third was Danny, a boy of 17 from Drumchapel in Glasgow, who shared a house with his girlfriend and their baby.

With all three participants I felt that guilt of maybe having burgled their privacy, of having taken from them something which they didn't know they had given. But I felt it most powerfully in relation to the boy from Drumchapel. George and Lynda had such a strong sense of themselves that I felt any unintentional damage we might do there would be minimal. Coming away from Danny's house, I was worried. He was so young, with the slightly desperate gallousness of the trapped, and he had an obvious tendency to arrange his life with all the forethought of a road accident. He didn't need anyone adding to his problems.

But these misgivings were to turn back on themselves a little later on. Since the programme was to be networked, it had to be submitted to London. Objections were raised. I'm still not sure where the objections came from. As a boy at school, I used to imagine a small man in an anonymous room somewhere, making up all the pointless dirty jokes that were going around. Maybe there are similar rooms for other purposes.

Certainly, the objection seemed like a joke to me. 'Balance', it seems, was what the programme lacked – this in a country where many of the newspapers might as well have been printed in Downing Street. The programme had been offered to me as a personal essay, and my first reaction was simply to withdraw, which would have meant no programme or at least the need to make an entirely new one.

Then I thought of how the past ten years of government had been carefully built of things not said, whether about the *Belgrano* or Anthony Blunt or the Health Service. I thought of a Secretary of State for Health who cavalierly answered the objections of dedicated doctors by telling them they were lying. Any speech against that state of affairs was better than none.

Then I thought of the three people I had spoken to. They had given of their time to try to say things that they meant. They deserved to be heard. The programme wasn't about me. It was about them.

Then I thought of the players of moshie, those young men burying their talents in the pavement – not much hope of significant growth from that place. They represented for me what the programme was finally about, the people left to measure their lives in the loose change that falls on the pavement while the entrepreneurs stuff their pockets with notes. It is their experience that is seldom heard, their lives that are usually ignored. It was worthwhile trying to point a pocket torch, however feeble, into the place where the media lights don't reach often enough, the darkness on the edge of town which may eventually engulf us all.

It is one of the happier attributes of censorship that it can only skim-read. Engrossed as it is in the letter, it misses the spirit. Peter Legge and I got together and made a couple of minimal changes that in no way affected the dynamic of what was being said, and we were through.

In a society where the government is dedicated to ignoring the damage its policies inflict on ordinary lives, and where even the news is largely an establishment construct, I'd like to dedicate the programme – small and marginal as it is – to the silent moshie players.

Another Six Whiskies, Please, Barman

EARLIER THIS YEAR, WHILE DOING WHAT WE ARTISTIC people call 'a reading', I read out a story I have written called *Death of a Spinster*. It's a very short story. It describes the routine of a virginal woman in her 60s, the repetitive narrowness of her days.

The routine is breached when she is hit by a car. She dies. In the hospital, as they strip her for examination, they discover that she is wearing very sensuous green underwear. The last sentence says: 'They went on with what they had to do, unaware that they were witnessing the stubborn resplendence of unfulfilled dreams.'

During the question-time that followed the reading, a woman suggested that the story was sexist. These are tricky times in which to talk or write about relationships between men and women or even, as in this case, the lack of them. The ambushes are everywhere. Round the corner of the most casual remark, stern-eyed women lie in wait, wielding self-righteousness like a very roughly hewn club.

'Why didn't you write the story about a man?' the woman wondered – a little sardonically, I thought. My answer was to the effect that, technically, the story hinged on the discovery of the underwear she was wearing. It was constructed like a slow fuse, the ignition point of which was the green silk underwear. That point was meant to illumine retrospectively the whole story, transforming its apparent significance. Were we to dress a man in this underwear, I suggested, we would have a story with altogether different implications.

But to such questions there is a more general answer, which I didn't have time to go into. It is that the prescriptive approach to writing is a nonsense. I remember Arthur Miller being interviewed on television several years ago – by Kenneth Tynan, I think it was. Tynan took Miller to task for not having dealt with the experience of the America Negro in his plays. As an admirer of some of Tynan's writing, I found that a depressing moment.

Only critics or ideologues would apply such a criterion. Serious creativity originates in a complex of compulsions. Writing for me often feels like trying to stay on a bucking bronco and go somewhere specific at the same time. Where you arrive at, and the grace with which you got there, will admit of critical judgment, but not where you set out from.

All writing inevitably inhabits silences vaster than itself. And just as intelligence is partly assessable by the skill with which it relates to the areas of its own inevitable ignorance, so creativity is partly judgeable by the implied stances it takes towards its own areas of inevitable silence. This does not mean it will have to articulate those areas.

Anyway, my questioner was unconvinced. Another woman in the audience, sensing one of those male-female impasses where each is wondering if the other has just stepped out of a spaceship, decided to help us. She asked another question. Wouldn't it have solved the problem, she wanted to know, if I had made the spinster's dream of fulfilment relate not to sex but to something else altogether – say, writing?

I must admit I found this a strange way of helping. She seemed to me rather like a woman who reaches forward to pat your head, misjudges the gesture and breaks your nose with the heel of her hand. I said that I didn't find the inability to write as potent a symbol of unfulfilment as the total absence of sexual experience. The woman seemed doubtful and I went further. Given the choice to live my life with either the full experience of a sexual relationship or the writing of many books but not both together, I said I knew what my choice would have been. Who needs royalties that bad?

We left it there and moved on to matters less fraught – such as do you use a typewriter or write longhand? But a residual gloom stayed with me. I had written the story partly as a compliment to the woman, an admiration of an appetite for life she had sustained against all the odds. I would have felt the same admiration for a man who had continued to nourish his dream in a similar situation, which is something I have written about in poetry and prose (for example, in a poem called *Brannigan's Song to the Wall of his Room*). For I think it is the humanity of our dreams that defines us more justly than anything else, whether they take a personal or a public or a political form.

Yet my attempted compliment had been construed as an insult. That's where the gloom came from. These days women's attitudes to themselves cover such a wide spectrum that direct communication can be difficult. One woman's compliment is another woman's sexism. One effect on men can be to make them feel that, conversationally, they live in a multilingual culture, since the idiom of address that may be acceptable to one group will be taboo to another. I once wrote a jocular song about the stress this can cause called *Another six whiskies, please, barman – and one for my friend here as well.*

I think one of the problems is that, under the undeniably just banner of the women's movement, there have enlisted some strange, not to mention downright loopy, social attitudes. There are the big flags, of course, beneath which any sane person would be prepared to rally, bearing legends like 'Women are discriminated against in our society'. But fluttering in among them can be discerned the small, daft pennants that declare things like 'Who needs men?' and 'Women should live with women'. For a woman to choose another woman as a partner is an inalienable personal right. For her to seek to make of this preference a social law for everybody is a plea for a straitjacket – as it would be if a man did the same.

The problem is compounded by the fact that in the interests of solidarity a lot of women refuse to break ranks with any of their sisters. She may be slightly extreme in wishing to terminate the species, their stance implies, but at least she's one of us. What can a man know about the experience of being a woman? (This has always been to me a strange one, since I have always felt that whatever it means to be a man is inextricably bound up with whatever it means to be a woman – and I had therefore assumed that the converse would apply, no matter what sexual expression you choose to give to the interconnection.) To restrict debate in this way seems to me equivalent to replacing conversation with monologue.

When I was being interviewed for a television programme some months ago, the woman interviewer asked me some questions about the women's movement with specific reference to women writers. At one point in my reply I made the observation that I thought the Kate Millett of *Sexual Politics* was a fierce and honest intelligence, presenting a body of evidence which the reader could check for himself or herself and drawing conclusions about sexual injustice that were largely undeniable, but that, in my opinion, Rita Mae Brown might well be having trouble with the joined-up writing.

The comment was edited out of the final programme. There is nothing sinister in that. They had far too much material and that was as good a thing to go as any. But what I remember is the slightly chilly feeling on the set, which was dominated by women, when I spoke. I may be misreading their reaction, and, if so, I apologise. But I suspected that I had blundered into a sanctum where I was seen to have no place, bringing my reprehensibly masculine sensitivity to an area I couldn't hope to understand. If that was the case, I would resent that.

We need, as they say, to talk. And we need to talk in a way that replaces propaganda with thought. And we need to think with attempted mutual understanding.

Anyone who has been seriously involved in a sexual relationship will have learned, I would have thought, humility. That relationship is the hardest and arguably the most important game in town. It needs mutual trust, which is only gained with difficulty and sustained with charity. What it doesn't need is the large number of people around today prepared to pronounce on the forms that sexual relationships should take, with a dogmatism that ironically suggests they're still waiting to have a real one.

The Death of Hunter Hollywood

IT WAS EDDIE WHO SAID IT FIRST. 'HE HAS TO GO,' HE SAID. 'You know that.' Andy nodded. He knew that. But he didn't like the way Eddie had said it. Sometimes Eddie could be callous. Maybe it was what he was wearing. Clothes affected Eddie that way. If he ever went to a fancy-dress party as a woman, Andy was keeping out of his way.

Eddie was wearing his early Marlon Brando gear, like an extra from *The Wild One*: tee-shirt, leather jacket and jeans. Eddie liked Marlon Brando. He had stolen all his videos.

'He has to go,' Eddie said. 'You know why.'

They were sitting in the long, narrow lounge of the Akimbo Arms. It was like drinking in the carriage of a train. The fact that they weren't moving made it more like the carriage of a train these days.

The place was almost empty. It was the dead time of the afternoon. It was too early for the kind of clientele who drank here to be out. You didn't start too early. That way, you were left nursing one pint through the evening. The regulars would be waiting till later, having found other ways to pass the time, like watching repeats of wildlife programmes on the telly or counting the number of flowers on the wallpaper.

Eddie and Andy were pacing themselves carefully, wetting their lips occasionally from stale half-pints. The gloom of what they would have to do hung over them like a small raincloud.

'I've got used to Hunter,' Andy said.

'You think I haven't?'

'How long is that he's been with us?'

'I don't know. Maybe a year?'

'It's more than that,' Andy said.

'So it's more than that,' Eddie said. 'He still has to go.'

Andy took a sip of beer.

'Hunter Hollywood,' he said. 'It's a cracking name.'

'There are better names than that,' Eddie said.

'Maybe. But what a name!'

'You're a sentimentalist,' Eddie said. 'You would let somebody live on past his usefulness just because of his name.'

104

Andy bridled slightly. There were times, he thought, when Eddie seemed to have no feelings.

'He's done us nothing but favours, anyway,' Andy said.

'I know that.'

'That's more than a year we've been having his housing benefit between us.'

'I know that.'

'And then there was the time we had his unemployment money too.'

'That didn't last too long.'

'Whose fault was that?'

'All right, all right.'

An old man had come in. He ordered a whisky and a half of beer in a quavering voice that made it sound like a last request. He took silver from a battered purse. He laid the money on the counter as if he collected old coins and these were rare ones. He stared a moment at the two glasses he was given in return, seeming to find it hard to believe that this was all the coins were worth.

'He's probably just in here to try to save the cost of heating his house,' Andy said.

'That's right,' Eddie said. 'The traditional form of Scottish central heating. Out of a bottle.'

The old man carried his drinks over to a table. He settled himself with difficulty. He took a ceremoniously delicate sip of the whisky and sat back gently, staring at the wall ahead of him thoughtfully, as if the liquid was a drug that regressed you.

'Proust with the madeleine,' Andy said.

'What?' Eddie said.

'When are you going to read more?' Andy said. 'Proust with the madeleine. When Proust bit into a cake once, it suddenly summoned up his past. Became a kind of return to childhood.'

'Oh yes,' Eddie said.

'Some man!' Andy said.

'Who? Proust or the old guy?'

'Hunter Hollywood.'

Eddie pursed his lips in annoyance and shook his head. But Andy was inside his own thoughts.

'Some man,' he said. 'Makes no noise, never complains. Eats less than a sparrow. Never asks for any money. I mean, he's selflessness on legs.'

'And he has to go.'

Andy nodded.

'He's become a menace to us now,' Eddie said. 'They come round to check out whether our place was worth the rise in rent, what do we do? I think they're suspicious already. Hunter has to have left by that time. I'm going to see him off.'

Andy looked up at him.

'Like now,' Eddie said.

Andy nodded.

Eddie got up and went out through the door that led to the toilets. He was gone a little while. When he came back in, he was smiling widely.

'That's it,' he said. 'I've just seen our best friend off to the coast. In little pieces.'

Andy started to smile too.

'That's everything?' he said.

'All documentation pertaining to Hunter Hollywood. Forms, National Insurance number, the lot. I tore them into little bits and flushed them away.'

Eddie sat down. They raised what was left of their half-pints in a mock toast.

'To the man who never was,' Andy said.

'Creativity's a hard business,' Eddie said. 'That which you have made out of nothingness you may have to return to nothingness. Sorry, Hunter. But this is a tough world.'

'We'll always remember you with affection.'

There wasn't much left of their beer.

'What now?' Andy said.

'It's obvious, isn't it?' Eddie said. 'Look, we're students trying to get a degree in a system that despises education. We're going to get that degree and try not to die of malnutrition in the process. Where the system stinks, subvert it.'

'You mean?'

Eddie nodded. Andy smiled.

'We invent someone else,' he said. 'And draw his money.'

'Well,' Eddie said, 'you're the one that's good at names.'

Andy was relishing the challenge. He felt playful.

'Donnie Largent,' he said.

It took Eddie a few moments to translate the name from French into 'give the money'.

'This is a serious business,' he said. 'We don't need schoolboy jokes.'

'Okay, okay. Something plain and elemental. John. John Adamson?'

'Never invent somebody,' Eddie said, 'who lives too near the front of the alphabet. That way, when they check things out, you're among the first to go under the microscope.'

They finally settled for Ronnie King. It had a credible ring to it, so that after a couple of minutes they felt they really knew him.

'At least we've given Hunter an heir,' Andy said.

'Let's get two more half-pints to toast the newborn,' Eddie said.

106

They went to the bar.

'And let's get the old man a whisky,' Andy said, 'to wet the baby's National Insurance number.'

And they did.

Well, it happened something like that. This has been a true story rendered fictive to protect the guilty – a fable of our times. But before you stoke up your comfortable indignation and set the sleuths of hypocritical rectitude on their trail – the DSS snoopers and the modern Means Test men – consider how fully they are a product of their society.

These, too, are modern exemplars of initiative and enterprise. These, too, are Thatcher's children – illegitimate, maybe. We may not know their fathers, but we sure as hell know who their mother is.

Lotus Land

'IS VANCOUVER BEAUTIFUL?' A COUPLE OF PEOPLE ASKED me during my first week in the place. They asked it the way a politician asks a question, knowing there's only one response. 'Is Vancouver beautiful?' Is Sophia Loren a woman?

I came into Kitsilano, not that I knew that's where I was coming into. I had been 12 hours on the plane, and I left my brains, if not in San Francisco, then somewhere over the North Atlantic. I had reached the point where standing in the queue for the lavatory was beginning to feel like an event. The attractive elderly woman beside me and myself had become dangerously confessional. She knew so much about my innermost secrets that I was wondering if the only way to guarantee discretion would be to marry her. When she got off at Calgary, my head was hazy enough to feel as though I had known her all my life. When I got off at Vancouver, the haze had become impenetrable fog. I wasn't sure I had known me all my life.

I wandered through Immigration, having managed to perform a reasonable imitation of who I was. Out on the concourse, I saw a man standing with a piece of paper on which was written: 'McIlvanney'. Some deep tribal memory stirred within me and I stumbled towards him, lugging the cases. He was a professor from Simon Fraser University. If you're going to get a chauffeur, get a good one. He drove me through the light-spangled darkness to the house of a friend of his, where I was made welcome and shown a bed that looked like the Promised Land, and sleep fell gently on me like manna.

Next morning, I saw Vancouver for the first time. I had wakened in a house in Balaclava Street. If you go north from there across West 4th and Point Grey Road, and are as keen to reach the ocean as a lemming, you will eventually find a flight of stone steps leading down to the water's edge. If you're as lucky as I was, you will look towards English Bay and see Vancouver floating gently on a compound of mist and water and you will have the company of a sweet-faced, contemplative Indian.

He was sitting on a rock. He wore trainers and denims and the check jacket that so many Canadians seem to share, like a national anthem, and a baseball cap. He was smoking and he was drinking from a brown paper bag. Strange customs here, I thought. They sell bags of alcohol?

Vancouver looked like somebody's dream of a city. That looked like stone all right, glinting in the hazy sunlight. But it almost seemed to waver in the mist and you had to wonder what the foundations were. Maybe it was the vastness of the setting Vancouver inhabits that made it seem somehow insubstantial, as if it wasn't sure who it was or how long it would last before the natural scenery it clung to overwhelmed it.

The Indian and I talked a little, quietly, the way people will in a place that makes words seem as significant as mayflies. He didn't contradict my reactions, which were just fancy ways of expressing 'ooh' and 'aah'. But he didn't particularly agree with them either. He nodded and offered me a few polite monosyllables and consulted his paper bag occasionally. He studied me with eyes that might have been saying his people knew this place before the contractors landscaped it. He gave me the impression that he knew something that was older than the hundred years Vancouver had been around.

'Don't trust your first impressions,' people say, but I do. We may build on them, overlay them, modify them, but we should never quite dismiss them. From here on, an integral part of my sense of Vancouver will be that dream city being patiently watched by the waiting Indian.

I lived in Vancouver nearly a year. It was a good time, give or take the odd visit from the moody glooms. I enjoyed working with the students I had at Simon Fraser. I had a nice ground-floor apartment on Chilco, near English Bay, until I did a two-month reading tour across Canada. When I came back, I rented on Comox until I could return to the apartment on Chilco.

I was lucky. Really to enjoy travelling and living in foreign places, you have to be a lucky traveller. So far, I have been. In Vancouver, I came to know a lot of people I liked, both at the university and socially. Most importantly, I was able to have a kind of surrogate family life that mitigated my loneliness.

Jim Lawton, a British sports journalist working with the *Vancouver Sun*, was friendly with my brother, Hughie. Jim and Linda Lawton had me at their house maybe a couple of days every week. Their three daughters were good company. Jim would hire some videos and we would all eat and watch and talk. Linda made Gaelic coffees that were very Gaelic – 'ludicrous coffees', we came to call them. Those were good times.

When Jim and Linda returned to England, Ron and Marna Paton took over, as if it were sentry duty. They were originally from Ayrshire and Ron made contact with me the week Jim and Linda left. I became a frequent house-guest, got to know their family and enjoyed some wonderful hospitality.

Come to think of it, Vancouver was so beautiful and so friendly, where was the problem? For there was one, at least for me. I couldn't locate it at first. Then one day I had a phone-call from a man I had never met. He was to lead me towards a clarification of what was troubling me.

For someone like me who comes from Kilmarnock, his name was a good omen: Johnny Walker. He was a Scottish psychologist who worked with the police, helping them cope with the stresses of the job. He had used two of my books in his work – *Laidlaw* and *The Papers of Tony Veitch*. I think he found my number from the university. He offered to buy me a drink.

It was pleasant to meet him and have one of those long, combative Scottish conversations. Scartin' and nippin' is Scots folk's wooin'. At the end of the evening he told me he could arrange for me to spend a night with two policemen whose patch was in and around Granville Street in downtown Vancouver. The drink said yes.

That night on Granville began with a visit to police headquarters where I signed a form indemnifying the Vancouver Police Department should anything unsavoury happen to me while I was with their men. I then met my guides to Vancouver's underside.

Dave was originally from Yorkshire, big and powerful and with quietly troubled eyes in which you could see the questions surface and sink, surface and sink. Dan looked as if he hadn't been born in Alberta, but hewn there. Even his hair looked strong. It was the black, curly type you suspect might have muscles. He did a lot of weight training, I was told, rather like Atlas taking anabolic steroids. Dan's eyes didn't go in for questions. He had a gaze like a security beam. It only broke for trouble. Dave told me on the quiet that anyone who tangled with Dan was being foolish. He had never seen him lose a fight. Dave had to tell me that the way you have to tell a watch the time.

We went in the unmarked car to the Granville Street district. I don't think Dan fell in love with me at first sight. He addressed a significant silence to me, occasionally flicking me with his eyes in the mirror as he drove. I decided not to challenge him about it. After all, I could understand his point of view. Who needs tourists on the job? Also, I didn't want him to knock me out with his hair.

The first thing, apparently, is to park the car discreetly and wait in a service doorway in a side-street. I have no idea what we are waiting for, but obviously Dave and Dan know. They are peering out, looking up and down the street, like urban woodsmen reading mysterious signs that mean nothing to me. Suddenly, we're all walking briskly. Even more suddenly, we've unlocked a door and I am bundled inside with them. We take an elevator and come out on to a polished wooden floor, gleaming eerily in the light that comes through the venetian blinds.

110

We are in a dance studio, mistily mirrored. One side of it looks down on Granville Street, opposite McDonald's. McDonald's is said to be one of the two main centres of drugs on Granville Street. The other is a café called Jo-Jo's. Jo-Jo's is later on our schedule. Dave has binoculars with him. He and Dan are studying the street in front of McDonald's. I am allowed to watch too but, since I am wearing a red jacket as subtle as a bonfire, I must stand back from the windows in case I am seen.

What is going on out there is about as clear to me as sheet-music. I need someone to hum the tune. Dave obliges. The seedy-looking white man in denim, the one who gives the impression of having been born with a two-day growth, is a drug-dealer. So is the long thin black man in the leather cap. Dave dislikes them both, but he dislikes the black man more. It's not a racist decision. Even at first sight, from this distance, I dislike the black man, too. He looks as if he's trying to win an unpopularity contest. He seems to be attending a private disco, making love to himself as he dances on the spot, clicking his fingers and staring provocatively at passers-by. Whenever anyone comes up to speak to him, he looks down on them as if he were the Sheraton Landmark.

He is, Dave tells me, a homosexual who befriends some of the young boys and girls who tend to gravitate to Vancouver, hooks them on drugs and then puts them on the street to pay for their habit. But he doesn't seem to be doing anything at the moment except advertise how wonderful he is. The man in denim is more active. He is definitely pushing hash, Dave and Dan decide.

Dan leaves to go down to the street. The idea is that he will make his way unobserved into one of the side-streets behind Granville. Dave will keep watch from here. They will be in touch through walkie-talkies. When Dave sees a sale being made, he will identify the purchaser and intercept him, take the drugs as evidence, get from him details and the promise that he will testify in court. Then Dave will arrest the pusher.

That's how it happens, in spite of less than full co-operation from Marconi. The walkie-talkies sound like people trying to make contact from separate planets. But Dan somehow absorbs an accurate description of the buyer, has to run and stop him as he's getting into a car. He is a student due to graduate from Simon Fraser University. He wants no trouble. He will co-operate.

Dave can make his move. The pusher has gone into McDonald's. I wait outside, staring in the windows like a visitor to the aquarium. The arrest is accomplished with minimum fuss. In the alley behind McDonald's where we wait to be joined by Dan and the paddy wagon that has been summoned, I am surprised at how young the pusher is, almost certainly not out of his teens. He has the slightly staring look sometimes seen on the face of the arrested, perhaps trying to see beyond what is happening through to what it's going to mean for him. He has no more drugs on him, only the money from his sales and not very much of that.

When he has been taken away, Dave and I resume our vigil, with Dan on the streets, but no more arrests are made. If a gun goes off, it can take the birds some time to resettle.

After a while, we move out on to the street to check a few places. I have turned my reversible jacket until it shows a less conspicuous dark blue. As if responding to the quieter colour, Dan seems to have accepted me by this time. He is a pleasant man though destined, I imagine, never to be effusive. He and Dave interpret the passing scene for me but even their formidable knowledge can't do much to lessen the weirdness of the experience, the sense of having stumbled into a series of undiscovered sketches by Goya in a bad mood.

We walk around for some hours. My reception system is overwhelmed. Painful experience affects me that way. I become like a computer on overload. Input goes automatic and, in order to have any clear awareness of what I have experienced, I have to wait for feed-back to unfreeze, abide memory's haphazard print-out of what has happened.

From that time I remember mainly a maelstrom of bleak prostitutes and down-and-outs with faces as dead as the moon and mean-featured men whose eyes come at you like switchblades. Human wastage is so easy to find. It hides in such plain sight that we learn not to notice it. It is the ubiquitous vagrant we refuse to give a home among us. That night I learn two of its addresses that are etched on my mind beyond forgetting.

One is Jo-Jo's. To call Jo-Jo's a café is like calling hell a holiday resort. Such Gorgon faces could turn your charity to stone. They seem to live in a contempt for any attempt to reach them. They have the bleak pride of the damned. They loll at grubby tables and sneer at us as we come in. They do not care why we are there or what we intend to do. They let their eyes erase us, each locked in a dark dream of the self we cannot enter. In the filthy toilet, Dave and Dan show me the machinery of their vision: scattered and scabrous needles, burnt pieces of tin, syringes flecked with poisonous-looking blood. It seems to me that any vision which creates such obscene detritus in its wake can't be worth having.

Then there is the Regal Hotel, a sad misnomer. You enter by a glass door from the street, climb a straight, narrow staircase to another glass door. Both doors are controlled by the man in the cubby-hole at the top. He is thin, ageing, grey-faced. He looks as if the world has done just about all it can to him. He has a smile he uses like a flag of truce.

We start to climb a warren of stairs and walk tight corridors where the smells seem as solid as furniture. Dan has a set of keys and he is opening doors, after knocking, as we go. He is checking to see that no one in any of the rooms is in trouble – say, from an overdose.

Some of the doors are badly buckled. This may be partly from the warping of age and neglect. It is also in some cases from a popular local pastime. Prostitutes use the hotel a lot as a place to bring their tricks. Then the idyll is suddenly disrupted by the prearranged arrival of a pimp who kicks the door in and robs the client of more than his ecstasy.

That hotel: catacombs for the living. Here people lie in the stinking cerements of futility, enduring a banal horror, staring daily into the emptiness of their lives. Who needs Dante? Each room here is a little bolgia of its own where the modern sins of social aberration and ill-health and loneliness and financial incompetence are endlessly atoned for. The atonement *is* endless. When a room is emptied by death or disappearance, it will be filled by another whose features will be different but whose hopelessness of spirit will be the same.

Most people here are on Welfare. It gives them enough to pay the rent and not much else. They are nailed to this place, trapped in an unending repetition of the same day. Aged lumberjacks who thought the good money would never stop, travellers who lost the map of whatever treasure they were seeking, they sit brooding towards death like migrant birds which have lost the power of flight.

Their rooms are places you would rather not see. The eyes wound themselves in looking. The surfaces are painful enough: the mouldering mound of unwashed socks on a table; the discarded, discolouring cans that lie about a room; the old book on a floor that looks as if the pages have fused together; the accumulated dirt. But it is the undertow of implication these bring with them that drags the heart down so deep you feel it must drown – the utter and seemingly irreclaimable waste of human potential.

In one room, a man lying on an unmade bed opens his eyes to look at us when we come in. He has not responded to Dan's knock. Now, asked if he is all right, he nods. The movement is as small as the trembling of a leaf. His eyes watch as we go out.

In another room, a thin, bald man, who may be in his 30s, is outraged by our presence. He is screeching like a parrot, one that is well versed in swearing. I am the object of his special contempt. He seems to know me from somewhere or perhaps he just knows that I don't belong here. After Dan has closed the door again, the man's hysteria continues eerily, conversing with itself in the shabby smallness of his room.

As Dan knocks at another door, I recognise the unmistakable tones of a countryman. 'Aye, what is it?' As we enter, he is sitting up in bed and swinging his feet on to the floor. Except for the bare feet, he is fully dressed. He looks in his late 50s, heavily-built and tousle-haired. He recognises Dave and Dan. 'Hello, boays. How's it gaun?' Dave asks him if he has been eating. 'Aye. Ah had a plate o' soup earlier the day.' As we go out, he says, 'Cheers,' and we leave him sitting, one hand clasping the

113

back of the other staring at the floor. He retains an impressive composure among chaos.

To wander through that place is to endure a mild and temporary stroke of the spirit. You move with difficulty. Your speech is paralysed. Later, at the end of it all, we sit in the Château Granville Hotel and have coffee, which Dan pays for. Dan takes a note of some of the titles of my books. I don't feel especially enthusiastic about Dan reading them. I fancy he could be a hard critic and, anyway, the continuing impact of what I have seen makes my books seem not especially relevant at the moment.

We go back to the car and Dave takes the wheel this time. We drop Dan off at the station and Dave drives me out to my flat on Chilco. We say goodnight and agree that the three of us will meet for a drink sometime. The West End seems a long way from Downtown.

I think about Vancouver. Vancouverites are understandably proud of their city. It has one of the most spectacular natural settings in the world. Architecturally, I find it exciting. It's where a lot of Canadians come when they've made it or when they want to live as if they've made it. The city and the superb West Coast around it are referred to by other Canadians as Lotus Land.

They have English Bay and the Stanley Park area and Kitsilano and Horseshoe Bay and one-bedroom apartments that cost a lot to rent and many people with impressive fortunes. They also have Granville Street and Hastings and Georgia and Indians on Welfare and people who spend their days systematically sifting the garbage skips.

Sitting in my rented flat as dawn approaches, I am aware of myself as an intruding alien. I try not to make too much of what I have just seen. Granville isn't the only place in Vancouver I have been. But I cannot shake the feeling that I have located what has been troubling me in living here. It has something to do with the relationship of Chilco to Granville. Wealth is always comparative. You don't have someone being rich without someone else being poor. I have seen the social mulch that underlies the lotus.

So what is the problem? All cities have their bad places. That is true. But there is something here with which I never could live comfortably. It isn't restricted to Vancouver. It may apply to all of North America. I enjoy being here. In Canada and America I know good places and good people. But I do not think I could ever be at home there. Why is that? It is perhaps that I am irretrievably European.

So how is Europe different? It has no Granville Streets? Of course, it does, and many. I imagine you could see Granville Street in any European city, certainly in any I've been in. But it seems to me there is a difference. What troubles me here is not that there is Granville Street and there is Chilco Street, but that there is no serious relationship between them. The lives experienced in these two places are not speaking to each other. They are separate monologues. The constant, deep dialogue that is community is lost.

I'm wondering why. I think that maybe those who cashed out of the ancient, social wrangle that was Europe were really saying, 'Separate dreams, please.' But the dream is shared or it's not worth having. I think in Europe the dream, however inadequately, however sometimes hypocritically, is still shared. I'm not sure how long that can last, for the Americanisation of Europe is far advanced and advancing farther.

But, for the moment, some piece of that distinction holds. Europe's history has tried to teach it that we all live in the same place, whether our address is Granville Street or Chilco Street. Other people's darkness is a piece of our own. I think North America has largely tried to deny that lesson. It tends to say: those who live in the light have earned the light, those who live in the dark have earned the dark. But that simplistic optimism is really a form of pessimism. It is really saying we can finally help only ourselves but not one another.

I don't believe that. That's why, although I can enjoy being here, I can have no sense of tenure. I don't want to measure my success against the failure of another but to measure our joint success against the failure of the world to match the humanity of our dreams. I am not now and I have not ever been – nor will I ever be – a citizen of the Lotus Land. I am with the waiting Indian in Kitsilano, looking at what is there and seeing what is not there, aware of the inadequacy of what has happened to match what might have been.

That first, double impression of a beauty in which the brash newness of the town is diminished a little by the brooding oldness of the place has stayed with me. Vancouver lives like a guest in a house that is haunted.

The ghost, perhaps, is Canada itself, the lost dream of our potential for shared fulfilment. For the West Coast is where Canada, like America, runs out of dream. The grandeur of the continent ends here in a last, vast spectacular flourish. The country was colonised from east to west and Vancouver is one of the last vantage-points from which to see the culmination of all that energy and adventurousness and hope. Almost everywhere here, when you look out from the city, the terrain reminds you of the stature of the dream. That's perhaps a hard thing for any town to live with. For how do you find a life that will match the place?

I have felt it, I think, most strongly at Horseshoe Bay. God overdid it, I thought. It's as if, knowing He was creating the coda to a continent, He pulled out all the stops. The place could use a bit more editing, like the Bible. As it stands, what is Vancouver to make of it? How to respond?

Possibly the implied answer lies in the relentless spread of individual houses that is most of Vancouver, in the sailing and the wind-surfing and the mountain-biking and the climbing, in the number of people who come here from somewhere else to live. Vancouver, or so it seems to me, is for a lot of Canadians as much an alternative to where they were as it is the place where they are. It lacks compulsion. It is less fulfilment than a refuge from the difficulty of fulfilment. It is the communal dream that Canada might have been, privatised and suburbanised, made into consumer product. It is where the great Canadian adventure came to retire.

'Is Vancouver beautiful?' Of course, it is. And so is a sunset.

The Shallowing of Scotland

1. Remembering McGorky

I CAME ACROSS AN OLD BOOK THE OTHER DAY, ONE OF those working-class equivalents of an heirloom; something that is kept and passed on, not because it is supposed to have any intrinsic value but because it evokes a labyrinth of memory to which it acts as the clue. I don't think I'll take it to the *Antiques Roadshow* in case I am led from the room in a net. But, holding it in my hands, I felt its worth beyond doubt. Like ashes, it doesn't look much. Like ashes, it testifies to an old fire – a passion for social justice that burned undiminished to the point of death in a man in whom I, as an admittedly naïve boy, found hardly anything that wasn't worthy of love and admiration.

The book is *My Childhood* by Maxim Gorky. With the passage of time, the title has acquired an extended significance for me. In writing about his childhood, Gorky incidentally created an object that has become for me a cipher of my own. Handling the book, I found summoned up in me, through the necromancy of touch, reminders of where I come from and why I think as I think and why I believe as I believe.

In accordance with the saying, it is not a book to be judged by its cover. It was, as far as I'm aware, sent naked into the world without benefit of a coloured jacket. The covers are of a dull, dark brown and rough in texture. This was a publication from people who believed that a book is a collection of words held together in the most convenient and least flamboyant form. I sympathise. The only lettering on the outside is on the spine. It gives the title and the author's name: M. Gorky.

It was that name which brought back the first memory. I remembered my grandmother referring, in her late 60s, to the fact that she was reading a book by 'that McGorky'. Whether that interesting linguistic conflation was the result of her fading eyesight or of her determined tendency to see Scotland as the paradigm of all experience, I'm not sure. But it has a certain aptness for me. She made Gorky a naturalised Scot in the same way that her son, who had given her the book to read, translated the ideological rigidity of the Russian political experience into a much more Scottish humanism.

My Uncle Josey was an unlikely manner of the social barricades. He had either been born with or acquired a chronically weak heart, a nice irony given the passion of his convictions. The condition wasn't accurately diagnosed until late in his life. But its effects plagued him from childhood. He was frequently housebound. He missed much of his schooling. He could work only intermittently and then usually only at manual work, to which he was desperately unsuited and which, presumably, helped to hurry on his death.

The death happened in hospital where he was undergoing treatment. It was during the visiting hour. He had asked to be made more comfortable on his propped-up pillows and, as the members of his family who were there reached forward to help, he said, 'It doesny matter' and died quietly. He was 34.

That day in the hospital I had been in another ward, seeing a school friend. As I entered the ward where my uncle was – having come down towards the end of the visiting time – I saw his raised body relax and his head droop, discreet as a closing flower.

Tragedy can be so quiet and casual and ordinary that sometimes it is gone before we fully know that it has been. We are left painstakingly to measure its enormity in retrospect. What I glimpsed that day in my first sight of a human death has stayed with me, not in any dramatic way. It was a quiet occurrence and it has stayed quiet. But sometimes without warning he will come again into my mind and I think not of what is lost, but of the privilege I had in being his nephew.

At first, with the innocence of boyhood, I had thought that my experience of him was who he was. He was tall and pale and thin and shy, with bottle-bottom glasses and a great rampart of crinkly hair. He cared about people with a passionate intensity, too much to let them off with less than the best of what they were. He did the same with me, young as I was.

Never having been married, he lived with my grandmother until he died and I used to like being around their house. My reasons for that liking were curiously ambivalent. Like most children I had worked out early that the climate around a grandparent is often more tolerant of unbuttoned behaviour than the presence of parents is. Your ego can go barefoot there without catching too many chills of disapproval. But I also liked the fact that my uncle would be around to provide some kind of guidelines for my experiential wanderings, for children like freedom benignly picketed by adults. My uncle provided limits all right, but he established them not with automatic authority but through reason and discussion. The only rank he ever pulled was logic. But he always did it by trying to understand your terms as well as his own.

For that reason I'm glad he was the one who often discovered my misdemeanours first. I'm glad, for example, it was down to him to find out

I had been stealing cigarettes, cunningly and stealthily abstracted one at a time from his current packet of Senior Service, as if silence in an empty room were a talisman against the fates. I'm glad he was the one informed by an all-seeing neighbour that a girl of nine and I (by this time a worldly, cigarette-smoking ten-year-old who should have known better) had been seen partially naked conducting a somewhat puzzled investigation of each other in a rockery. (The choice of venue suggests that even then I had an instinctive sense that the course of true love never would run smooth.) I don't think I would have minded too much if he had been the one to discover that I had been sampling – in the stoical manner of a boy accepting his punishment of manhood – my granny's sweet stout, thus tasting the meaning of misnomer before I knew it. But nobody ever did discover that one.

I don't want to give the wrong impression here. I wasn't so much a primary-school reprobate as an eager investigator of taboos. I never have believed in hand-me-down experience. If something was forbidden, I wanted to know why the establishment was keeping it to itself. Somehow my uncle seemed to understand that and, taking me aside after my latest transgression of a set of rules I couldn't see the sense in, he would talk to me.

I don't remember exactly what we said, but I remember the feeling those conversations have always given me. It is a feeling of arrival at a place of clarity and warmth, a free border of selves where nothing is contraband because whatever you declare will carry no hidden charge against you. Guilt was not the question. Why you had done it was, and how it had felt, and what you thought about it now that you had done it, and where did you go from here. The dynamic of what your experience meant was always given back to you.

That feeling was the essence of our relationship until his death. Not long before he died, when I was 14, he gave me as a present a copy of *The Loom of Language* by Lancelot Hogben. That book, seeming to me at the time roughly the size of Russia, became with hindsight symbolic of what he had done for me. He hadn't given me my self. But he had shown me how I might find it. He, more than any official teacher I ever had, gave me the future as a gift that I would have to unwrap for myself. He taught me to look in it not for material success or wealth or possessions, but for understood experience and the justice towards others to which it can lead.

It was only after his death I realised slowly that the gift was one he had made to others as well as myself. My increased awareness began in that extended conversational wake that follows a working-class death, the hoarded anecdotes brought out and passed around, the quiet shared wonder at what had been among us. I learned of the heroism of his self-education, of his mute suffering, of how he might, with Alexander Pope, have referred to 'that long disease, my life'. I was reminded of his skill in drawing, of the peace posters he made alone at night when my grandmother was in bed.

I learned of the time some chancer put the head on him at a charity dance because my uncle was on the door and wouldn't let the man brass his way in free. The man still didn't get in, but there were no recriminations. My father, five-feet-four but with a PhD in outrage, spent a long time trying to get the details so that he could trace the man and exact summary retribution. But my uncle wouldn't help. He was my mother's brother and like her he lived his principles to the limit, pain or pleasure. Pacifism was one.

I was reminded as well of what an awkward bugger he could be. He couldn't be intimidated, only convinced, and that was one difficult trick. He liked to argue the way Gargantua liked to eat. I remember once, during my Vaughan Monroe period, when I was trying to bring my voice from the soles of my feet and sing *Ghost Riders in the Sky*, he took me to task for singing such an ideologically unsound song. I knew even then that his attitude was ridiculous, like quarrelling with a vacuum. But I took him seriously anyway. I still do. He remains one of the small but bright and unnamed stars by which I steer.

Holding his old copy of *My Childhood*, I sense him as being like the book, unflashy but substantial – and out of date. The human stock he believed in so sincerely has crashed, probably beyond the point of recovery. For my Uncle Josey was a deeply committed Communist.

I didn't believe in his political philosophy then, I never did since, and I don't now. I am happy to see the present apparent liberalisation of Eastern Europe. But I hope I retain enough intellectual precision and emotional honesty not to be bullied by the aggressive rant of contemporary British and American politics into confusing Eastern Bloc communism with the humane and pragmatic form the same ideology found for itself in Scotland.

Since John MacLean, Scottish communism has remained its own animal, less bear than beast of social burden, helping hurt lives in the small ways that it could, given its continuously enfeebled state. It has remained almost entirely free from the theoretical rabies to which its English counterpart has sometimes succumbed.

Besides my uncle, I have met many Scottish communists. Sometimes they were boringly dogmatic. But then so have been many Catholics and Presbyterians and those of other faiths. More often they have been generous of spirit and deep in their concern for others. Disagreeing with their theory, I have found myself time and again replenished by their practice and renewed in my belief in a more habitable vision of the future. They have long been a benignly crucial part of our awareness of ourselves.

But these are meretricious times, in which slogan passes for thought and the intellectual scatter-gun is the favoured weapon of political precision. You may say with the mood of the moment that if one form goes, all should go. You may say, if you wish, that there was no distinctive baby in Scottish communism, only the same old bath-water.

You may say it. I won't. I owe these people. I pay my debts of gratitude.

2. *Conferring with Sad Captains*

'The hole in the ozone layer,' the man said, 'is the only serious issue of our time.' I could see what he was getting at. Who wants to live in a leaky universe?

He was a tall man with an untrimmed beard and a philosophical untidiness that suggested he was more concerned to have his ideas brushed and combed than to worry about his appearance. He spoke with a lecturer's *gravitas*, implying that if he told you the time it might be as well to make a note of it. When any of the others were speaking, as they were sometimes allowed to do, he held his head cocked slightly, maybe not wanting to miss any of the cosmic messages that might be coming in.

They were five at the table in the bar, three women and two men. The late afternoon sunlight shafted in through the windows as if William Blake had been given the commission that day, and it imparted an appropriate solemnity to the group. This was not a conversation. It was a seminar. Their intensity gave them the interconnecting fixity of people in a painting.

The three women were young and earnest and frank. If those sound like their names, they might as well have been, so basically a part of them did the qualities seem. The other man was one of these very reactive listeners, a nodder and an intent, forensic starer into statements, who said 'yes' like punctuation.

I wasn't eavesdropping. In the quietness of the place I was obliged to hear. I had no choice, short of wearing a Walkman. Their talk traversed the 'rain forest', was full of 'additives' and often came to the 'Greens'.

I was impressed and I was depressed. I was impressed because they seemed to live in a world where they knew where everything was, like a fitted kitchen. I was depressed because I didn't live in a place like that and most of the things that concern me seemed already to have been consigned to the pedal-bin.

Listening to them, my self esteem went through various, quick stages of decomposition, like a victim in a science fiction film. First, I aged alarmingly. How could I be so out of touch with the shining clarity of modern thinking? And the wrinkles came. What relevance did my beliefs and ideas have to the present preoccupations? And the grey hair cataracted round my head. Socialism was dead. And I collapsed. My life had been a long commitment to a discredited philosophy. And the wind blew my powdered bones into oblivion.

But I'm stubborn. Hold it, some atom in me said. Run this film back. And I reassembled suddenly, truculently solid at the bar. Let's think about this. Something was wrong with the way they were talking. I had to argue. But as well as being stubborn I'm polite, at least when I can remember to be. I didn't just want to crash their seminar.

So, while they all agreed, I conducted a discussion of my own in the ghostly reaches of the head. Like Mark Antony after Actium refusing to admit the death of his dreams, I called to me not all but some of my sad captains – three, in fact, from the host of honourable intelligences who have helped me over the years to decide what I think and feel about things.

George Orwell came first, coughing quietly and quoting himself, which is all the dead can do. He reminded me of what he had said about certain socialists of the '30s, how bright-eyed and self-convinced they were. They were hill-walkers and cyclists, middle-class intellectuals who recognised proletarians by their caps but not by anything that went on underneath them.

They would have led the workers out into the hills as into the promised land. Presumably, what they would have found there was deep breathing as a way of life. For those people, too, ozone was all.

Orwell was being quite bitter. But then he usually was. That was one of the reasons why I had recognised his benignly jaundiced presence so quickly. He'd mentioned 'the intellectual, book-trained socialist who understands that it is necessary to throw our present civilisation down the sink and is quite willing to do so'. He referred to 'all that dreary tribe of high-minded women and sandal wearers who come flocking towards the smell of "progress" like bluebottles to a dead cat'.

I was hoping that nobody else in the bar could hear him. I checked that none of the five at the table was wearing sandals. But, give or take a saliva fleck or two as always, I could see what he meant.

George, I said without moving my lips, I can see what you mean. These people are not as modern as they seem. This is an old tune they're singing, even if the words are new. It's not that I don't like the lyrics. It's just that they seem so narrow and so self-absorbed, rather like those love songs written by young people who like to imagine that they discovered love and that the millennia up to now were just going through the motions.

I really take your point about the '30s, I said. Those idelogical tourists – 'who are communists now, as they will be fascists five years hence, because it is all the go,' Orwell snarled. Okay, George, I said, okay. Don't blow a gasket. Those ideological tourists had a naïveté which has helped to land socialism in the mess it's in today. I can see that these people at the table are in some way their descendants.

But – and here I hesitated. It's awkward to start tutoring your teacher. This is something you won't know about, George. But I think they have another ancestry as well. They are also, to some extent, children of the '60s. They have connections with that time when flowers were power and the natural world was there to be communed with and day-to-day politics seemed like a seedy irrelevance.

What I think both parents had in common was a simplistic vision and I think they've passed their eyesight on to their children. They had a focus that excluded almost everything but their obsession. They knew where we should be going but how the hell were we to get there? Nobody said, beyond some mystical mumbo-jumbo. The practical realities of people's lives were insufficiently taken into account. The Utopian future they envisaged for all of us was largely a pre-empting of our present, not a development from it.

This was where Alexander Herzen came in. Along with the great, shaggy Russian head, as full of erupting energy as an active volcano, he brought his huge sympathies that had seemed symbolised by the name his aristocrat father had bestowed on his illegitimacy, suggesting that Alexander was a child not of the marriage contract, but of the heart. He had certainly lived as such, never cutting off his intelligence from the compassion that fed it.

He was waiting. I knew what he was waiting for. He had written something somewhere that was pertinent to the debate George and I were having. But locating one thing that Herzen has said is similar to looking for a specific leaf in a forest. His massive *My Life and Work* (part autobiography, part political tract, part philosophy of life) is a book like the Amazon basin. You don't read it, you mount expeditions into it. What had he written that was relevant here? He reminded me of his disagreement with Marx.

That was it. He argued that Marx's belief in the sacrificial present to achieve an ideal future was dehumanising. You must not ask people to forego the fullness of their present experience, that is real and certain, in order to create a blueprint for the future of others, that is uncertain and putative. That was it, wasn't it? Alexander nodded.

I think I can see the connection, Alexander, I said. These people have a just concern for the environment. But their concern has a visionary nobility to it that troubles me. It is all panorama and no foreground, in that one respect not unlike the overview of Marxism. What policies do they have to offer our more immediate problems? I will support anything that will lead to the green fields of what is to be, but only if it is combined with a way through the mud of now.

Then, dead on cue, came Miguel de Unamuno, with his urbane Spanish intensity and an interpreter. Having read *The Tragic Sense of Life* I knew what Miguel was going to say before he said it. He was on about his old obsession, which suited me fine because I never tire of hearing it. The man of flesh and blood, Miguel keeps saying, the man of flesh and blood.

It was music to my ears, as it has been since I first found him. I love his insistence that everything in life passes through the matrix of the individual. All grand ideas, all elaborate philosophies, all political theories must incarnate themselves in people or become inhuman. It is the nature of the animal that will provide the only means to the fulfilment of any theory and will, therefore, be the final comment on its practicability. That was where Saint-Just and those other fine intelligences of the French Revolution – great minds abstracted from their bodies and floating loose in a formaldehyde of theory – came to grief. That was how Marx saw inevitably happening what was not to be. They all tried to invent human nature instead of discovering it.

I followed Unamuno's man of flesh and blood into the present. What bothered me about the people at the table, I decided, was that they seemed to me to abstract one ideal area of our concerns (one with which none of us could disagree) and offer it as all of us, the essential aim of our lives. But what did they have to say about the rest, the daily scuffling, the legislated injustices among which small lives struggle to survive?

It is easy to choose one noble ideal and follow it through life like a Roman road. The hard thing is to carry with you many ideals and take them down the byways of sad lives and make them confront the hovels of hopelessness in our society and learn painfully from them. I would prefer to try the second way. I was a socialist still.

I thanked them – Orwell, Herzen, Unamuno – and they left without taking a drink. The dead have no thirst. But I felt better, as I always do, for their having been there.

The people at the table were still talking. I didn't disagree with them in kind, only degree. For there is a social ecology as well as a physical one. If we ever come to that fine, green place they envisage – and I hope we may – we will still have to worry about the lives our kind are obliged to live there. And that is a question for the present to address in its own urgent terms.

I left them talking and went out of the bar to buy a paper and see what was happening in Eastern Europe.

3. A Walk on the Wild Side

Man-made bad weather is the worst. King Lear knew that. He could abide the pelting of the pitiless storm better than he could the attitudes of people. I was walking in my home town of Kilmarnock. It was bright, if rather blustery – one of those spring days when the Scottish climate seems to be trying to remember what nice weather's like, and not quite getting it right. But it made for good walking.

My pleasant mood made me determined not to dwell on the mess the planners have made of the old place. I avoided the town centre, a pile of inconsequential bricks called a shopping precinct, which looks like a place made by a committee that was drunk at the time. Instead, I walked the old ways, mentally putting up my memorial plaques.

There was the wall Jim fell off and went into a coma and emerged from it to suffer alopecia. That was the path where possibly the ugliest dog I had ever seen used to lie in wait for you. Its name was 'Beauty' and, thinking back on it, I begin to wonder if dogs can appreciate irony and if the savagery of Beauty's temper related to its being lumbered with such a mocking monicker. There was the house where the primary school party took place at which I experienced the stunning revelation that girls are interestingly different from boys.

Just about there would be the scene of the great ice-cream fiasco. My father had sent my brother Hughie and me to the chip shop for ice-cream – six single nougat wafers, I think it was. On the way back we were taking chances each at doing tricks with the wrapped wafers when we dropped the lot on the pavement. A panicky debate ensued. My father was a man whose temper could be just slightly quicker than a striking cobra. Fortunately, he laughed and gave us the money to buy a second lot of ice-cream. On the way home we did the same thing again. I don't remember what happened after that. Probably we emigrated.

There . . .

It was then the voice shouted to me – a moment, although I didn't realise it at the time, akin to the first big splatter of rain that falls out of a clear sky. I hadn't seen him for years and it took me some seconds to connect the florid face in front of me with the past. I wish I hadn't bothered. The eyes were the giveaway – so self-assured they made puddles look like deep and troubled waters. His conversation was a small horror story.

Nuclear weapons, it seems, are a shrug-off. Unemployment is the creation of the unemployed. Apparently, they arrange their circumstances carefully and then blame it on the government. Who do they think they're kidding? South Africa is a much maligned society. How can I have any opinion about the country when I haven't been there? He has been there more than once – with the perceptiveness and sensitivity, I am forced to imagine, of a suitcase.

I walked on, wishing him a happy brain transplant. But the damage was done. The internal weather had turned sour. Maybe it was the sudden conjunction of old times with the present that made me feel it so keenly, but I started to brood on how dramatically the climate of attitudes we all live among has changed in the last ten years or so, so that any walk these days may turn into a walk on the wild side of reaction.

How is it, I wondered, that a government so utterly bereft of serious political thought, which can only talk in figures, could have caused such a radical shift in our sense of ourselves in such a short time? Part of the reason, I thought, might be the very shallowness of its policies. Everybody can understand selfishness and greed, and Thatcherism has constructed what passes for its political philosophy out of those two brute instincts.

But the speed with which it has happened still left me puzzled. How could the apparent progress we had been making over the generations towards a more socially-concerned society have been so swiftly reversed? Why has socialism so often seemed to take one step forward and two back in British politics? Apart from the Attlee administration, what serious socialist government have we ever had? Jostling after these questions came another: why has Scottish socialism, at least in spirit, usually appeared more radical than its English counterpart?

Searching for answers, I thought of Edmund Burke, who has been justly called the foremost Conservative British political thinker. That passionate and intelligent Irishman, coming in as a clear-eyed outsider, analysed English political attitudes with the precision of someone who had to find out how to belong. Under the threat of dynamic changes coming from France, he expressed that analysis most cogently in *Reflections on the Revolution in France*, a book he raised like a bulwark against the invasion of new ideas from across the Channel.

I thought Burke answered my questions. The reason he suggests to me is that since the Glorious Revolution of 1688, the British constitution (which simply means the English constitution assumptively extended to include the rest of the United Kingdom) has been a machine for the maintenance of reactionary attitudes. Brief spells of progressive government may occur, but, when these reach a certain point, reaction switches on automatically.

One of the keys to this process is, I think, that 1688 had created a monarchical pragmatism in Britain. The idea of kingship no longer carried the weight it had done. Monarchy had become a system, not a concept. What Burke understood – and sought to strengthen by giving it articulation – was that England wasn't susceptible to the ideas that were raging in France. Its constitution had developed antibodies to any dramatic form of progress. It was precisely because this element of lip service to kingship was alien to France, where the homage was more hallowed, that the Revolution was so violent. There it wasn't a case of tinkering with a system, but of the collision of ideas seriously lived through.

Burke understood this English suspicion of ideas very well. He celebrated it as the foundation of their political identity: 'All your sophisters cannot produce anything better adapted to preserve a rational and manly freedom than the course that we have pursued, who have chosen our nature rather than our speculations, our breasts rather than our inventions, for the great conservatories and magazines of our privileges.'

Any system so based on 'nature' and the hallowed accumulation of past practices is bound to be reactionary. New ideas are blocked by assumptions that guard the doorway to the sanctum of tradition, where such humility is demanded of us that we must remove our heads before entering. Thus, what English politics have tended to be concerned with is not human justice but national practicality, not political philosophy but political plumbing, not the rights of man but the acquired characteristics of Englishmen.

'You will observe,' Burke says, and we do, 'that from Magna Carta to the

Declaration of Right, it has been the uniform policy of our constitution to claim and assert our liberties, as an *entailed inheritance* derived to us from our forefathers, and to be transmitted to our posterity; as an estate specially belonging to the people of this kingdom without any reference whatever to any other more general or prior right.'

One of the problems here is that Burke – along with English politics – is very selective in defining who those forefathers are. The family tree from which the constitution claims descent has been very carefully pruned. 'We wished at the period of the Revolution, and do now wish, to derive all we possess as *an inheritance from our forefathers*.' Yes, but *which* forefathers? Dissent has its own genealogy.

What this leads to is a kind of intellectual *mortmain*: the dead hand of the collective past clenched round the possibility of serious change. 'Do these theorists mean to imitate some of their predecessors, who dragged the bodies of our ancient sovereigns out of the quiet of their tombs? Do they mean to attaint and disable backwards all the kings that have reigned before the Revolution, and consequently to stain the throne of England with the blot of a continual usurpation?'

Taken this far, reaction attempts to intimidate completely the possibility of change, not through reason but through accusing it of desecration. It is a form of ancestor worship that would make us the intellectual equivalents of the slaves who built the pyramids, consecrating our lives to the dead.

It creates a terminally static society, founded on the perpetuation of a historical injustice that can only be compensated for by the hope of an afterlife: 'The body of the people must not find the principles of natural subordination by art rooted out of their minds. They must respect that property of which they cannot partake. They must labour to obtain what by labour can be obtained; and when they find, as they commonly do, the success disproportionate to the endeavour, they must be taught their consolation in the final proportions of eternal justice.'

One thing, I suspect, that Thatcherism has effectively achieved is to provide a shallow, mindless echo of this impressively articulated and inhumanly vicious stance, one deeply – perhaps terminally – ingrained in the English political psyche.

I realised as I walked on, that Thatcherism has never been required to articulate anything like a coherent, serious political ideology. It has only needed to mimic the attitudes of the past. It has only needed to show its wooden head and mechanically open its wooden mouth and let the dead letter of tradition emerge, worked from the back (no matter how far back) by people like Burke. Such is the power in English politics of unexamined assumption and conditioned reflex that you only have to imitate the familiar reactionary attitudes, no matter how insubstantially, and the Pavlovian response is waiting by which the present will re-ingest its own past, sickness and all.

127

For the past ten years that is essentially what Britain has been doing. The only difference from the past in recent times is that the old assumptive aristocracy has been displaced to some extent by a narrow and spurious meritocracy. The new meritocracy is narrow because its sole criterion is economic. The only balance in which the quality of the new élite can be weighed will be found in a bank. The new meritocracy is spurious because it disenfranchises most of the nation from the possibility of fulfilling its terms. To participate in its promises, most of us must find money that we do not have and lose the wider moral and communal concerns that we do have.

The old reactionarism had at least a vision. It was a dead vision, sure enough. Born of superstition and the dread of change, it left us haunted by a graveyard sense of ourselves in which a past that had never been stalked like a ghost on stilts, intimidating us out of our progressive instincts. But it gave a certain macabre stature to our dreams. The new reactionarism has no vision. It has only sight, endlessly acquisitive eyes that can see nothing but the main chance. It would give us dreams that would disgrace an ant in an anthill. It would teach us to keep our horizons in a wallet. Given acceptance, it will destroy idealism.

This must not be. We have a right to the stature of our dreams and to the search for the political means to realise them. English politics seems less than ever likely to accommodate that right. The greater radicalism that has at least nominally persisted in Scotland may be partly attributable to the fact that the country has been for a very long time virtually powerless. It is easier to have noble ideals when you are not obliged to live according to their terms day by day. But that greater radicalism is also partly attributable to a tradition of taking ideas seriously.

We must not lose that. Taken seriously, ideas are dangerous but not as dangerous as the absence of taking them seriously. They must modify experience and be modified by experience. They are the means by which we harness pragmatism to idealism. The pragmatism must come first, certainly. It is the horse and not the cart. If we reverse this priority and simply give idealism its head, we will find ourselves in a place that is humanly uninhabitable, where the idea is all and the human being is its slave (as has happened to a great extent in Eastern Europe). But if we give pragmatism its head without making it carry any chastening luggage of idealism along with it (as has been happening in Britain for the last ten years), it will eventually take us to a place that is humanly not worth inhabiting, because we will have had to leave the richest aspects of our nature behind in order to get there.

Scotland need not go there, if it will rediscover the idealism of its own past. It is hard to see how Scotland can rediscover that fallible and fragmentary idealism while it remains yoked to the galloping materialism of English government, at present in full flight from humanitarian principles.

It must find the way to direct its own political destiny. And it must do it as quickly as possible, for idealism is constantly eroding in disuse.

Some such were my dark thoughts on a day of bright weather. I continued walking, scouting carefully for the psychological footpads of our time, the robbers of mood, the vociferous purveyors of shallow opinion, that I might either avoid them or shoot verbally on hearing.

4. All You Need is Love?

They've stopped holding the Sixties Nights in a pub I occasionally go to. Those nights seemed joyful enough for a time. Among the drinks and conversation people would get up and do twists and shakes and other imminently geriatric gyrations.

Music, the nostalgia machine, was continuously evoking another time, another place; while the talk might be of delayed giros, employment training and the poll tax, we would be listening to the quaint injunction that, if we were going to San Francisco, we would be well advised to wear some flowers in our hair – and, those who had a post-*Dirty Harry* cynicism about California might have added, a Magnum in your suit. Looking round the bar, you might also have wondered what the baldy people were supposed to do.

I experienced a kind of pageant of recent history, personal and public, which the songs let pass before me. There, driving out of the music, was the imperfectly functioning bubble-car, in which the mini-skirted girl had given me a memorable lift. (Sitting in the tiny dome with her thighs, I kept wondering if the car would break down first, or I would.) There was a dead musician floating in a pool. There were John Lennon and Yoko having a love-in. (That was the event that, for me, gave a whole new meaning to the term 'a long lie'. Was that when John mistook great talent for messianism? Can love, perhaps, neutralise intelligence?)

I enjoyed a few hallucinatory moments there among the glasses and guitar sounds. Is this a beehive that I see before me? Come, let me touch thee. (Not 'clutch' – you didn't clutch a beehive. Your hand would have skidded off the lacquer.) Is that a Maharishi I hear giggling faintly and inanely behind the music, offering phrases of wisdom that would have embarrassed a Christmas cracker? Anyway, it felt like fun for a while.

Then, like the 1960s themselves, the party was over. It seems that there were fights. People kept wandering in who weren't *au fait* with flower power and eastern mysticism. They spoiled the mood a bit. They offered an alternative culture, as it were, one that came from bad streets and run-down council housing schemes and wage packets that couldn't have weighed less if they'd been filled with bird-seed.

Disgruntlement ensued. Voices were, it appears, raised. Blows were struck and various rollings around the floor occurred. Meanwhile, the records went on turning, trapped in their repetitive innocence –playing, I like to think, something like:

> 'Those were the days, my friend.
> We thought they'd never end.'

In spite of the harmless pleasure those evenings were giving, there seems to me a certain poetic justice in the way they ended. Those disgruntled party-poopers came in off streets the times we were celebrating had tried to bypass. They were to some extent the foundling descendants of that generation that wore flowers where their brains should have been, and sang, as if their culture had taken one acid trip too many, *All You Need Is Love*. Those troublemakers could be seen as serving the '60s with the bill, one which all of us are still paying.

For the '60s, it seems to me, were a kind of irresponsible emotional spree that brought us close to something like moral bankruptcy. They were a colourful cavalcade that led us, dancing and singing, into a gloom that was as deep as the children of Hamelin's. There were great times then, of course. But I don't suppose Sodom and Gomorrah were especially dull places. It was just that the dark came early.

The psychedelic pied-piper-in-chief was pop music. Fifties rock 'n' roll, coming straight off the streets with a ferocious and innocent energy, had invaded our awareness like busloads of children at a funfair. In the '60s, that energy both peaked and declined with the Beatles. Having seen things with astonishing freshness and caught small moments of meaning in a lot of ordinary lives, they started to go after the big one: The Meaning of Life. It wasn't an edifying sight. Like a lot of successful and wealthy people who may feel that they have done it all and who start casting around for a purpose to which to put the rest of their time, they became half-baked philosophers. Since then, pop music has frequently been marred by its own pretentiousness.

To be fair to the Beatles, it wasn't a wrong turning they took entirely on their own. It was largely an effect of the climate of the time. For the '60s, not to put too fine a point on it, were full of many things, and one of them was crap.

That was the time when Timothy Leary was advocating drugs for all. His succinct contribution to the history of philosophy was 'Turn on. Tune in. Drop out', to which some kind of friend of his might have added: 'Shut up'. I remember reading *The Politics of Ecstasy* with a jaw so far dropped I was surprised I didn't bruise my kneecaps. Leary specialised in a mode of reasoning that had holes in it big enough to house a Boeing.

That was the time, I think, when the analyst R. D. Laing – who had been one of my most admired intelligences of the era (and the only person I wanted to treat me if I cracked up) – lost his way among the intellectual barrow-boys who abounded towards the end of the decade (including his friend, Timothy Leary), and bought too many dubious ideas that had fallen off the top of someone's hopped-up head. Seeing him on a television programme made not long before he died, I noticed that he still had his moments, but they were just moments – inconsequential, slightly oracular, decontextualised, very much in the idiom of the '60s, which I can't help thinking did him in in some way.

In literature, it was the time of the Beats, who have always seemed to me a band of travelling mountebanks, the snake-oil salesmen of the word, offering offensive simple-mindedness as simplicity, fluency as articulacy, and vociferousness as meaning. It is true they have become a part of history, but so did the Dark Ages.

In lifestyles, it was the time of the hippies. No wonder they were an essentially American phenomenon. Dropping out was the kind of luxury only a wealthy society could afford to give its middle-class youth. The romantic surface of hippiedom had a sad underside, the total abdication of social responsibility. It often involved the abandonment of other people to whatever society inflicted on them. You only have to read Joan Didion's *Slouching Towards Bethlehem* to see the effects of this.

The hippies were more wilfully naïve than any of us has the right to be. They really did act as if they had been born yesterday and human experience was a clean slate on which they could, with their lives, write anything they wanted. They didn't seem to realise that to opt out of the materialism and injustice of their society was to strengthen that materialism and injustice, since its most committed opponents were all away on an extended trip to nowhere. The opting out of society is the ultimate surrender to society just as to disown history is to give history total authority over you.

What these various aspects of the '60s added up to, I believe, was primarily the loss of continuity. They were, in social and political terms, a parenthesis so long that it became difficult to remember where we had been and, therefore, difficult to work out where we should be going. They had seemed to offer so many short-cuts – experientially and philosophically – which turned out to be dead-ends that many people were left to try to find their own way back to the mainstream.

The '60s had their own sense of politics, of course, and a very dramatic sense it could be. But those politics – whether manifested in a peace rally or a march on the Pentagon – were essentially the politics of event, never of process. And effective political power functions not through protest or public happening but through process.

The Glamorous Decade eventually left everybody in the lurch. After the party came the international hangover of the '70s, a time of nervous depression and dislocated thought and trying to gather up the debris. The '80s took the cure: the electric-shock treatment of monetarism; the beads giving way to the bright new business suit; philosophy simplified into finance; all you need is money. For the shallowness of where we are in Britain politically – and I consider it a very shallow place indeed – I blame in part the '60s.

All you need is love? And intelligence and constant vigilance and historical sense and political awareness and a knowledge of where the power is and an understanding of its workings and concern for the lives of others and endlessly renewed self-examination and a capacity to learn from experience and an ability to rethink today what you thought you knew yesterday and humility and passion and compassion and . . .

All you need is everything. Back to the drawing-board, everybody. Let's keep working on it.

5. A Scottish Socialism?

Sometimes, trying to understand the current confusion of Scotland, I am haunted by an image. It is a simple image but one precipitated out of a complex relationship with the past. Just as coal is created over a long time from the compressed life-forms of much vegetation, so that image achieves its crystalline hardness from a lot of subsumed experience. It is the found expression of many things beyond itself.

My memory can still separate some of those things. I remember my mother listening to the wireless while the results of the General Election of 1945 were broadcast. I remember labyrinthine arguments in my parents' house when it seemed undeniable that at the end of one of those corridors was waiting a doorway to the place we wanted everyone to get to. I remember small, heroic decencies practised by neighbours and friends in defiance of their circumstances.

Out of these memories and countless others comes the image. It is, as I say, a simple image. My father is sitting at the fire. With that power of imagination to facilitate the impossible, he is listening not to the news of his own times but to news of ours. He listens. I study hawklike, as I so often used to do, what his reaction will be. He smokes his pipe and stares at the hearth. He turns down his mouth and puts a spittle on the fire.

He was, like so many of his friends and his neighbours, someone politically passionate beyond his own articulacy. As his fancy-mouthed son, who used sometimes to infuriate him by having 'swallied a dictionary', let me say what the image means for me. Let me, as it were, analyse the spittle.

The spittle means contempt. The contempt is for the shallowing of Scotland. For his was one of several generations who out of hard lives constructed the serious possibility of socialism. They had a dream, those people. It was a confused ream but an intense one. Dreamed in hard and sometimes bitter places, it could have been forgiven for being simply a dream of self, of money, of comfort, of pleasures to be ingested like a meal alone. But it was not.

For the people like him whom I knew were not limited to the vision of a dung-beetle nor to the compassion of a piranha. No matter what happened to them, they tried to stay as big as their dream. That dream included everyone. Hard times had taught them not selfishness but compassion – the conviction that such injustices should not happen to anyone, not just themselves. Those generations blessed the bleakness of Scotland by transforming their hardships into vision, a shared vision. For they had learned together in a hard school things which today we seem to be forgetting.

They knew that people should be measured not just by success or material possessions but by the humanity of their aspirations. The more humane the vision, the bigger the person. They knew that the economy should be there to serve the people, not the people to serve the economy. They knew that a society where any section of the community is treated with systematic injustice is an unjust society and one which has been deliberately engineered to be that way, not some inevitable outcome of the nature of life.

They were no fools. Their education had been painfully and painstakingly acquired not just from standard texts but in factories and pits, from studying ration-books, from queueing at shops, from counting pennies. They knew how much easier it was to be a Conservative than a socialist. Any realistic socialist would, and they were first and last realists.

Socialism is a traveller whose destination remains uncertain. It seeks to explore the human possibilities for social improvement. Conservatism is a tourist with the tickets bought and the tour operator waiting. One seeks to go forward en masse. The other is only interested in individual upward movement. One wants to move into unknown country, where things could be better. The other wants to travel only the established network of routes, where the restaurants are listed and the stopping-places mapped. One carries a dream of the future, the other only the luggage of the past.

So they knew how hard the attempt to realise socialism would be. But in their hardships they also sensed their lives to be part of a worthwhile struggle, a relevant contribution to the deep dialectic of their country's development. If, like the image of my father, they could sit at a 1950s' fire and listen to what we are making of the committed debate that was their lives, what would they think now? I believe they would feel a fierce and just contempt. The contempt would find many things to fuel it into anger.

They would see a country where, over the past ten years, the debate which they believed the future would continue has been marginalised. They would find the parameters of political discussion dramatically narrowed. They would realise with incredulity that this has been achieved not by force of political thought, but by euphemism and double-speak and an appeal to the lowest common denominator in everybody and a revival in the United Kingdom of a base and pathetic jingoism. They would be appalled.

Looking for depth in the discussion around them, they would hear a political language in which the vocabulary has been melted down into a variety of synonyms for one word: economy. They would wonder where political morality has gone.

Thinking of socialism, they would be obliged to remember it, for they would not see it around them. They would have to remember that socialism is an attempt to develop the political system which will provide the optimum social circumstances for the fulfilment of what is best in human nature. It is rational morality. It is people choosing quite deliberately to develop what they consider the best aspects of their nature and to keep in check the worst. It is an attempt to evolve not from the good but towards it. Concern as opposed to indifference, kindness as opposed to cruelty, sharing as opposed to selfishness, experience as opposed to materialism – these are not just morally preferable. They are rationally preferable, because they create a society more humanly habitable, in which our natures can be experienced more fully.

Our lives are our experience of them. When we die, what we have achieved is the nature of our experience. It is our only significant monument, what we leave in word or thought or remembered action or attitude to those who come after, the pulse that beats for us beyond our dying. No amount of possessions or status will do that. We will become in death only the stature of our experience, the size of our humanity.

Knowing that – and they knew it all right, even if not in these words, for it was they who taught me – they would hardly recognise their country in its present condition: a country with 49 Labour MPs which is being Thatcherised so insidiously and relentlessly that the old bowdlerism of 'North Britain' is in some danger of at last becoming the truth.

The social advances they had waited so long to achieve they would see being eroded all around them, the hard-won machineries of compassion being dismantled. Unemployment wouldn't be new to them but the accepted scale of it would, and the unprincipled verbiage that surrounds it and the cynical manipulation of its statistics. They would be astonished to find that unemployment has become not the guilt of the government but an accusation against the unemployed.

They would look for the unions and see in their place mainly an assortment of shifty-eyed job-brokers. They would see most of the young demeaned to a pool of cheap labour, robbed of any shred of self-determination, given the choice of being penniless or wage-slaves. They would see the Health Service, the greatest single achievement of the Labour Party, being clinically dismembered. They would see disadvantage being studiously legislated back into education. They would see great universities, in which they had believed so much, treated like factories for processing business skills and told to make their product viable in the market place.

They would despair. Despairing, they would ask how this could be happening in Scotland. They would be shown a Secretary of State for Scotland who, seeing the way his land lay, followed not its contours but his career; who, knowing the groundswell of his country, went directly against it as his way of serving the people. Listening to his public pronouncements, they would hear in his tight vowels the sound of the last, admittedly confused broth of Scottishness being strained through a very narrow plastic sieve so that only the thinnest gruel might remain.

And what of the Labour Party? They might well ask. We would have to point out to them a Labour leader who, having lost two elections, has decided to do a Saatchi & Saatchi on the Labour movement. His emblem is a nice, placative rose. His logic with regard to Scotland seems to be: since it is one of our essential power bases, let's control its aspirations in case we lose it through them. He promises to administer capitalism more humanely. If you can't beat them, join them. His socialism seems to have all the substance of a flag. It remains symbolic but it goes whichever way the wind blows.

But what of the Scottish Labour MPs? We would have to admit that they seem virtually impotent. So diminished has their sense of their own mandate become that they have begun to construe the embarrassment of a government minister in the House of Commons as some kind of triumph. 'Effective opposition' they call it. Unable actually to *do* much, they have had recourse to being political pedants, playing a parliamentary word-game. In their desperation to score political points that might register at the ballot box, they have allowed themselves to become part of a process whereby the Labour leader has been opportunistically adding to the central definition of socialism (a society restructured towards justice) any vote-catching digression he can think of, as if politics were Scrabble. In spite of themselves, they have, with several honourable exceptions, simply become Westminsterised.

Why? Eh, well, we could mutter, glancing furtively at one another, what was that word again? Pragmatism. That's the one. You have to be pragmatic. Socialism can only be implemented through government. First, find how to get into power. Now, the Tories have won three elections in a row. If we find out how they did it and imitate them (always, of course, retaining just enough of our heritage still to use the words 'Labour Party', for we have to keep a different name so that people know who it is they're voting for), maybe we can get back into power. And, when you get there, what will be the purpose? If the point of socialism in power is to father a better future and the cost of socialism in power is emasculation of its principles, how do you reconcile the two? Well, we've decided to change our principles.

This is socialism? No, it isn't, we would have to confess. It is what we have instead of socialism these days. But you must understand, we could say. Socialism is brave and we have learned to be afraid. You see, there is a bully among us. And aren't bullies terrifying? They make so much noise and they seem to know exactly what everybody else should do. They reduce the complexity of things to the one dimension of their own insensitivity, as if the world were a lollipop given to them to lick. What they don't understand isn't there. So, really, we could say, socialism doesn't really exist any more. Does it?

And the answer, looming massively out of the past, would be so many small, underprivileged lives bravely shared and put together into a communal structure of honest thought and honourable belief. Before that awesome monument that will not go away such specious reasoning would evaporate like studio mist. And we would be obliged to confront the smallness of ourselves, the shabby personal compromises of contemporary Scotland. We would have to admit that if socialism is failing, the failure is ours.

For socialism does exist. Nothing in our lifetimes has happened to discredit it, except its own faintheartedness and inimical propaganda and the careerism of politicians and the selfishness of some people. But it can only happen, it can only emerge from theory into practice if we have the courage to make it happen. We will rediscover the commitment of the past or be haunted by it and shame the future.

Of course, that renewed commitment will involve a degree of pragmatism. But the point about pragmatism is that it should work. It has no other reason for being. The present pragmatism of the British Labour Party is not working towards the achievement of socialism and it cannot do so. The reason for this is simple. The British Labour Party has compromised its own creed to such an extent, has moved so far to the right that the choice between it and the Conservatives is essentially a difference in management styles. If the British Labour Party were to win an election, we would still not have socialism in power. We would have humane Conservatism. That would be an improvement, in the way that benign management of a bad system is preferable to malign management of the same system. But it would not be a great enough improvement. And it would categorically not be socialism.

Where is the pragmatism in achieving socialism by negating it? According to that logic, you can win a fight by not turning up to engage in it. After all, who can say you were defeated? But if Scottish socialism wishes to do more than play games of political chop-logic, it will have to develop a practical course of action distinct from the crowd-pleasing contortions of the British Labour Party. (Roll up! Roll up! See the old boy vanish up his own posterior and emerge as someone else.)

136

In developing that practical course of action, Scottish socialism will begin, as all pragmatism must, with the reality of its present circumstances. In Scotland it is nominally in power. In Scotland it has no real power. How can it make this nominal power real? It could wait and work with the British Labour Party towards the next election. But the British Labour Party no longer seriously represents socialism. Whether the name of the next Prime Minister is Thatcher or Kinnock, the result will be a greater or lesser attempt to dilute the comparative radicalism of Scottish socialism into something else. Either way, we lose. Thus, we cannot wait and remain neutralised by the British Labour Party.

Therefore, Scottish socialism, if it is to attempt to realise its potential for power, must separate itself in some way from the rest of the United Kingdom. Those socialists whose internationalism makes a decision like that abhorrent should reflect that there is a world recession in the movement. The only way for it to survive in a serious form is to retrench. Scotland is one of the places where it could effectively do so.

There are only two forms such a separation could take: devolution or independence. Practically, devolution would seem to me the more promising choice, for two reasons. The first is that more Scots at the moment support devolution and, presumably, most of those who favour independence would back devolution in preference to the present situation. The second is that devolution need only be an interim measure. It does not preclude the further possibility of independence.

Either way, time is running out. We will, over the next few years, work together across party borders or we will be left squatting separately in the ruins of our heritage. We will refuse to let the political debate in our country remain determined by the shallowness of current Conservative ideology. We will honour our past by attempting to connect it seriously to our future.

And if we don't, that imaginary spittle from the past shouldn't go in the fire. It should be on our faces.

6. A Socialist Scotland?

Distance can give perspective. Fairly recently, I spent a year in Canada. I travelled across the country. I met a lot of interesting people and I enjoyed my time there, but towards the end of my year I came down with a bad case of Scotland-starvation. I saw clearly what it was about the place, apart from individuals, that made me hungry for it.

It wasn't its lochs and bens or the West Highland Way, though they are impressive enough. It was the deep commitment of its people, at least some of the time, to matters beyond the material. I was ravenous for a conversation that didn't end in who owned a Porsche and who a Mercedes or what was the best place to have a winter break. I was salivating for one of those interminable arguments that lead like a Marco Polo caravan into wild places and leave you wanting to find God's address and chap him up and ask him to explain what he was on about when he made all this.

For Scotland is one of the most intense talking-shops I have ever been in. Here the Ancient Mariner haunts many pubs and Socrates sometimes wears a bunnet, and women at bus-stops say serious things about the world. The talk may touch on anything from the essential Scottish sporting hero to politics. But, in my experience, two common factors will tend to recur regardless of the subject under debate: the talk will at some point connect with non-material values and it will, frequently at the same time, challenge current social orthodoxies. There are reasons why this should be so.

Scotland was born poor. There are two main ways to react to poverty. One is to fall in love with money, since that is what you do not have. The other is to generate values beyond the economic, since otherwise you acknowledge your own inferiority unless you can acquire wealth. Scotland grew up with the potential to do both.

The country contained that implicit division within itself, like the internal striations in an apparently solid rock that only needed some natural calamity in order to become a fissure. Scotland's calamity came in 1707. The Act of Union made a separation in the nation that created a unique and confused historical legacy. The people were separated from their legislature. This meant that insofar as democratic government is the fulfilment of the people's will, Scots would be denied the means of self-government. Yet they retained the characteristics of a nation without the political identity of one.

This situation had one major side-effect. The Act of Union had not been brought about by the will of the people. It had been brought about by the will of a few entrepreneurial spirits. They traded in the sovereignty of Scotland for two gains: money in hand and the opportunity of advancement. That opportunity lay primarily in London. It was the rationalisation and consolidation of a trend that had begun with the removal of King James's court to England in 1603. The division in Scotland had become explicit. There was on the one side an Anglicised minority, a controlling establishment whose motivation was accepting the materialistic values that made sense of the English connection. There was, on the other side, a more radically Scottish majority whose motivation was the maintenance of a distinctly Scottish identity and for whom the cost of realising that motivation was adopting the deeper, non-materialistic values that were needed to make sense of their determined Scottishness.

The division has never been a clean one. Each side has infiltrated the other. The self-interest of the minority has often been tempered by the weight of community values ranged against it. The community values of the majority have often been compromised by the secession of greater or lesser numbers of Scots to the pursuit of materialism. That is why the Scots have been simultaneously both the furtherers of English materialism and imperialism and potentially its greatest subverters.

The results of this dichotomy, which had been foreshadowed by the intensity of the Reformation in Scotland, were cultural as well as political. This ambiguity in the nation's sense of itself helps to explain why two major Scottish writers, who have achieved international reputations, have a status so dramatically different in their own country. Sir Walter Scott conquered Europe but he remains marginal to most Scots' sense of themselves. Robert Burns still represents Scottishness so effectively that he retains for many, even today, the authority of a talking icon.

But the greatest single effect of 1707, the year of the Great Divide in the Scottish psyche, has been felt continuously for nearly 300 years. You can take the people out of the parliament but you can't take the parliament out of the people. In that imaginary Scottish Parliament without powers that has been sitting in uninterrupted session for so long in some dark corner of Scotland's dream of itself, one brute fact has been re-enacted again and again: it is the majority who form the opposition, the minority the government.

That is a trauma-inducing state of affairs in a democracy. No wonder the Scottish psyche is a strange place. No wonder Scots are called argumentative. No wonder a union representative in Vancouver, an expatriate Scot, told me his union wouldn't allow him to speak on television because the sound of a Scottish accent in a political context sent householders off on a quick search for the Reds under their beds. If Scots have a long history of being agin the government, it isn't surprising. The government was never theirs. That was the shattering result of 1707: the majority of Scottish people were disenfranchised from their potential rights. They have not yet won them back. The Act of Union effectively put Scotland politically in a time-lock, moved it aside out of the mainstream so that by the time universal suffrage arrived it couldn't mean as much as it might have. For Scots it was circumscribed by the events of 1707.

The growth of the British Labour Movement seemed to offer a way out of the impasse. Much of the movement's energy and most of its radicalism came from Scotland. The majority in permanent opposition had found a vehicle for their discontent. That vehicle has certainly carried the aspirations of the Scottish people forward, no matter how often it has stalled, but now it may have broken down completely.

And these days as Scotland looks around for the umpteenth time to try to work out where it is, a disconcerting truth emerges. The view, despite the energy expended, despite the distance travelled, is oddly familiar. It may not be precisely where we were but it more closely resembles where we were than where we thought we were going. Look. There, still dominating the landscape of our consciousness, is that same ugly, depressing landmark – political powerlessness. In fact, look more closely. Someone's been adding to it. It's bigger.

Of course, it would be when you think of it. Since 1707, Scotland's tenuous awareness of its political identity has depended upon a tacit agreement that refused to descend to anything as coarse as a clear constitution. Such an agreement was nice but it did not foresee the arrival of a Home Counties Valkyrie wearing hobnailed veld-shoen.

For the past ten years we have had a Prime Minister (name her not, lest a vision of her come) who thinks consensus is a way of falsifying the voters' roll. She is insensitive enough not to see any insult in vowing to take socialism off the agenda, thus glibly disenfranchising the majority of the Scottish people. Her answer to the awkward difference of Scotland is to steamroller it and make it a motorway into England (no doubt reassuring open-mouthed Scots the while by informing them that tarmacadam is a Scottish invention). She is aided in this lofty endeavour by a British Labour Movement the dominating present principle of which seems to be conformity to the mood of the moment, rather like a revered but troubled philosopher volunteering for a lobotomy.

1707 is with us still. How could it be otherwise? The most significant development is that its effects have become more chronic, closer to the terminal – thanks to the present government. Because of the peculiar ambivalence of Scotland's political position, the commitment of many Scots to the British Labour Movement has so far taken our aspirations (towards some kind of self-government) mainly round in circles. We are still essentially where we were. When you go round in circles, all you do is use up time. We've used up most of ours. And look. Here comes the night and we are stranded here, still in political no man's land. As darkness threatens to descend on the serious possibility of Scottish self-determination, will it be for the last time? For by the time we waken into renewed possibilities, they will be different possibilities, as we – if this government succeeds – will be a significantly different people. Will we rediscover ourselves too late, wandering down differing but not dissimilar convictions that at one time almost converged into a coherent nation? Before that happens, what can we do?

We can gather separately round the separate hearths of our domestic preoccupations and forget it. We can halloo at one another through the growing dark from our mutually exclusive positions, demanding that it is the other who must make the move to get it together. Or we can gather under the one remaining light there is and confront one another honestly and try to agree on who we are and who we want to be. That light is called the Scottish Constitutional Convention. It is not a big light. But it's all we have. None of us should exaggerate what we can achieve with the help of its illumination. Of course, it will not give us devolution. But, of course, neither would it lead us to independence in Europe. There is only one thing the Scottish Constitutional Convention could possibly achieve. That is the clarification in the consciousness of the Scottish people of what it is they want.

140

The bulk of the Scottish people remain, after nearly 300 years of practice, profound political sceptics. They need an event traumatic enough to jolt them out of their scepticism. The Scottish Constitutional Convention, if it is representative enough, can supply that event. It can supply it by taking to Westminster a demand that represents a clear majority of Scots and then having that demand inevitably rejected. The result will be to precipitate a climactic choice in Scotland: give up your aspirations or make them happen for yourselves.

The true purpose of the Scottish Constitutional Convention should be pre-political. It should be there not to deliver anything to the Scots except the awareness of the contempt with which they are treated, the anger that will dynamise them into serious political action.

That is why it is specious politicking to make the point that the Prime Minister won't listen to any demand for devolution. The Prime Minister won't listen to anything she doesn't already agree with. The Scottish Constitutional Convention won't be seriously trying to tell the Prime Minister anything. What could possibly be the point of that? It will be trying to tell the Scottish people something.

What it tells them must, most importantly, be authoritative, an echo of a national conviction. The Convention can achieve that degree of conviction without the presence of the Scottish Conservative Party, that cuckoo in the nest of Scottish politics, living fat off votes that don't belong to it. But it needs the presence of the Scottish National Party. If the Nationalists continue to stay away, I think they will have misread the significance of the Convention. They will have seen it as a forum for the furtherance of specific party policies and will have missed the point that the precise nature of the demand ultimately made by the Convention will be less important than the weight that demand carries. At a time when it was crucial to come as close as possible to some kind of unity, no matter how uneasy, they will have emphasised division. Instead of helping to clarify Scotland to itself, they will have confused it further.

They are taking a gamble, of course, I think they will lose. I think they deserve to. This is no time for party political manoeuvres. This is a time when we are still trying to earn the means to make such manoeuvres relevant. The stake in this gamble is Scotland itself. For if the Scottish Constitutional Convention fails to generate among the Scottish people a widespread and dynamic awareness of what they must do politically to achieve some form of self-government, the country's future is bleak. Our distinctive sense of ourselves, sustained with such difficulty and determination since 1707, is likely to erode further. Scotland may become shallower and shallower until it succumbs to being just a further expression of the non-dialectical materialism of contemporary British politics.

X the Unknown

I CAME ACROSS HIM IN MY FIRST YEAR OR TWO OF TEACHING. It was before comprehensivisation, but the school I was in was not selective. He was one of those in what we called E classes, which were – among other things – flourishing knackeries for educational theory, places from which carefully contrived pedagogical attitudes emerged flayed to raw self-pity in 40 minutes.

X had bright red curly hair, as if his head was on fire. In a sense, it was. He was a social arsonist. His idea of making contact with other people was to abrade with them, not maliciously, just as a matter of course. It was a friction that influenced every teacher he came into contact with.

The simplest request would be greeted with an incredulous jerk of the head, as if he had just seen a meteor falling. 'Look at page 20,' you would say, and while 30-odd heads were lowered, one was jerking. You saw the mouth form '20', trying to penetrate its cabbalistic content. Arrived at the page, his eyes would scout it carefully, presumably looking for some explanation of your weird request, then he would check the page beyond it, then the page before, then he would glance around for confirmation of his astonishment, then he would study you with bewildered eyes, as if checking for antennae.

Twenty minutes of his relentless amazement could reduce any teacher to screaming at him – which always amazed him, of course.

Initially, I had felt some anger, too, but I gradually learnt to appreciate him. He was simply trying to tell us something and he had evolved a subtle and elaborate language for doing it. His art was surprise. He was a master of banal amazement. From beginning to end of the period, he was in un-interrupted communication with you through head-jerks, widened eyes, head scratchings, spread palms, puzzled glances. I came to realise that not only was he trying to tell me something, but that what he was telling me was right.

What I was doing *was* amazing. The assumptiveness of teachers *is* amazing: that tendency to make a series of predetermined offerings to the class on the basis of what the teacher thinks they ought to have. The tendency is inevitable to some degree but the important and constantly

142

adjustable decision the teacher has to make is: to what degree? It was in that crucial empirical area that X became my teacher.

He was well qualified for the job, having withstood the irrelevance of numerous pedagogues already, with his amazement at their wilfulness completely undiminished. The rest of the class seemed pretty well brainwashed into accepting whatever the classroom offered. I imagine if you had asked them to copy out *War and Peace*, they would have cynically pretended to comply, secretly mapping out the broken pencils, staved hands and mysterious astigmatisms they would depend on along the way like oases.

But X was different. His naïve capacity for amazement at everything that happened in the classroom was undentable. He kept it burnished like a shield in his crusade to establish the abnormality of education. I came to depend on him. At the moment when his vast array of tics and signals fell silent, like an army making camp, I knew I was no longer talking to myself but to the people in front of me. Contact had been established. With his help, I managed to achieve a rapport with the class which would otherwise have been impossible.

He was a genuine educational pioneer. Singlehanded, he laid the foundation of what little I know about the teaching of English: that it is first and last a human relationship, founded, like all valid relationships, on mutual respect, and where the teacher has no respect for the pupil, the pupil's rebellion is to be admired; that, similarly, where the pupil has no respect for the individuality of the teacher, the teacher's anger is to be admired; that if for both it isn't a learning situation, it won't work as it should; that it is simply a matter of trying to elicit and develop such abilities as the pupil may have – it has nothing to do with obliging him to conform to invented criteria.

Regardless of the countless other aspects involved, I believe that the indispensable core of it lies in that honest relationship. X was the first to demand it of me.

I am grateful to him and so I remember his quirks with that affection we all feel for those teachers who have really got through to us. I remember him playing chess, for example, on the last day of term. After he had made a move, he sat with his head bobbing back and forward, like somebody on a terracing trying to get a better view of the game. He had only just learnt how to play but already he had developed his own distinctive approach: the muffler-and-nicky-tams method, you might call it.

The basic philosophy, as far as I could see, was simple: rape the queen and the other sods will surrender. I still remember the way his pawns drummed across the board towards their doom. You could imagine them shod in bovver boots. I remember, too, the unselfconscious courage with which he handled the most ferocious stammer I have ever heard. He demanded the chance to answer questions. Having given him the floor, I used to watch helplessly the preparatory twitch of his face and the raising of his right shoulder like someone getting ready to bump his private cross, as he set out on his lonely safari towards meaning.

For me there have been so many since him, of course, as there must be for every teacher – a great host of those unsung pupil-educationists who teach teachers how to teach. Short on theory but massively adept in practice, they teach purely by repeated demonstration of those skills the teachers must have, such as instinct, subtle honesty and a patiently acquired understanding of the person they are dealing with.

They offer no certification to those who accept their tutelage. In any case, in the difficult terms which they lay down there can be no final success. There is only the daily barter of success and failure. What the honest teacher gets out of it, apart from the money, is an uncomfortably shifting sense of his ability. Now you have it, now you don't.

There are no satisfying finalities in this profession. You cannot walk round the finished building and say, 'I designed that.' You cannot even lift the paper and read a mixed review of how you taught *The Old Man and the Sea*. The air into which our efforts vanish is very thin. Having tried to do it today, you will have to try and do it again tomorrow – which is perhaps why some teachers set too much store by examination results. In a wilderness even a wooden compass can be reassuring. Beyond that, the most significant guides you have are the class that is in your room and the pantheon of definitive moments your experience has given you, the laurel wreaths and the crowns of thorns.

Those moments are what the pupils teach the teacher. Exactly because they are utterly specific moments, experiential bridges between one person and another, it is hard to reconstruct them in the abstract and try to make them carry general conclusions. But if I were to attempt to express the significance of the sum of such moments in my own experience, I would suggest that they are all renewals of the same awareness: that, outside of educational theory, there is no such thing as a pupil. There are only people.

That's easy enough to acknowledge in the abstract. The problem is to learn it on your pulses, to entertain it not just as an intellectual cipher, some kind of liberal badge to be worn at educational conferences, but to acquire it as a difficult, daily practice.

This practice involves the rejection of school as an institution for processing people into predetermined roles. People who attend schools are too often approached as merely fodder to meet our society's needs. Education only begins in acknowledging what a libel on their natures this is. Teaching should be an attempt to meet the needs of the taught, not of the teachers. Illich's distinction between 'hope' and 'expectation' is relevant here. We should never, through a desire to equip them with the means for having expectations, forget that what they have a right to is hope. A career is a poor substitute for a life.

So let X, and every other 'pupil', be an unknown quantity. That way, by keeping our necessary preconceptions at least flexible, we may learn from them what it is we have to teach.

Gulliver's Last Voyage

AND SO IT WAS IN MY LATER YEARS THAT, CONTINUING insatiably curious about strange lands and strange customs, I quitted my house at Redriff and took shipping again. Having been condemned, as I have stated heretofore, by Nature and Fortune to an active and restless life, I was not to find on this voyage that my hunger for the incredible and my thirst for the exotic were to be disappointed. Here were feasts of strangeness and hogsheads of wonder.

For on this occasion I came upon a land more mystifying than Lilliput, more awesome than Brobdingnag and floating less substantially than ever did Laputa. But, being that I am advanced in years, I pray that my courteous readers will not desire of me the long and perhaps tedious narratives of my past. While youth is an endless conversation, age is but a series of remarks. I offer here the merest lineaments of a sketch.

I have found, I say, the strangest place that ever yet I came to. It is a country that is not a country. It has no borders, at least none that matter. It has a name but the name has no meaning, except in the passionately convinced utterance of its people. This is not a country but a mirage of one. These are not a people but the apparition of a people.

Consider their miasmic sense of their own past. All nations need a history. It is to a people what memory is to an individual. It sustains the continuity that is meaning. It is the shared sense of self that is identity. It is the very furniture of the people's minds, where they can live in comfort with themselves.

Yet in this strange land what is it that I find?

These people come as near to the absence of a history as any I have met. It cannot be that the history is not there (since when was there a present that was not at least in part defined by its own past?) but rather that they do not wish to know it. With a few very honourable and largely unheeded exceptions, those commentators on ages gone by do not discover history. They invent it.

Thus, the heroes and heroines that have been proffered to the people as a mirror wherein they may see themselves are no more than mockeries of the nation they purport to represent. In this fashion, much sentiment is expended on a princeling of dubious ancestry whose chief attributes, or so it appears to me, were a venality of spirit and a gargantuan capacity for intoxicating liquors.

Perhaps one reason for the place of high esteem he holds in the people's hearts is that he won every battle he engaged in except the one that mattered. In that final rout, he demonstrated all the military skill of a child in swaddling clothes and then fled, leaving many of his countrymen to perish. That the people still hold him in affection and, indeed, yet sing songs in memory of his disastrous presence among them may betoken their hidden disbelief in their own powers. They show for certain an inordinate loving of grand failure.

Similarly, there is a queen much talked about and written about among them. Dramas are sometimes enacted on her sad fate. Tears are shed. Yet, as far as my confessedly-limited researches in the matter have led me, I cannot but conclude that her silliness conspired with her circumstances to undo her. She had an intelligence wayward enough to make a butterfly seem constant and, if the observation be not too cruel a one, I am obliged to think that the losing of her head – as was in fact the case – must have been no more than a minor inconvenience to her.

There is, too, an ancient bard who wrote in a language more venerable than the people currently use. Much has been made of him as a receptacle of the true spirit of the nation. His influence spread to many other countries and many famous men made obeisance to him. Yet if you will believe that he existed at all, you may soon be found trying to plot the exact location of a rainbow's end that you may avail yourself of the pot of gold.

Wondering why these things should be has furnished me with much occasion for thought. The result has been that I tend towards the belief, not generally held perhaps, that some terrible event has happened in this people's past, an event they find themselves not quite capable of facing. This event, if my supposition be allowed, may be likened in its effect to a childhood experience – let us say a profound betrayal by its parents – that ever after leaves the child seeking to avoid the memory and the implications of that experience, so that it grows into an adult denying the reality of its past.

Let me suggest what this event may have been. It is well recorded of this people's past that at a certain point in its history the country was sold. It was not conquered, it was not overrun, it was not occupied. It was simply sold – among many protestations, it is true. The salesmen in question were a very small group of persons called, quaintly enough, the nobility.

Now, since the common people did in no way concur with this selling of their sovereignty to a neighbour, they have continually ever since been inclined to behave as if it had not happened. There is something oddly moving in this spectacle. This people's ferocious belief that they still exist has a smack of heroism to it.

But heroism can be a usurer that charges exorbitant rates. These rates often take the form of deducting from us our sense of the more banal realities we live among. In the case of this people, the price they pay is twofold.

The first price is, as I have suggested, a losing of the reality of their past. So determined are they to hallucinate themselves into a nation that they see their history either in the events that preceded the selling or in such later events as imitated the time before the selling. In this they lose the essence of themselves. For, in truth, their real identity lies in what came after, in the time of the machines, when they stayed as human among the artefacts and as humanely concerned each with the other as any people I have known.

Yet they continue to allow that impressive, naked reality to be dressed in fictitious robes. There was a man who came among them, a man of great ability, who rendered much of their past into a doubtful fiction. He was less a sculptor of the truth than a tailor of lies. He dressed his people not in the reality of themselves, but in a national costume. It is sad to see them pretend to be who they never were. Not only their bodies are adorned in such mock regalia, but their minds as well.

The second price they pay is, after the falsity of the past, the agonising confusion of the present. For this place is abounding in such anomalies that, be they not resolved, the people perish.

For example, they have a most handsome city in the east of the land. This they call the capital. This is a fascinating usage which can only make you wonder what they can possibly mean. The city is the capital of the country in the same way that a statue's head is a real head, the brain of the place having been removed (by very clumsy surgery) and transported into the neighbouring nation. Thus, when you visit the part that they name Parliament Square, you will search in vain for any sign of a parliament.

Furthermore, strange customs still pertain. The natives intermittently engage in an activity they are pleased to call 'elections'. All the adults, as the people still call themselves, make marks upon pieces of paper and call it voting. Then, as soon as these votings are counted, they are rendered instantly irrelevant, since it is the neighbouring country that will determine the nature of the government that rules. Yet the natives continue to evince much excitement as to the outcome. Certain men of science have called this strange behaviour 'conditioned reflex'.

Such is the barely imaginable strangeness of the place wherein I find myself. But here I shall stay. I have completed my last voyage. Where else might I find a land so rich in oddity – unique, it is my suspicion, in all the climes of the world?

Also, there must soon be a resolving of this dilemma, an ascent or descent from the people's limbo. This is an interesting time and place. I shall abide the outcome. Either these people must ere long vanish into the very vapour of their dreams or crystallise into the unrealised reality of themselves. I long most fervently for the latter.

Wreckage that Floats

The Courage of our Doubts

A BOOK IS LIKE A FOREIGN COUNTRY. YOU TAKE YOUR identity with you, like a passport, but you have to give the author the chance to ratify it or to question it to some extent on his or her terms. Your intelligence is legal currency in that foreign land, as much of it as you can bring with you. But prejudices are contraband. You should allow them to be confiscated at the covers.

When the book is what is called a 'thriller' or 'detective story', there is one prejudice in particular you should try to get rid of before you enter. This is the assumption that such a book is automatically inferior to 'literature'. As someone who has written both detective stories and 'serious' fiction, I have been made aware of the prevalence of this attitude.

Before I wrote *Laidlaw*, I had written a long novel called *Docherty,* which was critically well received and won the Whitbread Prize. With the subsequent publication of *Laidlaw*, I discovered to my surprise that I had offended some of my former supporters by degenerating, in their eyes, to the level of detective fiction. It was as if I had committed some social gaffe. One man who had read all my stuff went so far as to chastise me for doing something as 'worthless' as a detective novel. I suggested in the heat of the moment that, if brains were food, he could be suffering from malnutrition.

Good writing occurs where it occurs. If you are alert enough and appreciative enough, you will learn to know it when you see it. There is no other way to guarantee its presence.

Of course, a lot of detective novels are pretty dire. But then so is a lot of established literature. It is true that Agatha Christie often writes as if the human species were made out of cardboard. But it is also true that D. H. Lawrence often writes as if they were made out of ectoplasm.

The only honest test is in the reading, line by line, while refusing to have your responses predetermined by generalised attitudes. The only reliable distinction between good and bad writing is to be found on the page and its effect, in how it involves, how it enlightens, how it moves, how it enlarges your sense of your own humanity.

The assumed, automatic distinction between detective stories and literature can only serve as a way for people whose reading habits have petrified to protect themselves from having to think afresh. Such a distinction is phoney, an intellectual attitude quite counterfeit and it will buy you nothing – in terms of the reading experience – but the unearned confirmation of your own sterile preconceptions.

Laidlaw is what people like to call a 'genre novel'. The label has a limited value in that it vaguely forewarns the reader of the kind of reading experience that may be inside the covers. But, like most labels, it conceals as much as it reveals, inviting comparisons with other genre novels that may have no significant similarity.

The result of this may be that, because of false expectations, the reader is so busy seeing what isn't there that he or she fails to see what is there. Putting the label 'genre' on a book can make readers decide what it's like before they have come to know it, or at least decide what it should be like. They will sometimes approach such a book the way a stranger will approach another stranger at a conference, reading the name-tag on his lapel as if it seriously informed him of who the other is. For an author that can be a depressing experience.

The scene is London. It is 9.30 in the morning. The night before, the second Laidlaw novel – *The Papers of Tony Veitch* – has been launched. There was a party. It was one of those parties so long that it began to feel like a way of life.

Now I am sitting in a radio studio, somewhere near the Tottenham Court Road, I seem to think. But, given the way I feel, it could be in New York. I am trying to reassemble my few remaining brain cells before I am interviewed by a woman in a radio studio in Edinburgh. The interview begins. Throughout the interview I will be sitting alone, staring at the brown perforated wall of the tiny studio. It will not help my state of mind.

Nor will the woman. The main thrust of her questions is to establish why I have written a 'police procedural' novel which has so few details about police procedures. I cannot believe the irrelevance of her questions and, in my fragile state, begin to feel the world is a plot against me. It is in vain that I try to suggest that the book I wrote was not, in fact, a police procedural novel. She knows what I've done okay and proceeds to interview me in detail about a book I didn't write. It's like being back at school in the bad old days and getting belted for a terrible essay that somebody else wrote, because the teacher mixed up the names.

When the interview began, I had been unhappy about the long-range nature of our conversation, about the fact that she was in Edinburgh. By the time it ended, I was delighted that she was in Edinburgh. I think I

154

would have preferred her to be in Outer Mongolia. I think I would still prefer her to be in Outer Mongolia.

And that's one problem I have found with having written *Laidlaw*. People keep judging it in terms that don't apply to it. It's like having done the long jump and finding yourself assessed on the height achieved.

Laidlaw has been called a police procedural. It isn't. It makes no serious attempt to deal in any detail with the technical procedures of police work, partly because such procedures have little to do with what I was after and partly because I find such procedures largely boring.

Laidlaw has been called a mystery. It isn't, at least not in the sense in which most people would understand the word as applied to a crime story. The book begins with a crime committed and the criminal identified. That, in the usual sense of a mystery, is the story over. It's not a whodunnit. It is a whydunnit – only in that area does the book contain any mystery.

Laidlaw is less an example of the traditional detective story than an attempted challenge to it. I don't read a lot of detective stories. With many of them, I suffer from reality-starvation after a few pages and find myself staring at the depicted events across a credibility gap as wide as the Grand Canyon.

This is not an objection to the genre, just an objection to the undemanding uses to which it is sometimes put. I didn't want to write a detective novel that was mainly a way to get through a long train journey, a substitute for an armful of newspapers with crossword puzzles in them.

One of the things that interested me about the detective story was its potential for development. Gore Vidal has written about 'colonising the genres'. This seems to me to make good sense, especially at a time when the falsely final division between 'quality' fiction and 'popular' fiction is being constantly reinforced by those cultural maintenance workers, reviewers and literary academics.

It seemed to me a division worth trying to cross. It wasn't a distinction which, in my experience, held good too often anyway. On the one hand, I could remember reading books which came to me garlanded in tributes, tipped to win the Booker Prize, sounding as if they ought to be read in a position of prayer, and I had found that many of them were a Gobi of disappointment, arid of almost everything except a certain self-conscious worthiness and without enough blood in them to feed a gnat. On the other hand, I had often felt that a lot of popular writers, ignored by intellectual commentators, were performing yeoman service for literature, maintaining the audience in an age of declining readers.

One way to try to cross the division would be to produce a detective story that hopefully made no deliberate concessions to the reader in the quality of the writing and which handled the subject matter as more than a means of titillating the reader's deductive powers. I saw the detective story as a popular form, capable of sustaining 'serious' writing. There were, of course, precedents for doing this.

I decided not to confuse solemnity with seriousness or fluency with articulacy. I wanted a book that dealt with the life of the streets and took it as seriously as any other matter of fiction. I wanted a book that wasn't intimidated into imagining that popularity equates with superficiality. I wanted a book that was unapologetic about the form in which it was cast. (*Crime and Punishment* is, after all, a kind of detective story.)

The impulse to write such a book might have remained one of the numerous ideas that lie about my mind like so many inert Frankenstein monsters in the laboratory of a mad scientist, waiting for the electrical storm that will galvanise them into life. The electrical charge that gives them animation is always compulsion. I have never written any book that I didn't feel at the time to some extent compelled to write. How that compulsion came about in relation to *Laidlaw* I'm not sure but I can suggest, in retrospect, some of its possible sources.

Having finished *Docherty*, a long novel about a West of Scotland mining family in the first quarter of the 20th century, I was hungry to connect with a contemporary theme. Like a short-term Rip Van Winkle, I woke out of my preoccupation with the past and found that I was fascinated with what was going on around me.

This interest in things of my own time focused most dramatically on Glasgow, probably my favourite city. There resurfaced in me a desire to write about the place. This was an ambition that had been with me for a long time.

The strength of my desire to write about Glasgow perhaps came from the fact that I am not a native of the place. I had been familiar with the city since my teens. A lot of people believe in Glasgow like a religion. For me, it wasn't a religion into which I was born. I was a convert.

As a convert I studied it carefully and examined the articles of my faith in it. I loved the people, the Socratic scepticism of them, the disbelieving looks they gave when they thought someone was shooting them a line, as if they were listening to a mouth that had declared independence from its brain. Most street-wise city-dwellers have developed a style – Cockneys, for example – the implied essence of which is that they know more than you. Their talk is full of jargon you're not meant to understand and questions that are invitations to make a fool of yourself and prearranged put-downs. Glaswegians tend to be different. They are great conversational counter-punchers. The implied essence of their style is not that they know but that you don't know either. It makes for some very democratic exchanges and a continuing process of mutual learning.

I loved the place. The city has always given me a working-class variant of the feeling I get in Paris. It isn't hard, when walking in Paris, to imagine that just about every corner should carry a plaque to one formidable intelligence or another. A lot of the most influential ideas of modern life have lived there at one time or another in transit to all over the world.

What I feel in Glasgow is the accumulated weight of working-class experience. The streets of the former Second City of the British Empire are haunted by what the Industrial Revolution has meant to us, the tensions it imposed on the human spirit and the resilience that grew out of the tensions. There, more intensely than anywhere else, you can sense the force that shaped the nature of modern Scotland. It was a brute force but, like a gallous lion-tamer with a chair (and a table and some other bits of furniture), Glasgow men and women domesticated the beast and made it part of their way of life. Their history, I believe, tells contemporary Scots most clearly where they have been and who they are.

No wonder I wanted to write about the place. But the idea remained lifeless. The electrical charge that would transform a possibility into a compulsion was still missing. Then, if it doesn't sound too much like Joan of Arc, I heard a voice. I noted down what it was saying.

The voice was saying random things. I had no idea of the wider context in which it was speaking. It was an abrasive voice, not saying what it was supposed to say but what it believed, things it had worked out with difficulty for itself. I knew that the man the voice belonged to inhabited a hard place, some kind of front line of life. Whatever it was he did, it didn't allow him to hide from the harsher things. Slowly, from jotted remarks and tentative notes, the man behind the voice emerged. He was a detective in Glasgow and his name was Laidlaw, Jack Laidlaw.

The previously uncertain impulses formed into clarity around him. Traditionally, plot grows out of character. In any novel that – as Forster puts it – 'oh, dear, yes . . . tells a story', events only become meaningful in relation to the people involved in them. It is *precisely* those people in relation to *precisely* those circumstances that generate the plot. Exactly the same set of circumstances applied to a different group of people would yield a quite different story.

With the arrival of Jack Laidlaw, the possibility for a book that had lain dormant in my mind jerked into life. He stood aggressively at the centre of a vaguely imagined novel and invited me to construct it around him. By being who he was, he suggested ways in which I might challenge some of the conventions of detective fiction and hopefully deepen them. His nature would to a large extent determine the nature of the book that would carry his name.

Laidlaw says, 'A crime you're trying to solve is a temporary mystery. Solved, it's permanent. What can the courts do with this then? Who knows what it is? It's maybe just another love story.'

Laidlaw says, 'I'm not just suspicious of the people I'm chasing. I'm suspicious of the people I'm chasing them *for*.'

With these remarks, which are central to his sense of himself and what he is trying to do, Laidlaw negates two of the common conventions of the detective story. The first is that the story fulfils itself in the solution of the crime and the apprehension or dramatic death of the criminal. The second is that the straight world is morally right and the criminal world is morally wrong.

By coming to realise what motivated Laidlaw, I began to realise how a detective story that centred on him might subvert some of the conventions. Like all conventions, these aren't just technical matters. If the premise of a book is that there is a complete moral division between legitimate society and the underworld, the impulse of that book is liable to be reactionary. It will serve to shore up social preconceptions, unexamined attitudes, complacent assumptions.

Any book operating within that convention will be a cosy conspiracy between the writer and the readers. Here we will sit like Olympians, the implied contract between writer and reader says, and watch *them* get their come-uppance. Society will be conceived as static. Readers will be protected from the more disturbing elements of criminal activity (how it threatens their values) and their reactions will be delivered to them like pre-cooked food.

But if that convention is challenged, if the perceptual barriers between the legitimate world and the criminal world are broken down, the assumed space between them can be infiltrated with doubts and readers may lose the bearings they started out with. Then their relationship to the material they are reading may become dynamic, as it should be. They have a chance of seeing both the criminal world and their own world from new angles, each one mirroring the other strangely. When that happens, the detective novel can become not a means of reinforcing unexamined prejudices but a way of undermining them.

Laidlaw, by his very character, spearheads this endeavour in the book. He believes that a measured doubt is the most fructifying force in the world. His wife is aware that even their relationship is obliged to inhabit this uncertainty: 'The trouble was, it occurred to her, that with him you never knew whether you were the maiden or the dragon.'

It is a doubt which doesn't just move outwards into the case he is investigating but forever inwards as well, into the terms of his own life:

> He was a policeman, a Detective Inspector, and more and more he wondered how that had happened.

158

'I mean if everybody could waken up tomorrow morning and have the courage of their doubts, not their convictions, the millennium would be here. I think false certainties are what destroy us.'

Milligan: 'That's Laidlaw. He's running about no man's land with a German helmet and a Black Watch jacket.'

And, if the book succeeds, he will to some extent take the reader there with him. (The extent to which Laidlaw manages that, of course, isn't solely dependent on the book; it also partly depends on the reader's capacity to come out from behind entrenched attitudes.)

The central mystery of *Laidlaw* is Laidlaw. It is a detective novel in which the detective is at least as mysterious, and as difficult to be comfortable with, as any of the criminals. Through him, the assumptive certainties the reader might want to depend on keep refracting into doubt.

Since it is Laidlaw who solves the crime, even the solution partakes of his nature. The significance of the crime does not end in identifying the criminal. Solved, the mystery is permanent or at least is left in the mind of the reader, lives on past the bringing to trial of the criminal.

The specific mystery of the crime proves to be merely a code which – once it is broken – becomes a key to unlocking a larger mystery in which we are all implicated, of which all of our lives are a part. At the same time as he is investigating the crime, Laidlaw is investigating the terms of his own life and is offering readers a paradigm for the investigation of the terms of their lives.

Laidlaw, I believe, is an unusual phenomenon in detective fiction. He is a subversive policeman. Laidlaw doesn't patrol and check out the readers' sense of their position in society in order to ensure its security but in order to burgle it.

But his is a strange kind of burglary. I have found that the commonest immediate reaction to burglary by its victims is not to count the insurance money or to wonder how they can ever replace the unusual ring that was given to them by Auntie Jemma. Such reactions may be in the post. But the first stomach-chilling response tends to be much more primitive. It is the feeling that their very sense of themselves has been invaded.

If Laidlaw succeeds, if he manages to neutralise the elaborate alarm systems of automatic response by which we maintain a privacy of comfort in the midst of public confusion, he should leave the reader with a benign variant of that sense of invasion. The feeling should be benign, firstly, because it is safely contained in a book (in other words, it is not experience but para-experience) and, secondly, because Laidlaw is a psychic burglar who should give as well as take.

If the Laidlaw effect were to work to its fullest, the reader would waken into a slightly changed awareness, which is not so much about an insult to your sense of yourself as about a possible partial reassessment of it. The comfortingly familiar furniture of the mind would be rearranged a bit and rifled. Assumptions as intimate as a hairbrush would either be missing or no longer as comfortable, since they had been handled carelessly by another and were therefore less definitive of you.

But there would also be new, unfamiliar presences: an insight which you hadn't known was yours and which you weren't sure you could devise a use for; an odd idea that you would have to find a place for; maybe a motivation made in a working-class housing scheme sitting strangely in the sitting-room of a suburban bungalow. You would have to work out anew, to however minimal a degree, where it is you live.

To make that happen isn't easy. It requires not just a lot of goodwill and generosity of spirit from the reader but a difficult search for an appropriate technique on the part of the writer – a search rendered more fraught by the familiarity of the genre, a form where so many people will have decided what it is you have done before you do it. But the difficulty of achieving a purpose was never a valid argument against trying to realise it.

Basically, I agreed with Laidlaw. I should do – I had created him from some part of myself. If that was the quarry he was after, the mystery beyond the mystery, it was up to me to try and help him to catch it. He needed a trap that was appropriately selective, that would let the smaller, domesticated species of the form pass through unmolested and only close on the big game.

He needed a plot.

For me the commonest crime in a detective novel is the crime against the nature of experience. This is a crime committed by the author. It results from making the dynamic of the book the resolution of a puzzle.

The effect of this attitude is to push the reality of human experience, its passion, its pain, its grief, more and more towards the abstract. The smaller irritations of this effect, like a recurring astigmatism, abound in detective fiction.

There is the detective who is beaten up, abducted, shot at, threatened with death and yet appears to experience no significant trauma. He comes to, shrugs and carries on, as if his head were made of ferro-concrete and his nerves lagged with asbestos. He has ceased to be significantly a person and become a vehicle for carrying the plot. There is the relative of the deceased whose grief would seem inadequate to the demise of a budgie, because the writer has reduced his or her humanity to the cipher that is necessary to further the story.

These are, of course, conventions but, as I have suggested, conventions are never merely technical. They are ways of determining how we see experience. Beyond the robot detective and the relatives who react to the death of a loved one as if they had come upon a broken cup, there is a kind of insult to our lives. These devices can lead us, seductively and almost imperceptibly, towards a sterile place where the reasons for which we commit the ultimate enormity against one another become an intellectual pastime. Murder can become no more than a conundrum.

In that way, one of the harshest realities of our society, which our complacency might choke on, is processed into a nice, digestible lie. Violent death is filleted of its hardness and sauced with superficiality and served up as cuisine.

I didn't want to write a book like that. In order to focus the readers' attention away from a trivialising concentration on human actions as a puzzle, I began by presenting them with the crime and the criminal. It was a way of serving notice that this book wasn't a whodunnit. It was about something else.

Also, the nature of the crime itself was important. The crimes the thought of which I find hardest to cope with are all abuses of the person. Reading of the molestation or physical abuse of a child in a newspaper, for example, I often have to put the paper aside. I feel all my liberal attitudes threatening to collapse into atavistic anger, a manic rage against such inhumanity. Rape appals me as much as murder does. It is, effectively, the murder of the self without murdering the person.

By making the crime one of sexual abuse and murder, I put myself and my own attitudes under pressure, which is where I think the writer should be. I was in no danger of merely playing lowbrow intellectual games with an imagined set of circumstances. This wasn't murder at the vicarage. At the centre of the book was a harsh, immediate and brutal action, the appalling imagined reality of which would oblige me – and hopefully the reader – to continue to take it seriously.

These two factors, the nature of the crime and the abandonment of the whodunnit element, put the book at once into that area of creative hazard where for me all worthwhile writing must take place. Creativity is risk. By working without two of the common safety nets of the genre ('let's-concentrate-on-the-puzzle' and 'here-crime-will-come-deodorised'), I was trying to generate a more dynamic relationship between the writer and the reader through the story.

There would be tension but it wouldn't be the tension of wondering who would be next to die or which of several suspects was the murderer. It would be, first of all, the tension of wondering what will happen to the murderer (will Harry Rayburn get him out or will the police get there first or the vigilantes who want him dead?) and, growing out of that, the secondary tension in the reader of how he or she feels about that outcome, and why.

That secondary tension is really what *Laidlaw* is about. As the narrative progresses, the crime should become not less real (distanced by intervening issues of who did it or who'll be next) but more real to us. The surface story of three different attempts to decide the murderer's fate should, like an iceberg, carry with it a lot more under the surface: different reactions to the crime, a deepening understanding of what has happened and why, a changing of the way we see the criminal. In that sense, the subject of the book is the reader's reactions.

In this attempt to explore the complexity of our responses to a murder, Laidlaw is the guide. It is his own complex nature that reflects the complexities around him and holds them in some kind of human balance. He stands between the totally unforgiving vengeance of Bud Lawson and the totally forgiving absolution of Harry Rayburn and comprehends both. ('I'm sure I'd be in the Bud Lawson stakes if it happened to one of my girls.' 'How many people have you ever loved like that?') But he also understands the dismissal of humanity in both attitudes – one in dismissing the life of the murderer, the other in dismissing the life of the victim. He realises that to be fully human he must daily inhabit the tension between the two.

Laidlaw invites us to join him in a place where there is no them and us. There is only us. It is a place where murder may result from a still-born attempt to love, where in the ugliest moments we may catch a momentary reflection of a part of ourselves, where protectiveness may be a mode of destructiveness, where we may feel a little lost among the shifting borders of good and bad, of right and wrong, of normal and abnormal, where a 'monster' may be given a cup of tea.

That is a dark place to go to. A French critic who was generous enough to call *Laidlaw* a masterpiece also described it as 'a book as black as night'. I'm not sure about that. But even if it were true, night is where the dawn comes from. Hope begins in confronting the reality of ourselves.

Where Greta Garbo Wouldn't Have Been Alone

PEOPLE TRYING TO BE HONEST WILL HAVE A CLEAR SENSE of cities in inverse ratio to the time they have spent there. The longer you are acquainted with a place the more you know you don't know it. About New Orleans I'll give you some instant impressions, gleaned in about a week. If you're in a hurry – and if I'm talking about New Orleans, you probably should be – you might be fooled. But five minutes' casual probing would find me out. My clarity about New Orleans is born of ignorance.

Paris I'm more vague about. I wasn't always like that. From a fortnight's trip made as a teenager, I carried a neat sense of it around with me like a postcard. Then I lived there for several months. Don't ask me about Paris. Vancouver's worse. I lived there nearly a year. Glasgow? What I don't know about Glasgow would fill several books. Some people might say it has. What I think and feel about Glasgow, after more than 30 years' close acquaintance, is very involved: the onion, memory. I peel it.

The cafeteria of the Students' Union in Glasgow University: evocative place, my Grand Central Station of the mind. From here you can catch ideas that will take you just about anywhere. The condition of the serfs in 19th-century Russia. The pibroch as the essential Scottish art form. Is abortion murder? Arnold Toynbee's *History of the World*. What do you think will win the 2.30? Was Marlowe Shakespeare? Outline briefly the attributes of your ideal woman. Who was Jack the Ripper?

Here, more than at lectures or tutorials, my mind will be stripped of the fustian of prejudice, the shoddy of preconception, and sent out to abide the pelting of a pitiless storm of wild ideas. It is my subversive university within the University. Maybe I'm particularly lucky in my timing. I arrive here in the mid-1950s, by which time the fabled fortresses of deep thought have been breached by fairly large numbers of working-class students. The Visigoths are here. They bring a refreshing common sense and scepticism to some of the more arcane studies. Anglo Saxon sound-changes will take a terrible pounding.

After lectures we convene in the café of the Students' Union, often for hours. We have epic conversations. No sacrosanct precept is safe from our desire to scramble all over it and hopefully reduce it to rubble. The size of the group is constantly changing. We can be anything from four round a table to maybe a dozen, with chairs being pulled up and later left empty. New voices arrive from the Reading Room. Someone who has raised an interesting question may have to catch a train before the poll of answers is finally taken. The ashtrays look like pit-bings.

I am among such a group now. I am taking part in an impromptu group lecture on Yeats, whom we read last week. I, who arrived like an urban Johnny Appleseed in the groves of academe, am already, towards the end of my first year, a sophisticated smoker of Player's (bought in packets of five from the kiosk in the Union), a placer of daily bets with Strachan the bookie (maximum stake: one shilling) and a fearless purveyor of opinion on all matters (knowledge of subject under discussion not an essential).

Around me are my friends. One of them has been reading Freud and is going through a phase of seeing sexuality in all things. A cigarette is a mammary substitute. If you stir your tea, he's liable to accuse you of intercourse in public. Another is developing a betting system that will make his fortune when he becomes a professional gambler. Another is seriously questioning his Catholicism. Another is a Rangers supporter who likes to say that he hates bigotry and Catholics.

But, at the moment, everything is concentrated on Yeats. He is our man. We marvel at his wisdom, savour individual lines as if they were nectar. We are endlessly trying to analyse the magic of his words.

At the edge of our group is a rare attender. He comes to university on a motorbike. He is wearing a crash helmet now, perhaps as a protection against the sleet of insubstantial opinion that is all around him. He observes us from his casing like an extra-terrestrial trying to work out what these earthlings are up to. During a rare pause in the conversation, he speaks.

'It's all right for youse bastards,' he says. 'Youse like poetry.'

The inference is that we are cheating. For he, too, is a member of the first year English class and he seems to have a sense of being disadvantaged because some people taking the course are actually enjoying it. This may explain the abstracted way in which he has occasionally sat in on our debates, like a Rabbi attending a course on bacon-curing. It may also explain the infrequency of his visits to lectures. He has opened a second-hand shop, it seems, and he is more interested in driving his motorbike to salerooms all over Glasgow, buying used furniture.

At the end of the academic year, he is refused a class ticket, not surprisingly, since the English Department have no very clear idea of who he is. We hold a hurried council of war in the Union and he decides he will go to the English Department and speak to Professor Alexander, a man of great benignity and kindness. When Professor Alexander confronts the non-poetry-loving entrepreneur, accoutred as is customary in his crash-helmet, he apparently says something like this: 'With your attendance and performance, sonny, when you come here to ask for a class ticket, you shouldn't be wearing a crash-helmet. You should be wearing a suit of armour.'

Professor Alexander, ever humane, gives him a class ticket. But he either doesn't pass the exam or doesn't turn up to sit it – I forget which.

Glasgow University was for me not a bad vantage point from which seriously to begin my studies of the city. Unlike some seats of learning, it was no hermetically sealed chamber of self-defining scholarship. It abutted on the very real world. You could step out with a headful of Chaucer and see the Wife of Bath Street on a tram.

I learned more than degree courses during that time. I laid the foundations for a kind of inter-disciplinary study of the place. Glasgow has always been in my experience a city where boundaries are not very rigorously observed, full of socially mixed blood. The forensically precise mind of the lawyer may also accommodate a fanatically irrational belief in the divine right of Celtic to win the Scottish League. A philosophical debate may be resolved with a fist fight.

The crash-helmeted tearaway who was reading selected parts of Spenser's *Faerie Queene* was found to have many counterparts, like the working man playing pool in a Rutherglen pub and simultaneously extolling the quality of *Anna Karenina*. I once had some difficulty escaping from a cab in which the driver hadn't finished outlining his plans for writing a modernised version of *The Ragged Trousered Philanthropists*. At least he turned the meter off. I have heard two drunk men discussing their lives in The Royal Scot bar in Central Station, with one of them insistently quoting Socrates.

Those seminars that began in the Union have continued casually for over 30 years. A group of us have been meeting intermittently in Glasgow pubs, conversationally unravelling our entrails, while jobs were changed and children grew up and marriages broke. We have discussed everything we could think of and a few we probably seriously couldn't. But the sub-text to those discussions has always been Glasgow, and therefore Scotland – for Glasgow, lochs and bens and talk of Gaelic bards notwithstanding, has forged much of the essence of modern Scotland. It reveals most dramatically the basic features not of who we were but of who we are.

Our meetings were often gently haunted by a need to work out Glasgow: to come to terms with the ferocity of its sectarianism, that weird, warped creature that haunts the Scottish psyche, sustaining itself on the iron rations of Rangers-Celtic games and offering meaningless aggression like a Japanese soldier lost for years on some Pacific island and still fighting a war that is long since over; to understand the strong, instinctive socialism of the city, a socialism that seems not to have achieved much that is more concrete than calling a part of itself Nelson Mandela Place and putting up a statue of La Pasionaria on Custom House Quay.

But even as we tried to catch the place, it was changing in our grasp, like Proteus.

I'm on a late-night train leaving Central Station. I have the compartment to myself until the train begins to pull out. I can hear the scuffling sounds in the corridor outside that announce the man with drink taken who has just made it. Experience tells me he will soon be my travelling companion. He soon is.

He has slid the door open with a force that leaves it jammed. He nods ambiguously, a kind of friendly belligerence. His face is florid, perhaps with running. His eyes are aggressively blank and have a tendency to fix themselves fiercely on a perfectly ordinary object, like an upholstered arm-rest, as if it is the only one of its kind in the world and he will have to report back to a committee on his findings. For a short time our reflections manage to avoid each other in the window as first the edges of the city and then the darkened countryside slide past. But I know, short of taking a header through the window, I won't avoid a conversation.

'Just made it there,' he says.

I acknowledge the information it seems to have taken him some time to glean and a conversation has begun. It proves to be an interesting conversation. He lives and works in Coventry but comes originally from Glasgow. He has been paying a visit to the old town. His stay there seems to have followed a not uncommon pattern for such visits: quiet at first (seeing his mother, failing to make contact with friends) but building towards a series of jolly thrashes that have climaxed in this evening's impromptu party. Thinking of the party and the time he's just had, he brims with nostalgia.

And then, finding his moment as we rattle through the night in the tatty compartment, he delivers an ambiguous but moving elegy on the Gallowgate. The ambiguity is unintentional. He speaks of the old Gallowgate with a genuine love that few outsiders who have seen it might expect. He sees no irony. He lays the memory of it before me as reverently as a pressed rose. It's just that he doesn't seem to notice that it still has the thorns attached.

The old Gallowgate, he says, was a marvellous place. Everybody helped everybody else. The sense of neighbourliness was total. He is searching for the clincher, the moment held in a shaft of remembered light that will convince even me, find another convert. He decides he has it. It is a story.

This is the story: when he was a boy, he loved snooker. But snooker, say ninepence for half-an-hour, or it may have been one-and-three (he remembered but I don't), was expensive. He and a couple of his mates did devious things and saved up until they had enough money to pay for a half-hour on the table. They were maybe 12 at the time. They duly were given a table. They set up the balls. They chalked the cues. They were ready to break when three local 18-year-old heavies cut in. They shoved them away from the table and told them to get lost. They would be playing. He and his mates had no way to deal with the situation. They went outside. A small man that they knew, a local, a 'nice wee man', was standing at the door, smoking. He knew they were supposed to be playing a game. They weren't. He asked them why. They told him. The small man went in. Shortly afterwards, they played their full half-hour.

The man on the train speaks of three people 'carried out'. I doubt that. But I believe the gist of his story.

'That was the Gallowgate,' he says in the voice of one who once knew Eden. 'Kind people in the Gallowgate.'

Kind people who batter unkindness – the rose with the thorns. The man from the Gallowgate introduced into our compartment, like a tangible presence, one of the great Glasgow legends – the hardman – and reminded me how in recent times the sharp edges of the legend have become blurred. The fact that something has become legendary, of course, doesn't mean that it isn't rooted in reality.

Glasgow is a hard town. I know Glaswegians who get instantly annoyed if you say that, their faces acquiring a 'here we go again' expression, just as I know New Yorkers who are tired of hearing how dangerous their city is. 'Look, I've lived here all my life,' a free translation of their general reactions might run. 'And I'm lucky if I've seen two fights in that time. Sure there's violence here. But there's violence everywhere.'

They have a point. Violence is more dramatic than passivity and, therefore, constitutes a kind of news. Few interesting anecdotes begin, 'I was at a Rangers-Celtic game on Saturday and nothing happened. Let me tell you about it.' Nevertheless, only people who have observed Glasgow exclusively through the windscreen of a car or who arrange their social diary as a means of censoring their own awareness or who take the pronouncements of the Scottish Tourist Board as hard reportage could pretend that part of the reality of Glasgow has not been a potential for casual violence. The legend may have been fed on the steroids of publicity but it originally earned its muscles on the streets.

There are reasons for it. Glasgow, more dramatically than any other part of Scotland, experienced the brutalising effects of the Industrial Revolution. Edinburgh might partially side-step it by becoming a place where money, more than machinery, was deployed and a centre for tourism. Glasgow stood four-square to the whirlwind. The ensuing varieties of deprivation had their results.

One was the development of a fierce physical pride, fed partly on circumstances that often left room for little else and partly on the democratic traditions deeply embedded in Scottish life. The combination meant that in Glasgow people who frequently didn't have much more collateral than their sense of themselves weren't prepared to have that sense casually burgled by passing strangers. Standing up for yourself, sometimes against improbable odds, became a Glaswegian convention.

The late John Rafferty, sports reporter with the *Scotsman*, used to tell a story of the time when Jacky Paterson, flyweight champion of the world and regarded by many as pound-for-pound the hardest puncher in boxing at the time, was training for a fight. I repeat the story from memory and, if I get it wrong, I apologise to a very fine reporter. The way I recall it, Paterson was training in Glasgow and having trouble making the weight. He was heavily clothed in the gym, trying to sweat off the excess poundage. This meant there was a risk of dehydration and they were having fruit delivered from the Fruit Market. The small man who delivered it looked as if he could make the eight stone flyweight limit with his clothes on. He was pleased to be in the presence of the world champion and became unnecessarily fussy about where he should put the fruit, prolonging his stay and checking with Paterson where exactly he would like the fruit to be. Shipping sweat and understandably irritated, Paterson told him roughly to put the stuff down and get out. The attitude of the fruit-deliverer changed immediately. He was for the jacket off and inviting Paterson to step outside. Nobody spoke to him like that. Only the intervention of John Rafferty and a conciliatory handshake from the world champion mollified the small man.

It hasn't been an entirely malignant convention, though often so. For a long time at least, one aspect of it was a discouragement of casual bullies. When you don't know where the aggression may come from, the quiet man at the bar or the innocent-looking punter in the bus queue, you should walk warily, especially since a lot of Glaswegians are not averse to taking up arms in causes other than their own if they see what they think is an injustice. Even allowing for the fact that memory is a seductive talker who sometimes makes us forget to check his sources, I find the reminscences of the man from the Gallowgate largely confirmed by personal experience and things I've heard.

While I was teaching, a mature student who had joined the English Department of the school told me about a night in an East End pub. It illustrates what I mean.

There were four students, not from Glasgow. The main protagonist of the story came from Troon, one of those douce – at least on the surface – coastal towns about which I sometimes wonder if they toilet-train the seagulls. Every Thursday the students, in search of the real Glasgow, would have a night in an East End bar. They must have fitted in perfectly, carrying their briefcases.

This night they were drinking at the counter and listening to Engelbert

Humperdinck on the television singing *The Last Waltz*. The man from Troon started to sing along and, noticing a woman sitting in a corner singing too, he began to harmonise with her. The woman was amused. Her large male companion was not. He came across and demanded that the student come outside with him, presumably regarding singing with his woman as some kind of sexual approach. The student at first, not unwisely, refused. But he found himself outside anyway with the large man saying very severe things about what was going to happen to him.

But another man had followed them out from the bar. He forbade the large man to touch the student and produced from his coat pocket, as a reinforcement of his point of view, a hammer. The large man withdrew. The man with the hammer was reported to me as saying then, 'Now, son. You go back in there an' have a right good night.' The student apparently remembered he had a train to catch.

Robin Hoods with hammers in their hands are probably less likely in Glasgow these days. It's always hard to gauge the changing temper of the times in these matters but the very fallible readings that emerge from newspapers and talk and personal experience would appear to suggest that there has been an erosion of the admittedly confused ethic of the non-criminal hardman. Drugs may well have played a part in that.

But perhaps just as significant a reason for the apparent decay of honour among hardmen is the sub-theme in the talk of the man from the Gallowgate: the dispersal of the sense of community. The post-war annihilation of the tenement in Glasgow wiped out not only buildings but a way of life. As Bertie Auld, then manager of Partick Thistle, once said, 'If they'd given Hitler the contract, he couldn't have done a better job.' Often what was put in their place suggested a novel interpretation of 'progress'.

Outside Queen Elizabeth Court on the South Side: there's a photographer and a young journalist and myself. We're looking for high views of the city to go with a piece in the *Glasgow Herald*. The concrete block of flats looks good as a place from which to take photographs. But that's all it looks good for. I can't believe that this building has been conceived as an improvement. An improvement on what? Alcatraz? The journalist is telling me that this sort of work has won an architectural award for Sir Basil Spence. He does not specify which award. It was presumably the Bomber Harris award for architecture, since it looks like vertical rubble.

We go inside. Outside the lift, two older women, a younger woman and two boys are waiting. The boys are playing keepie-uppie headers with a tennis ball. They don't look ready for the first team. The ball has a dangerous tendency to wander close to other people. One of the older women promises mayhem if the ball so much as touches her.

'No problem, missus,' one of the boys says unconvincingly.

On the way up in the lift, they all leave except the young woman and the three of us. We talk to her, explaining what we're here for. We want to get out on to the roof. She's visiting her mother on the top floor and knows that there's a door out to the roof but she doesn't think it will be open. It's kept locked for obvious reasons. On the top floor she directs us to where the door is and goes into her mother's.

We find the door and the young woman is right: it's locked. As we're wandering back along the corridor, thinking janitors and jemmies, the young woman is standing outside an open door. She is signalling the three of us in. She has mentioned us to her mother and they both wonder if we couldn't use their balcony to get our photographs. We could.

Ensues a happy time. We take our photographs. We come back in to cups of tea and biscuits. We talk for almost an hour of governments and high-rise flats and how the family's doing. We look at the album of the daughter's trip to Canada to see her sister and her family. We're all pleased that they're doing so well out there.

These are impressive people. They're trusting. They make us feel instantly that we have a right to be here. As we leave, the mother says to be sure and look in again if we're passing. The whole occasion is an unexpected gift from strangers. Never mind the photos, I'm just glad I came.

The woman and her daughter were practising an old Glaswegian art form: the transformation of your circumstances with humour and pride. Never mind the buildings, see the people. It's a skill in which the people of Glasgow have had to become expert. It's also a skill which has been under increasing pressure over the past 40 years.

A lot of the old tenements were hardly fit to live in but they did have a strong sense of community. Changes had to be made but they were frequently made by people who seemed to have all the imagination of a soldier ant. Mainly, what had been fairly coherent communities were either shipped out to housing schemes like penal colonies on the edges of the city or incarcerated in high-rise flats. Presumably, they had committed being working class. The buildings themselves usually looked like the result of some Dada school of architecture, cunningly created with built-in obsolescence, so that they would turn scabrous in ten years or so.

The philosophy, shared supposedly by a lot of Labour councillors who should have known better, appeared to be that working-class aspirations stopped at the inside toilet. The malignant implication behind it was that there was no such thing as a working-class culture and, therefore, nothing would be lost by thoughtlessly unstitching the fabric of a way of life put together over generations.

However unintentionally, that attitude suggests contempt and contempt

170

makes distance between people. The distances that housing policy helped to create were not just geographical.

La Laterna, Italian restaurant in Hope Street: three of us at table. The waiter brings the menu. One of us is distinctly fidgety. He studies the red-checked tablecloth, the cutlery, the surroundings. He shifts his position in his seat. He lifts the menu and glances at it, puts it back down. He shakes his head. His unease is uncontainable.

'Ah'll have tae go, Wullie,' he says.

'What's the problem?'

'Nah, this is no' for me. No way. Ah canny sit here.'

We rise and make our apologies and go out. We look for a less intimidating place to eat. The fidgety man is Hughie, a friend of mine from Possilpark, and I have just demonstrated how socially insensitive I can be.

I have recently been spending some time in Possil, trying to understand what's happening there, however inadequately. What's happening there wouldn't be out of place in *Last Exit to Brooklyn*. I've found how freely heroin is available in pubs, how protection is rife, how just about any article within reason can be ordered at lunchtime and delivered at teatime, having been stolen in the afternoon. I've met a girl who was raped at fourteen and soon after turned on to heroin by her addict brothers and put on the streets to feed all their habits. I've met a former social worker so shell-shocked by what he has to deal with that he outlines a scheme whereby local tearaways would be given handouts to buy good suits so that when they go to Bearsden to break into houses they won't be conspicuous. I study his face for irony but am not convinced I see it. I've also met a lot of good local people whose decency seems incredible, given the circumstances they live among. I've stayed overnight at Hughie and Annie's house with another friend, enjoying a few drinks, home-made soup and a sing-song.

The Italian restaurant was my way of offering a gesture of thanks but Annie couldn't make it. I was at first surprised by Hughie's reaction in the restaurant. And then I was surprised at my surprise. I should have known. Eating out is not what Hughie does.

My surprise gave way to annoyance at myself for forgetting for the moment where I come from. If anyone should have foreseen Hughie's attitude, it should have been myself. All I had to do was remember my own former awkwardness in such places, an awkwardness that can ambush me occasionally still and makes me regress to those times when I sat at weddings determined not to be the first at the table to start on the next course.

But it was a salutary experience, a neat hook on which to hang my awareness of that other Glasgow that lies behind the increasingly yuppie image of the city. I had noticed the outriders of that image some time before.

A group of us go one night for a drink in The Gay Gordon, a downstairs pub in Royal Exchange Square. We feel slightly out of touch with that part of the city and will renew our acquaintance with old haunts. The bar is closed and the exterior is concealed behind the wrappings that denote renovation. We go off, muttering vaguely among ourselves, and have a drink elsewhere.

Another night we come back and behold the transformation. What was The Gay Gordon, a pleasantly scruffy talking-shop, is now a French restaurant called, if I recall, L'Auberge. (It has changed since.) Upstairs is something called Charlie Parker's. We stare at the new black chic door and look at one another, feeling our arteries harden. We push open the door and are confronted by two very tall young men who have the threatening suavity that seems to earn you your bouncer's card these days, as if they have been to karate finishing school. Whatever obscure test it is these gentlemen are taught to apply, clean collar, deodorised oxters or a full set of teeth, we seem to pass it. We are allowed to enter the sanctum.

Gloom, not only ours, abounds. Nearly everything, furniture, bar, ceiling, walls, seems to be black. There is even a black bandstand, peopled by black metallic figures. There is one emaciated figure with a saxophone attached. This is presumably 'Bird' himself, living up to his nickname – in this case maybe a heron or flamingo. My first impression, admittedly perhaps rancorous with the apprehended encroachment of old age, is that this is somebody's confused impression of a speakeasy remembered from the back row of the pictures during a heavy necking session.

But it is not the place so much that makes us grope abstractedly for our Rip Van Winkle beards and wonder where we have been during the last several years. It is the people. Where do they come from, these people? This is Glasgow?

They are mainly young and dressed in an interesting variety of styles but, no matter how eclectic the gear they wear, what they are all mainly dressed in is a kind of hand-me-down self-assurance. They know they're with it because their clothes are with it. They're sure of their identity because they're wearing it. By pushing open a door, a group of post-war conversational artisans have found that the time of the poser has arrived.

For these people are here to be seen, not to debate the failure of socialism for three hours over a beer-stained table and then apply old songs like bandages to the mental wounds. They stand with their interesting clothes and their different drinks and laugh tunefully and count the house. The phrase that keeps forcing itself into my mind, as I survey the scene like one of Yeats's wrinkled men in *Lapis Lazuli*, is communal pretentiousness. Showing off on such a scale and in such borrowed styles (gallousness is one thing) is not something I have expected to see in Glasgow, which has always seemed to me to be to pretentiousness what Wimpey was to empty houses. We stand around for a while, like people waiting for a bus that doesn't pass this way any longer, and pay what we feel are inflated prices and talk in an awkward, conspiratorial fashion, as if ideas might be contraband. Then we repair to an older bar where people talk to strangers they don't want to pick up.

Being an insistently analytical group, we all have theories. The disco, that peculiarly modern art form where living statuary meets and attracts mainly by gesture and stance, has invaded the pub. Just as the old humanising and individualising patter of the dancing seems to be going largely by the board, so maybe the pub as talking shop is under threat. Innocence has gone. You can't call a pub 'Gay' any more. The American influence has always been strong in Glasgow. We have seen the future and it's largely kitsch.

We were over-reacting, of course. Isn't that what pubs give you a licence to do? The truth was that not only had Glasgow been changing, so had we with it. And I have since developed a certain affection for Charlie Parker's for I once had a life-affecting lunch in there. Any place can be transformed by circumstances.

But that night remains important in my understanding of Glasgow and the door into Charlie Parker's led to a couple of reminders about the place. Firstly, the city always has been changing significantly since I've known it, whether in the big ways like the miles of internal motorway and the Gorbals becoming a different place or in the small ways like Alice's Restaurant disappearing or the amazing acrobatic fiddler in St Enoch's Square giving way to the one-man Wham Bam Boogie Band. You glance away for a month or two from a place you've known and you look back at a stranger. Writing about the city and wanting to use real places in a novel, I have had to keep checking, between conception and execution, that the places were still there.

Secondly, I was reminded of what is the essential direction of that change. It has been a movement, superficially at least, towards a softer image. That's all right, as far as it goes. The question is: how far does it go?

It's good that people should realise how architecturally beautiful Glasgow is. The handsomeness of the city has too often been underplayed. It's good that the fever for demolition seems to have passed its crisis and some of the fine tenements are being refurbished instead of destroyed. It's good that the Merchant City and some points further east begin to flourish again. But there's a danger in handing Glasgow over lock, stock and Burrell to the brochure writers.

Many of those who bemoan the old exaggerated image of Glasgow as a kind of Somme in civvies are busy giving it a press that is just as phoney. That is bad news in two ways.

First, to gloss over the existence of a problem is to feed the problem. Cosmetic surgery never cured a cancer. 'Glasgow's Miles Better'? It depends which direction you go in. If you head towards Possil or Blackhill or Easterhouse or Garthamlock or Drumchapel, you couldn't take that ad-man's slogan as more than an ad-man's slogan. And if you're not prepared to go in these directions, you're missing Glasgow.

Second, the selling of Glasgow as some sort of yuppie freehold is a diminution of Glasgow. It's a lot more than that. It's fine that business and tourism should come to the city – as long as the terms are right – but let's not confuse the press release with the reality. The reality is much more complex. Glasgow is a great city. Glasgow is in trouble. Glasgow is handsome. Glasgow is ugly. Glasgow is kind. Glasgow is cruel. Some people in Glasgow live full and enlightened lives. Some people in Glasgow live lives bleaker than anyone should live – and die deaths bleaker than anyone should die.

I am sitting in my reasonably grotty Glasgow bedsit being a writer. I have done my statutory spell of staring at the wall. I am now making notes towards making notes that may lead to an idea that may lead, eventually, to the clarification of what it is I want to say. Then perhaps work can begin.

Outside it is a dull day. But, given the state of my windows, any day looked at from here is going to be a dull day. To be absolutely accurate about the quality of the weather, I'd have to go out and check.

There is a knock at the door. This is unusual. Apart from the fact that my self-imposed isolation has been making me feel recently like a one-man leper colony, my bedsit is in one of those divided Victorian houses. What was presumably one big happy family has become a series of separate units where some students and other migrants and myself hang out. I know them mainly as people nodding on the stairs and records playing and flushing cisterns and ghostly ripples of half-heard laughter. But the point is that our divided household means a list of names outside and a series of bell-pushes and one of those crackly devices through which you identify yourself as not being a mugger.

So who can it be? It must be somebody from inside the building. I suppose the best way to find out is to open the door.

It is a woman I have never seen before. She has a small girl hovering at her side.

'Could ye dae me a favour, son?' she says.

Any half-baked quips about women always appearing at my door with such requests are forestalled by the sense that something is wrong. Later, I'll be glad they were. The small girl is the sign. She is ill at ease without seeming to know why, in that instinctive geiger-counter way that children have.

'Certainly, love. What is it?'

The woman is already moving away, talking as she does so, with the small girl holding her hand. When I'm asked to surface quickly out of work, it can take me a while to focus. I'm not entirely sure where I am, I tend only to hear part of what's being said. I won't say I'm coming back from a deep place but certainly a far one. I'm like that now. The woman is leading me through the open door of a flat and talking. It will only be in retrospect that I'll be able to decide clearly what she has been telling me.

It's about wee Tommy being the tenant of the flat and she cleans it for him and he's out at work just now but last night he had somebody staying with him who was drunk and he was still there this morning and Tommy phoned her and told her to make sure the man was out by the time she left but the man still seems to be drunk and could I help her to get him out?

It sounds like a commission not without its risks.

'He's in there,' she says, pointing to a bedroom door that is ajar.

There's the woman and the small girl and myself. It's John Wayne time. I go into the bedroom. At first I don't see him. The bed is mussed but empty. Then I see him. He's in underpants and tee-shirt. He's lying on the floor, quite still. He is a short and powerful man, say late 20s, with dark curly hair. There's a record player on the floor beside him and his right hand is poised over it in a strange way. His head is slightly under a sideboard. It looks as if he's passed out while putting on a record. I cross towards him and bend and touch his shoulder. It feels like cement.

'Excuse me,' I'm saying ridiculously.

I can hear the girl beginning to cry out in the hallway. The woman is standing at the door. I try to look into his face and I touch his head gently. The hair is very cold.

'He's dead, love,' I hear myself saying and the woman begins to cry as well.

I say we have to get the police and does she want me to phone. The woman says no, if somebody has to stay here it won't be her and the girl. She'll phone the police. While she does so, I realise that what I had thought was an identity-bracelet was a piece of wire round his wrist with a ring of blackened skin beneath it. I realise that he wasn't changing a record. He was plugging himself into the socket.

Later, during questioning, a policeman, who knows my occupation, says, 'You're our first suspect. We think you did it to write about it.' Later still, at the inquest in the Sheriff Court, I'm shown photographs of the dead man with his tee-shirt off and can see how he has wrapped himself round and round with wires. I'm asked what kind of shoes I was wearing at the time. They were rubber-soled. It's a good thing for me, it seems. The dead man was, ironically, live and I had two chances at being electrocuted.

In the time between the finding of the body and the inquest, I will think about the dead man quite a lot. But on the evening of the day of touching the utterly innocent coldness of his head, I just go out alone into Glasgow. I get drunk.

The calculated savagery of the young man's act against himself was appalling. So, imaginably, was the loneliness that led him to do it: the sewers of self-contempt he must have crawled through to bring himself to the place where he wrapped himself so meticulously in his own death that there would be no possibility of escape; the utter absence he must have felt of anyone with whom he could share the bleakness he had come to.

His action expressed a condition so extreme as to appear eccentric, a grotesquerie of experience faced with which all you could do was turn away. But only the extremity was eccentric. Milder forms of the loneliness that became in him terminal were observable all around. Thinking of him, I thought also of the lesser species of loneliness in the city: not just the more obvious ones like the bearded winos who seem to have taken a short-cut to old age and make you wonder where they come from (being, as my mother would say, 'somebody's rearin'') or those descendants of the ancient mariner who wander companionless streets imparting urgent gibberish to the world, but also the more discreet and self-contained loneliness of people in damp basement flats and hardboard-partitioned bedsits who tend fragile hopes like potted plants.

That, too, is Glasgow. In my quite wilful map of the city, I tend to place them roughly around the Byres Road area, in Hyndland and behind the Botanic Gardens and off Great Western Road. They are dreamers of small, lonely dreams. I remember a conversation in a café in Byres Road with a young man who had read something I had written and who recognised me. He came across and we talked for maybe half-an-hour. He was living in a bedsit with his girlfriend and doing, I think, translations from Spanish and wanting to be a writer. Our talk was for me a peephole into a fierce and private obsession sustained on meals that came pre-cooked in tinfoil and long talks into the night. I remember a late night with a taxi-driver friend and his mates in a room with bean-bag seats and posters on the wall, and a joint circulating, and the names of foreign cities evoking a future that would be different from this. I remember a flat in Hyndland where I turned up with an ex-fisherman I know and all the Highland voices were melodiously evoking images in haunting contrast to the city outside.

The dead man in the bedroom reminded me of such places and such times and later I tried to put the feelings in a poem I called *Bless this house: a sampler for Glasgow bedsits.*

> Bless this house, wherever it is,
> This house and this and this and this,
>
> Pitched shaky as small nomad tents
> Within Victorian permanence,
>
> Where no names stay long, no families meet
> In Observatory Road and Clouston Street,

WHERE GRETA GARBO WOULDN'T HAVE BEEN ALONE

Where Harry and Sally who want to be 'free'
And Morag who works in the BBC

And Andy the Artist and Mhairi and Fran
(Whose father will never understand)

And John from Kilmarnock and Jean from the Isles
And Michael who jogs every day for miles

And Elspeth are passing through this year:
Bless them the short time they are here.

Bless the cup left for a month or more
On the dust of the window-ledge, the door

That won't quite shut, the broken fan,
The snowscape of fat in the frying pan.

Bless each burnt chop, each unseen smile
That they may nourish their hopes a while.

Bless the persistence of their faith,
The gentle incense of their breath.

Bless the wild dreams that are seeded here,
The lover to come, the amazing career.

Bless such small truths as they may find
By the lonely night-light of the mind.

Bless these who camp out in the loss of the past
And scavenge their own from what others have lost,

Who have courage to reach for what they cannot see
And have gambled what was for what may never be.

So turn up the Hi Fi, Michael and John.
What is to come may be already gone.

And pull up the covers, Jean and Mhairi.
The island is far and you've missed the ferry.

The thoughts provoked by finding the man dead crystallised another small awareness. The man was Iranian. Rumours circulated about why he had taken his life. One theory was that his parents were still in Iran and he was in despair about what would happen to them under the Ayatollah. Whatever lay behind his death, it reminded me of the small ethnic groups that enrich the city and tend too often to be overlooked when those who love the place are taking a conversational census of its characteristics.

I thought of the musically named Ladipo Banjo, whom I had known at university. Thinking of him, I found myself guilty of that same oversight. I knew Ladipo was African. I thought he was Nigerian but I wasn't sure. All I could be definite about in my memory was that he was marvellously sweet-natured.

I thought of drinking coffee and discussing being a Pakistani in Scotland with Ahmed Choudry in his leather shop near Partick Cross. I remembered the late Jonathan Meadows, an intense and intelligent man whom I had met in a bar when he couldn't resist joining in a discussion a group of us were having about Norman Mailer. We became friends and he gave me some insights into the experience of the Jewish community in Glasgow. I thought of the Poles and the Italians and the Chinese. I thought of the Irish, whose positive contribution to the nature of Glasgow and of Scottishness is so deeply ingrained that its importance is often overlooked.

It's no wonder Glasgow is such a vivid city, ready to surprise you at any time.

It is raining at the taxi-rank opposite the Botanic Gardens. It is doubtless raining in many other places as well but this is the only one I'm interested in at the moment. I don't have a coat on and turning up my jacket collar is no substitute. I'm cold and wet and getting wetter. Everything seems dark, including my mood.

A taxi comes off Great Western Road and makes a u-turn into the rank. I climb in, discontinuing my mental tirade against all Glasgow taxi-drivers and reflecting more charitably on the number of times in my experience hackney cabs have justified their Glaswegian nickname of 'black ambulances'. I tell the driver my destination and we set off through grey rain, along grey streets, under a grey sky. The driver studies me in the rearview mirror with the eyes of a man who has never lost his curiosity about things.

'Have ye ever wondered,' he says, his eyes still flicking on to me more frequently than seems consistent with maximum concentration on his driving. 'Have ye ever wondered whit would win in a fight between a crocodile and a shark?'

I am, as they say, nonplussed. In all my deep ponderings on the world and its many manifestations, this is one I've missed. It seems such a natural,

even inevitable question the way the taxi-driver says it, I can't imagine why
I've never asked it myself. Shamefacedly, I acknowledge how unthinking my
progress through life has so far been.

'It's an amazin' thing,' he says. 'Ah'm sittin' in the hoose the other night
readin' a book. An' Ah shouts to the wife, "Hey, hen. See the way Ah'm
always sayin', 'Ah wonder what would win between a crocodile an' a
shark?'" (I have an eerie flash of the kind of conversations that must take
place in his house: 'See's ower the paper, hen. Bet ye there's nothin' in it
aboot crocodiles an' sharks the day again.') "Well here's the answer here."'

I sit tensed in the back of the cab, no longer a mere traveller to an address
but a journeyer into esoteric knowledge. But the taxi-driver, like all true
gurus, knows the path to wisdom is a winding one.

'Seems there's this river in Australia. Right? An' at the mouth of it ye've
got yer crocodiles. An' then yer sharks are swimmin' in. Into the estuary,
like. Fair enough. Wallop. A square go.'

He seems to need for the first time to concentrate totally on a tricky piece
of steering. He knows he has me. I try to ask him nonchalantly, to make sure
my voice isn't quavering with suppressed emotion.

'So what would win?'

He glances at me in the mirror, looks at the road.

'Ah suppose it's obvious when ye think about it,' he says. 'The crocodile.
Seems it bides its time, one bite, holds on, ta ta shark.'

So there we are, another nibble at the infinite apple of knowledge.
Brooding in my back seat, I decide daringly – for David Attenborough I'm
not and what do I know about crocodiles and sharks? – that I don't believe
him. Isn't it true, my scepticism is whispering like a wee boy in the back row
of the class, that crocodiles are freshwater creatures?

But I am very glad he told me. He has, as the poet says, saved some part
of a day I had rued. We've been exploring together to other climes, he and
I, however briefly. The rain receded just then and it was like the moment
when Dorothy leaves the black and white farm and walks into the
technicolour of her search for Oz.

The memory of such experiences brings me nearer to the essence of my sense
of Glasgow. No matter what harsh anomalies I find in the city, no matter
what misgivings I may have about what's happening to it, no matter what
changes overtake and alter what I thought was final, a moment like that is a
familiar landmark and I recognise the place again.

I stood once at the bar of the Gowdoc in Great Western Road, feeling like
a tortoise that had just been de-shelled. I no longer remember what troubles
I had then but I had decided they were big ones. I was standing in for Atlas.
Nobody knows the trouble I've seen. A small man at the bar beside me
suddenly spoke.

'How's it gaun, big yin? Ye don't look that happy. You think you've got problems? Listen.'

It seemed that a few days ago he had met a friend he hadn't seen for years. They had gone on the skite together and the wee man hadn't been home for nights, three, I think it was. He was asking my advice. Should he go home tonight or, since he was bound to get laldy anyway, should he have another night at it?

Always at such times I know that this is Glasgow: land of the unsolicited confidentiality, country of the unasked for information, city where Greta Garbo wouldn't have been allowed to be alone – 'Who's the big wumman wi' the funny hat? Get ower here, ya big stoater, an' jine the comp'ny. Charlie, gie 'er a piña colada.'

It is lunchtime in The Horseshoe Bar in Drury Street. Several tall lights on tripods have been focused on one of the wooden tables. A man sits at the table with his back to the door. A television camera has been set up. It is trained on the door into the bar.

My moment has come. For I will be entering through that door. The camera will catch me as I enter, follow me to the bar, where I will order a drink, and doggedly pursue me as I sit down at the table opposite the man with his back to the camera. The interview will begin. It is for a film about Glasgow to be shown in West Germany.

I stand outside, waiting for the shouted signal. It's just like being in the pictures, isn't it? This is really a kind of acting, isn't it? I hope the rain doesn't plaster my hair to my head the way it usually does, making it look like a greasy balaclava. 'Okay!' Camera, action, shoot.

I enter. I walk over to the bar in a manner I hope is casual and ask for a whisky. The manager, who has obviously given us permission to invade his bar in the first place, smiles and hands me a huge whisky which he has had sitting ready under the counter. My quest for method-school naturalness, an inhabiting of the part, is thrown by this. Why not use the optic? I have reached into my pocket and pulled out some money but the manager smiles again and turns away, commendably refusing to hog the camera. But what do I do with the money? Donate it to charity? I put it back in my pocket.

By this time, as I stumble towards the table, I feel the omens are not propitious for an interview in which I'm supposed to try to give a real sense of Glasgow. We've already, in about 20 seconds, managed to depict Glasgow as a city where casual strangers entering a bar are given bowls of free whisky. I envisage legions of outraged German tourists picketing Glaswegian pubs. I sit down and nod to my interviewer, who smiles reassuringly back. Even this part, now that I'm doing it, feels daft to me. Won't it convey the impression that people meeting for the first time in Glasgow bars conduct interviews with each other? But it's not my programme.

'Tell me,' my interviewer says, 'what, do you think, is the special quality Glasgow bars like this have? What's typical of them?'

This is probably my chance to explain that what has just happened isn't typical and that, for example, you usually have to pay for the drink. But the remorseless eye of the camera is on us and I chicken out. Instead, I go into a spiel about the communal nature of at least some Glasgow pubs, the likelihood of being engaged in conversation, of having your privacy benignly invaded, of being interrupted – at which exact point I'm aware of a shadow across our table and the lighting man dancing like a dervish in the background and I hear a voice saying: 'Oh-ho, whit's gaun on here, then?'

A fairly elderly man has joined us at the table and is interviewing the interviewer. The interviewer is English and there seems to be some language difficulty. Offering my services, I ask the man what the problem is.

'Oh, no problem, son,' he says, his eyes assessing what size of coffin I'll require. 'Ah jist want tae know whit's gaun on here.'

We continue talking and, while he studies the lights and checks out the television crew, I explain that we're conducting an interview.

'Interview?' He holds up a stiff, leather-gloved hand that is obviously made of something other than flesh. 'Interview? Ah'll gie ye an interview. How about interviewin' the war-wounded?'

The man said more, much more. I've never seen the finished film but I understand the director intended to cut that moment of interruption. Certainly, the cameraman stopped filming very quickly, which was a pity. The scene was Glasgow in action, far more eloquent than any conversation we could have had.

The man wasn't just the incarnation of the point I had been trying to make. He was an interesting user of Glasgow speech, that aspect of the city in which I see most hope for the survival of its identity undiluted. For Glasgow's soul is in its mouth. Anyone who wants a quick and painless introduction to the essential Glasgow should read Michael Munro's excellent dictionary of Glasgow speech, *The Patter*, full of superbly creative examples.

Even a cursory acquaintance with that speech will reveal that it is not merely a collection of slightly different words. It is the expression of a coherent attitude to life, a series of verbal stances as ritualised as one of the martial arts. But it is also continuingly inventive, an established style within which individual creativity can flourish.

The salient features of that style emerged directly from the hardness of life in the streets of a major industrial city. Such a life demands the frequent application of painkillers and so there are many ways in which you can be drunk. You can be wellied, plootered, steamboats or blootered, among others. Drunkenness can lead to insults and the designation of someone as a bawheid, a doughheid, a chanty-wrastler, a heid-banger or a bampot whose patter's mince. Insults beget violence and you may find yourself banjoed or burst or rattled or melted or invited to come ahead.

But, in fact, many Glaswegian insults and threats are as much a way of containing violence as of causing it. They are like the warning signals animals emit. Perhaps part of the reason for Glasgow's reputation for being a threatening city is that much of the violence has been codified into speech that is highly skilled in drawing demarcation lines of behaviour. These can make certain conversations a complex map of grid-lines and markings the wise cartographer can interpret: 'No Go Area', 'Dead End', 'Bears Crossing'.

But these are the outer edges of the significance of Glaswegian speech. The core of its style is two main qualities: deflation of pomposity and humour. It's hard to be pompous when you have a geggie for a mouth and a bahookie for a posterior. The humour takes many forms but I believe that the commonest of these is the humour of disgruntlement – that central source of laughter to which we have been led by such diverse practitioners as Evelyn Waugh, Groucho Marx and Woody Allen. So much of Glasgow humour is disbelief under anaesthetic. It is anger with the fuse snuffed but still smoking.

Glasgow speech, like so much of Glasgow itself, expresses partly incredulity at what life offers, partly a way to make the best of things, partly an invitation to seize the moment and to hell with the formalities.

The late-night train has left Waverley Station in Edinburgh and is headed towards Glasgow Queen Street. I am slouched in my seat, flagellating myself silently for another failed Festival. Every year I go through determined this time to gorge myself on the arts. Every year I retreat feeling culturally emaciated. It's the sheer number of possibilities on offer that always paralyses me: so many exhibitions, recitals, plays, films, so many Fringe shows in out-of-the-way places that are 'stunning' and 'magical' and 'riotously funny'. I usually end up as one of an audience of nine, trying to remember where I read the review that was presumably written by the actors and wondering where the action is. It's always fun to go there but is it art? This year has been no exception.

The door to the compartment opens and two women in their 40s enter. One of them is calling to someone behind her: 'Come oan in here, hen. They're a' snobs through there.' They are followed by a girl carrying a violin-case. Throughout the long car, somnolent people quicken into apprehension, knowing that, whatever is going to happen, this is not part of the normal service of British Rail.

'Right, hen,' one woman says. 'You sit here an' gie 's a wee tune.'

The girl unlocks the lid of the case and, removing a violin from its velvet bedding, transforms it instantly to a fiddle in her hands. A spontaneous ceilidh occurs. Music, that old subversive of the senses, insinuates its way past inhibitions and darts like a pyromaniac from person to person, igniting faces into smiles. Hands clap. Heads bob rhythmically. The place is jumping. There is dancing in the aisle. Whirling there with a black man she has unceremoniously 'lifted', one of the women shouts to me: 'Ever had two Blue Lagoons? This is what they do for ye.'

The jollity continues until we have almost reached Glasgow. Then the two women go round the compartment taking a collection for the girl. She makes a nice bit of money. As we pull into Queen Street, I realise that Glasgow has had its own unofficial mini-festival.

If someone has a violin, you say to them, 'Gie's a tune'. If a dignified black man is sitting on a train, you get him up to dance. If you've had a drink, you announce it to anyone who'll listen. If you think a young girl deserves some money, you take a collection from a carriageful of strangers.

The core of the onion. Does an onion have a core? This one does. I come at last to the heart of my Glasgow, boil it down and freeze it in two words: humane irreverence. Those who are, for me, the truest Glaswegians, the inheritors of the tradition, the keepers of the faith, are terrible insisters that you don't lose touch for a second with your common humanity, that you don't get above yourself. They refuse to be intimidated by professional status or reputation or attitude or name. But they can put you down with a style that almost constitutes a kindness.

A group of us are leaving Hampden after an international match. There's my son, three policemen, Sean Connery and myself. I've met Connery twice before, once when I interviewed him in the Dorchester Hotel and once, in a James Bond way, at Edinburgh Zoo, where he talked of trying to get the money together to film one of my books, *Laidlaw*. But with that authentic charm that he has, he has connected as if we all saw one another last week. We're going to run him to the airport to catch an early flight. We're walking and trying to find the car, which has been parked some way from the ground.

'I can't believe I'm here,' Connery says. 'I'm sitting in "Tramps" at two o'clock this morning when Rod Stewart walks in. He's chartered a private plane and why don't I come to the game. So here I am.'

It's a straight enough statement, just a genuine expression of surprise at the way things have happened. Sean Connery doesn't need to drop names. But, anyway, one of the policemen puts one quietly in the post for him.

'Aye,' he says. 'It's a small world, big yin. Ah was in a house at Muirhead at two o'clock this mornin'. It was full o' tramps as well.'

The man who says this comes, in fact, from Ayrshire but he has been a policeman in Glasgow for years, is an honorary Glaswegian. And he picked the right place to say it.

Humane irreverence: more than the big ships, Glasgow's greatest export. I just hope they don't export it all away. May the Mitchell Library, now so handsomely refurbished, always have its quota of sceptical readers finding out for themselves, noseying into things that are supposed to be none of their business. May the Citizens' Theatre and the Tron and the King's and, yea, even Scottish Opera always find among their audiences some of those perennially disgruntled faces that could be captioned: 'They ca' this art?' May the Burrell and the Glasgow Art Gallery and the Third Eye Centre always have their equivalent of the wee man I once saw standing before 'Le Christ', seeming to defy Salvador Dalí to justify himself and shaking his head and glancing round, as if looking for support. For if they go, Glasgow, except for the bricks, goes with them.

They – not the image-makers, not the bright-eyed entrepreneurs, not those who know the city as a taxi-ride between a theatre and a wine-bar, not those who see it as Edinburgh on the Clyde, not the literary cliques, not those who apply the word 'renaissance' to a handful of movies and a few books of poetry and some novels and plays – they are the heart of Glasgow: the quizzical starers, the cocky walkers, the chic girls who don't see a phoney accent as an essential accessory of attractiveness, the askers of questions where none was expected, the dancers on the train, the strikers-up of unsolicited conversations, the welcomers of strangers, the deliverers of deadly lines in most unlikely places, the people fighting decency's rearguard action in Possil, the unpretentious, the unintimidated. Glasgow belongs to them.

The Sacred Wood Revisited

(Preface to *These Words – Weddings and After*)

THE FOLLOWING IS A RESPONSE TO RE-READING *THE Sacred Wood* by T. S. Eliot. The book was written a long time ago (First Edition, 1920) and I should perhaps explain why it seems important to me to re-examine it and why it seems relevant to offer that re-examination preceding a book of poetry being published more than 60 years later.

One of the reasons why it still seems to me important is that the cultural élitism of which I accuse it in this essay remains with us, I think. It has usually a less abrasive manner now, has learned a few placative tricks and mock concessions but still lives, I believe, in a good health that connotes, comparatively, the poorer cultural health of many of those whose can't share in it. Another reason why I believe in the continuing importance of the book is that I have never found a more erudite or, much more important, a more intelligent defence of that élitism.

I am aware of T. S. Eliot's criticism subsequent to *The Sacred Wood*. I have decided to deal exclusively with *The Sacred Wood* for two reasons. The first is that no criticism he wrote after *The Sacred Wood* seems to me to overthrow the basic principles he was outlining in this book. I detect in much of the later criticism a mellowing of tone but no significant change of mind. He may modify his voice a little but its pronouncements come ex the same cathedra. Therefore, it seems fair to confront him in the precincts of *The Sacred Wood*.

The second reason is a matter of personal history. When I arrived at university as a first generation university student, I became progressively dismayed at how much 'literature' seemed neither for nor about most of the people I knew outside. As I suggested later, it was like being asked to study a body of evidence in which 90-odd per cent of the witnesses were never called. The book that crystallised my misgivings for me most fully was *The Sacred Wood*. This essay is partly an attempt to acknowledge that debt, since I think we are indebted to those who most clearly define what we can't agree with, because they oblige us to try to define our own positions.

The very name – *The Sacred Wood* – is like a warning, implying a place where the uninitiated had better not venture. And so it proves. Here be mysteries, age-old rites the form and purpose of which are truly understood by a very few. One of them is our guide. But he is no chatty tour-operator who wants to show himself anxious to answer all our questions. He will simply tell us what he knows, realising before he speaks that most of us will not be able to grasp what he says. Given the nature of the place he believes himself to be and the attitude he has towards it, he would behave like that.

I first came across *The Sacred Wood* as an undergraduate. My mind went barefoot in awe and probably should have done. I was recently a schoolboy who had 'read a lot'. When the king of the paddling-pool sees his first ocean, awe is appropriate. Since then I have 'read a lot more' but I return to *The Sacred Wood* with that original awe not so much diminished as peopled by other considerations which are no longer content merely to gaze in wonder at the feeling but want to explore it and perhaps colonise it with questions.

Coming back to the book with my somewhat increased competence, I'm struck by two things: how often, where my judgment is adequate to the task, I agree with his observations on specific writers: a nagging worry about agreeing with him on anything. Mr Eliot has that effect on me.

I find his comments on Swinburne and Blake generally agreeable and illuminating. I have a clearer sense of Ben Jonson because of him. His remarks on *Hamlet* are interesting, even if they do seem a hardly adequate account of what is happening in the play, like a still photograph of an earthquake. His brief study of Marlowe's blank verse is arresting, if not wholly convincing. His seems a just assassination of Professor Murray. So where does the unease come from?

Part of it, of course, may relate to the unavoidable realisation that, as a critic, T. S. Eliot was a man of breathtaking pomposity, frequently giving the impression that he probably left not a note for the milkman but an illuminated manuscript:

> In a world which is chiefly occupied with the task of keeping up to date with itself, it is a satisfaction to know that there is at least one man who has not only read but enjoyed, and not only enjoyed but read, such authors as Petronius and Herondas. That is Mr Charles Whibley, and there are two statements to make about him: that he is not a critic, and that he is something which is almost as rare, if not quite as precious. He has apparently read and enjoyed a great deal of English literature, and the part of it that he has enjoyed most is the literature of the great ages, the 16th and 17th centuries. We may opine that Mr Whibley has not uttered a single important original judgment upon any of this literature. On the other hand, how many have done so?

Still, Eliot himself was aware of this. In the preface to the 1928 edition, he says: 'especially I detect frequently a stiffness and an assumption of pontifical solemnity which may be tiresome to many readers. But these, like the other faults of the book, are too well diffused throughout to be amended. I should have to write another book.'

And, although apology isn't reparation, it would be churlish – in the light of his quality as a critic – to make too much of this. This can't be a serious objection, although it is perhaps a symptom of one.

The unease, though, persists. It surfaces from time to time in the way he quotes lines and knows you must see at once the point he is making about them and must agree. Sometimes I don't feel quite so sure.

'There is no conclusive evidence that he realised all the difference, the gulf of difference between lines like:

> En l'an trentiesme de mon eage
> Que toutes mes hontes j'ay beues;

and even the very best of Ronsard or Bellay, such as:

> Le temps s'en va, le temps s'en va, madame;
> Las! le temps, non, mais nous nous en allons
> Est tost serons estendus sous la lame.'

That, of course, is part of the Eliot critical method. That gulf is obvious to him. If it isn't to you, you're wrong and that's your problem. He intimidates with learning. He is, in his quiet, pernickety way, an intellectual bully, less obstreperous with it than Pound but no less dismissive of possible opinions other than his own.

The assumptiveness extends to more general statements:

'Qua work of art, the work of art cannot be interpreted; there is nothing to interpret. . . .'

'The emotion of art is impersonal.'

'He has not the austerity of passion which can detect unerringly the transition from work of eternal intensity to work that is merely beautiful, and from work that is beautiful to work that is merely charming.'

I leave the first two to yourself. The third purports to be about Mr Whibley again, who has been unfortunate enough to incur Mr Eliot's praise. You may have noticed that it isn't about Mr Whibley at all. It is, by implication, about Mr Eliot. For how could Eliot see this lack in Mr Whibley, how could he even know such an amazing quality resided in anyone, if he didn't possess it himself?

And what is it, this amazing quality? It is an 'austerity of passion'. It can 'detect unerringly'. It recognises 'work of eternal intensity'. It is the process of patient erudition inexplicably transubstantiated into a godlike capacity for judgment.

At the end of *Tradition and the Individual Talent,* Eliot says: 'This essay proposes to halt at the frontier of metaphysics or mysticism, and confine itself to such practical conclusions as can be applied by the responsible person interested in poetry.'

Eliot may speak in a quiet, meticulous voice but the statements it makes patiently add up to an unexaminable belief in the basic infallibility of his own judgment. He has erudition but the conclusions it has brought him are not seriously for questioning. They have to be taken on trust, and that's the way he likes it. If it weren't, he might not only pass judgment but pause to clarify it.

'But this is the case when such a man plants himself firmly in his awareness of caste, when he says "The gentry must not abdicate". In politics this may be an admirable formula. It will not do in literature. The Arts insist that a man shall dispose of all that he has, even of his family tree, and follow art alone. . . . But there is only one man better and more uncommon than the patrician, and that is the Individual.'

Eliot suggests somewhere that those things we read casually (like advertising), when we are less on our guard, may get through to us most effectively. Perhaps a corollary of that might be that those things we write when we are least on our guard, when the subject about which we are writing is someone to whom, say, we feel superior, may reveal us most significantly.

The above quotation is from a section of *Imperfect Critics* called 'A Romantic Aristocrat'. The subject is George Wyndham. Mr Wyndham is someone to whom Mr Eliot is offering, as he does to Charles Whibley, what you might call a small pension of reputation, nothing too substantial, just enough to let him eke out his immortality in a kind of genteel poverty of esteem.

These seem to me a very revealing few pages. It is from them that the 'gulf of difference' already quoted comes. It is also in this small essay that Eliot says:

'We cannot grapple with even the simplest and most conversational lines in Tudor and early Stuart drama without having diagnosed the rhetoric in the 16th- and 17th-century mind.'

Notice that he doesn't say that a knowledge of such rhetoric will enlarge our understanding or appreciation of those lines. He says that we cannot so much as 'grapple' (which is a pretty basic activity) with 'even the simplest' without 'having diagnosed' – a very weighty matter, indeed. Only scholars need apply. And then who's to say they'll get it right? Aware that he does sometimes tend to be exclusive, he makes a concession to non-scholars in *Tradition and the Individual Talent*: 'Shakespeare acquired more essential history from Plutarch than most men could from the whole of the British Museum.' Apart from the dubiousness of this statement, it can hardly be said to widen the field a lot. It still leaves most of us troglodytes hanging about outside, presumably reading the papers.

But it is in that part about the non-abdication of the gentry that what is going on here becomes clearest, as far as I'm concerned. And for me the key sentence is: 'The Arts insist that a man shall dispose of all that he has, even of his family tree, and follow art alone.'

To modify one of Mr Eliot's own statements: we have heard of this abandoning all for art before. And we didn't believe it then. For what does it *mean*? Does it mean materially? If so, I'm not aware of many great artists who did, outside of novelettes. Does it mean in some more spiritual way? If so, how can you tell what they abandoned?

But even if the truth of the statement were conceded, what would still dismay me about it is the tone of implied heroism. Borges says, 'Who can pretend to be merely an impostor?' By the same token, who can pretend to such purely high-minded motivation? What about the possibility that someone who chooses such noble dedication is so anaemic he'd rather do this than hassle with living as well? It seems to me mainly just another way of bolting the door on the plebs.

I don't think that Individual with a capital 'I' is just any individual. It may be an unworthy suspicion of mine that he is a patrician of letters, someone like T. S. Eliot or Ezra Pound or James Joyce. But, assuredly, there aren't too many of him to the epoch.

He represents the malignant premise I think underpins Eliot's criticism, a kind of literary capitalism: your heritage belongs to me because you wouldn't know what to do with it and I'm the one with the erudition in the bank.

This attitude seems to me something which permeates *The Sacred Wood*. I suspect that it comes from a quite impossible high-mindedness, a kind of lay sanctimony of the self-elect, further expressed, for example, in:

'The two directions of sensibility are complementary; and as sensibility is rare, unpopular, and desirable, it is to be expected that the critic and the creative artist should frequently be the same person.' (*The Perfect Critic*)

The belief in this mutually sustaining clique which the artist makes of himself (with the possible inclusion of such others as prove 'rare' enough) may not have been invented by Eliot but *The Sacred Wood* is assuredly one of the books of its apocryphal bible. It is a belief which was one of the basic tenets of what has been called modernism:

189

I join these words for four people.
Some others may overhear them.
O world, I am sorry for you
You do not know these four people.

Causa, Ezra Pound

Anyone who, being told this, can give such an attitude mind-room has abdicated his brains.

The Sacred Wood is the work of Eliot as critic, not as poet. The separation of the two functions is one insisted on by Eliot himself: 'This gives us an intimation why the artist is – each within his own limitations – oftenest to be depended upon as a critic; his criticism will be criticism, and not the satisfaction of a suppressed wish – which, in most other persons, is apt to interfere fatally.' (*The Perfect Critic*)

This is a statement which has a pleasing neatness and is quite unverifiable. Still, that is the nature of comments on the arts, where educated assurance of assertion must stand in for the absent possibility of proof. In relation to this statement, I would make my own assertion: such separation as he implies would have to be questioned insofar as he uses the criticism as a mechanism for the release of the poetry, a self-conscious means of clearing the way for the poetry to happen as he thinks it should.

He may not be writing surrogate poetry when he criticises but he will presumably be justifying by implication his own poetry when he does so. Unless the poet-critic is inhumanly self-disciplined or has discovered the means of spontaneous cloning, his poetry and his criticism will be interdependent in this very significant way.

The implied disinterestedness, the claimed purity of response have to be questioned. In *Tradition and the Individual Talent* Eliot refers to 'my programme for the métier of poetry'. I find it questionable that a practising poet who has evolved such a programme should claim, when he looks at other poetry, to be seeing more purely what is there than someone who is solely a critic. I would suspect that he is more liable not to see what isn't there (which he suggests the critic may) but to fail to see what is there if it doesn't conform to the terms of his programme.

The question appears to be more complicated than Mr Eliot perhaps allows. For all those academic critics who engage in acts of conspiratorial pedantry with the writer of their choice, evincing galaxies of significance from atoms of meaning, there are all those poet-critics who see only what they need to see to prop up their own creative prejudices, reacting the way Auden confesses to when looking at another writer: 'My God! My Great-Grandfather! My Uncle! My Enemy! My Brother! My Imbecile Brother!'

The unaligned layman might do well to be suspicious of both, keeping with him as a kind of compass in the weedy wilderness of literary opinion the certain knowledge that art is usually more arbitrary than either its practitioners or its commentators admit.

There have, of course, been critical reappraisals since Eliot's criticism. But I believe the assumptively dominant minds in these matters are still those conditioned by the aesthetics of élitism which Eliot championed.

There are obvious reasons why this should be so. The people who have a voice in establishing the fashionable criteria, who pronounce publicly on what is good and what is bad, are themselves an élite. They are poets and critics and university men. It is, therefore, not surprising that their preferences should tend towards the intellectually arcane and the experientially effete. Such poetry mirrors many of their own lives. Then again they are likely to be a very conservative group, having invested heavily in career-shares of long established stock. Fluctuating markets worry them.

What Dire Straits call 'a whiff of the street' is seldom their favourite smell. The questionable image of T. S. Eliot, prim and clerical, pontificating on the wildness of Villon, one of life's dishevelled vagrants, like a chemist analysing a cupful of cataract and purporting to give you the essence of the phenomenon, is one paradigm of academia. Further, there is no surer way to put in suspension the common sense of academics (a commodity sometimes in short supply among them because so many of them in a sense make a career of disproportion, a living from obsession) than to intimidate them by having more learning than they have. What you do with the learning will be of less importance than the fact that you have it. What I think T. S. Eliot has done with his in *The Sacred Wood* is to use it quite deliberately as a weapon against those who have less. I see him as a monopolist of literary heritage.

Such élitism might be said to be inevitable. Eliot himself has said, 'for there is no method except to be very intelligent'. That seems fair enough but it does leave unanswered the not unimportant question of what constitutes intelligence. I can't answer it either. I can only affirm my belief in two of its crucial pivots: the continuing capacity for growth that is oiled by self-doubt and some awareness of the dimensions of the ignorance your knowledge inhabits.

Anyone who, in matters so open, can trust his own judgment to the extent that Eliot does isn't to be trusted himself. And that 'ignorance' doesn't only apply to books; it applies to the nature of experience as well, which is, after all, the proper subject of poetry – not 'truth' but a true sense of ourselves, the only kind of truth we can seek to inhabit without hypocrisy.

'The end of the enjoyment of poetry,' Eliot says in *The Perfect Critic,* 'is a pure contemplation from which all the accidents of personal emotion are removed.' I wonder who could achieve such a condition. I doubt that Eliot ever did. I don't know a single human being I can imagine reaching such a state of mind. It seems to me literary mysticism: I can imagine the attempt but not the achievement and I think we should always suspect the impossible ideal – it's a way of blinding us to the possible, so that we lose our share of it.

Imagine a bon viveur of massive influence, a prophet of the palate, a gastronomic Billy Graham. He has, through years of tasting and trying and purification of his taste buds, concluded that veal is the finest food, the only meat for the truly discriminating. He disseminates his wisdom. The food purveyors of many countries hearken to his words. Think how many people with a taste for steak would have to forego it. Think how many people with no taste for veal would be turned off altogether. And it wouldn't help the experience of cattle a lot either. To convince a lot of its practitioners and critics that poetry is an activity for the élite doesn't just falsify their own tastes, sending them in pursuit of a bloodless refinement, it kills the potentiality for a more varied taste in others. For there is nothing to feed it. To insist that sensibility is such a rare, rare thing is a demand for philistinism in others. You are, after all, giving them no option.

Something analogous to this has been done, I believe, by Eliot and others who have come to poetry with a similarly religious zeal, as if it were an escape from human nature and not an intensification of our sense of it. The tendency seems all the more regrettable to me because it has coincided with the growth of other media which have been making it progressively harder for poetry to get much of a hearing anyway. Perhaps the inroads made by these other media into its sacred domain constitute one of the reasons why poetry has turned in on itself, become to some extent a cabal of poets talking to themselves. Maybe it's the pedants' revenge on all those parvenu art-forms. If so, it's about as logical as going on the attack by committing suicide.

A time when cinema and television and popular music were making great progress as majority media seems to me a time when poetry might have been trying to see what relevant voice it could still have in a more complicated dialogue. Perhaps T. S. Eliot, publishing in 1920, can be forgiven his ignoring of other media and his one sniffy reference to the existence of an art-form other than literary in *The Possibility of a Poetic Drama*: 'a mute theatre is a possibility (I do not mean the cinema)'. But it remains ironic that while he was intoning his highly personal interpretation of the scriptures ('For mine is the kingdom', 'Blessed are the few') in his sacred wood, the trees were being chopped down round about him.

Yet *The Sacred Wood* remains a very valuable book. For one thing, to be in the company of an intelligence as fine and as disciplined as T. S. Eliot's can only do us good, provided we keep our wits about us and don't blink once. To appreciate the concentration and seriousness with which Eliot looks at literature you only have to turn, say, to W. H. Auden's essays in *The Dyer's Hand*. Read, for example, the first two pages of his essay on Byron's *Don Juan* to see that his critical intelligence is essentially frivolous and the rest of it to see that it is assuredly intelligence. In comparison to Eliot, Auden is a dandy of ideas, concerned more with the cut of his thought than the substance it contains.

A second reason follows for me from this one. In *The Sacred Wood* Eliot formulates more forcefully and clearly than any other critic I know what might be called the capitalist aesthetic of literature. Its criteria work to exclude as many people as possible. Its general effect is to teach most of us that our lives can at best provide fodder, raw material for that marvellous art which will eventually feed the esoteric sensibilities of a very few. Eliot lets us have it admirably straight, with no misleading mock concessions, no politic rhetoric for the plebs. What the devil, he won't speak 'em fair. He's the Coriolanus of critics.

If, like me, you feel yourself ranked among the plebs who confront Coriolanus, if you identify with the vague and partially inarticulate many whom Eliot rather loftily dismisses, whom he declares in his patrician way to be inevitably excluded from the 'end' of poetry, you've got problems.

Anyone who, like me, wants to suggest an alternative approach to poetry, to postulate the exploration of what might be called a socialist aesthetic (which might simply mean a way of appreciating poetry that keeps its contribution to our understanding of ourselves accessible to many more people than at present) will have to proceed with discipline. Flabby liberal sentiments about the rights of readers will not do. If you want to breach that sanctum, vaguely egalitarian impulses aren't enough. Nor is happy proletarian philistinism. It's no good trying to throw bricks through the window. It doesn't have any windows. It's no good shouting obscenities. Nobody can hear you in there. It's no good storming it with screwtops. It's too well guarded. You have to learn the passwords.

And there's a danger in that. The key password to that sanctum is 'sensibility'. What is it? How can it be acquired? It isn't easy to define. It's something vague. It has to do with intelligence, certainly. What *can* be said about it is that only those who have it can recognise it and it is utterly individual. It is presumably acquired from the process of applying intelligence rigorously to the reading of literature, preferably all literature.

There's the danger. The process of acquiring such sensibility is a process of isolation, leaving you able to identify in literary terms only with the few who share it. The only way to gain access to the sanctum is to become one of its guardians. It is analogous to the classic dilemma of revolutionary politics: how do you penetrate the modes of established power without becoming part of them? How can you make such ideas a part of your system and preserve immunity to their élitist effects?

It's a problem compounded by the intimidatory effect of established systems. Eliot's interpretation of the past is *fait accompli*. He may say 'the past should be altered by the present as much as the present is directed by the past' (*Tradition and the Individual Talent*) but, given the fixity of that past as he conceives it and demands that it must be, any possible alteration seems about as dynamic as repositioning some of the parts of an ambiguous jigsaw. Anyone trying to penetrate to the core of such critical theory to test the possibility of an alternative aesthetic finds, in the nature of things, that he has to confront an elaborate structure of postulated certainties, ostensibly hallowed with time, with a hopefully fructifying doubt. It's a hard struggle, like pitting a dream against masonry. Imagine a sensitive Visigoth (if, of course, you can't imagine such a thing, the dream will be one you can't have in the first place) arriving alone in a perfectly intact Roman villa. Won't the various mysterious facilities be awesome? Will it not be easier for him to take lessons from a Roman in their uses than to try and find out for himself and perhaps discover new inventive purposes? And won't the comfort they afford him be likely to make a Roman of him? And might his conclusion not be that only such Visigoths as become Romans are full participants in his culture? The significance of the Visigoths will become that they are not Romans.

For sophisticated assurance, no matter how dishonestly arrived at, has an apparent dignity of presence that honest doubt will seldom achieve. In such a presence honest doubt is all too likely to feel itself naked among the well dressed and put on borrowed precepts to cover its reality, simply because the other is so commandingly *there*. Too reverential an awareness of the past, of how it has been done, will habituate the potentially new voice at best into imitation, at worst into silence. I've known many university students who came to university with the determination to write and lost it there because they became intimidated by their awareness of what had already been written. They lost their belief in the primacy of experience.

It seems to me that the primacy of experience (the need for literature to judge itself not merely on its own closed terms of beauty and rhythm and form but most importantly in terms of how far it expresses and clarifies the realities of our lives as we have to live them) is in much need of acknowledgment. One thing the advance of a medium like television has done is to make all of us far more conscious of the bewildering varieties, frequently hardly tolerable, of human experience. Such an awareness is no longer just a concept in the mind of an experienced and sensitive person. We are bombarded with it daily. In the light of that, poetry as a privately cultivated ornamental garden of the spirit seems to me unacceptable. I think the literary idealism of the past is past.

But the hold it has on our consciousness and on the view we have of literature is still present. The critical method of T. S. Eliot and others forms a very effective security system against the invasion of their privacy by others, leaving them in peace to enjoy the 'end' of poetry. I think poetry has potentially other ends than the one to which they put it. I think poetry is required for other uses by a great many more people. I think, in order to free it effectively so that we can begin to test its efficacy to meet those uses, we have to try and dismantle that security system.

'On the other hand, poetry as certainly has something to do with morals, and with religion, and even with politics perhaps, though we cannot say what.' (Preface to the 1928 edition of *The Sacred Wood*.) Like the make-up of an actor, the statement isn't meant to be obtrusive. It is made and forgotten about and it should allow us more effectively to accept the terms of the rest of the book. Thereafter, poetry will be presented as 'poetry and not another thing'. (Preface to the 1928 edition.)

The desire to maintain this clinical isolation of the phenomenon of poetry is understandable, especially in someone who refers to 'the pernicious effect of emotion' (*The Perfect Critic*) and to the fact that 'social emancipation crawled abroad' (*Euripides and Professor Murray*). Poetry may be 'excellent words in excellent arrangement and excellent metre' (Preface to the 1928 edition). The difficulty is that the excellence isn't automatically decided by the words and the arrangement and the metre in independent conclave. Their relationship to our experience is somewhat relevant. Poetry is an adjunct of life or it is nothing. It only lives through an immensely complicated relationship with our experience. That relationship has many aspects more dynamic than 'pure contemplation'. To isolate poetry in this way, to seek rigorously to refine away its natural impurities to achieve this 'end' of 'pure contemplation' is like auditioning for the role of the mad scientist in an old Hollywoood movie ('I haf discovered ze secret of poetry. All ze stanzas vill belong to me'). Once you build a laboratory round poetry, the only kind of investigation left to carry out is an autopsy.

The error lies in that phrase 'though we cannot say what', which is the sound of the laboratory door closing. It is true that we cannot say what, and it is the fact that we cannot say what which calls in question so much of what Eliot and others think they *can* say. It is precisely what we cannot say, what is unknown that for a serious application of intelligence is not dismissible. It is precisely that capacity of the known to qualify its stance in relation to the unknown that constitutes the continuance of intelligence.

I think Eliot's sense of tradition, judged against that criterion, is morbid. In spite of his remark that 'the past should be altered by the present', I cannot see the signs that he believed in this in any significant way. His sense of the past is of something to be submitted to with a terrible rigour in order 'to ponder collaboration to the utmost line . . . to distil the last drop of it [this pleasure], to press and press the essence of each author . . .' (*Philip Massinger*). Why? To be a dutiful servant to other people's pasts? What about the present and the future? Is our chief function as readers to revivify that past through our understanding and appreciation of it? Pharoah lives: let us labour to make pyramids of appreciation to house the great dead spirits of the past. Aren't we as well to loot them, each of us as best we can?

Even looters, of course, should be discriminating. In trying to achieve that discrimination, we will have recourse to some of the techniques Eliot makes use of. But need we apply them in the same ways or to the same ends? Erudition itself, the basis from which he starts, has a value that shifts in relation to the intelligence and experience that inform it. Cultivated for its own sake, it becomes merely a morbid hobby which can lead to a kind of inflation of the intellect. The more self-consciously esoteric it becomes, the more carefully the mind should ingest it, like a potentially unhealthy diet, because it can encourage you to form unearned opinions free from the vigorous opposition of other minds, giving rise to an inert complacency. The metabolism that transforms it into relevant energy is the intelligence, and that energy will seek dialogue.

Intelligence is the most crucial element in Eliot's critical method. It is, indeed, the method itself: 'for there is no method except to be very intelligent'. This intelligence is, of course, separate from the erudition. Knowledge is never intelligence, it is what intelligence reacts to; the way in which intelligence reacts is how it shows itself. A man with much less knowledge than another man may not only be more intelligent but may often demonstrate the fact. I would suggest that, for intelligence, knowledge is most significantly a means of more precisely getting a fix on what it doesn't know, so that it locates the way in which it may grow; that intelligence is most properly gauged by the (intellectual) justice and honesty and skill with which a mind can inhabit its own inevitable ignorance.

Eliot, of course, is referring to intelligence as it applies to language. The first indication of morbidity I find in his sense of this intelligence and how it applies itself is the assumption he seems to make that it must of necessity remove itself from any very wide or significantly public dialogue. The energy seems, first of all, turned inward and at best shared only with a few like minds. That seems to me a singularly undynamic application of intelligence based on a quite unwarranted assumption. Where does the idea come from that the highest expression of critical intelligence lies in understanding or appreciating what very few can understand or appreciate? What is literature – some kind of eleven-plus of the spirit?

Intelligence as it relates to language inhabits an area with a characteristic that distinguishes it from, say, the sciences. It operates in a public domain, is a commodity of which almost everyone has some knowledge, is a consciously deployed factor in all our lives. Therefore, I'd suggest that linguistic intelligence is properly measured not just by its capacity to articulate but by its capacity to communicate. Writers may begin by talking to themselves but that self-articulation contains an implicit dialogue. A relevant criterion must be the extent of that dialogue, the extent to which the writer can make his words comprehensible while sacrificing as little as possible of the complexity of what he is trying to articulate.

The remit any writer takes on isn't merely to 'have been there', as Americans say, to have undergone with understanding the extremes of internal experience (whether you see that in terms of Hemingway-Mailer machismo or the more spiritual contemplation of someone like Eliot). It is also to have come back. Like the black box in an aeroplane crash, the writer's function is not just to discover the nature of experience but to bring back an expression of what it is like that is relevant to the experience of as many others as possible.

The width of that relevance seems to me crucially important. The more people to whose appreciation you can honestly submit your findings, possibly the more validly they are tested, because just as experience is shared by all of us, some significant appreciation of the expression of it is potentially so. Such appreciation can't be total, of course. It has limitations. But it should at least be an important principle of writing that the writer should not wilfully or self-indulgently preclude the wider possibilities of that appreciation. The complacency with which Eliot accepts the inaccessibility of the best poetry seems to me a narrowing of the craft's potential. Such an attitude has rubber-stamped a fair amount of charlatanism in modern poetry, arcane utterances that merit Roy Campbell's comment *On Some South African Novelists*:

> You praise the firm restraint with which they write.
> I'm with you there, of course.
> They use the snaffle and the curb all right.
> But where's the bloody horse?

The attempt to achieve such appreciation and relevance must remain, of course, something which involves the reader in effort as well as the writer. There can never be a licence for the reader – no matter how intelligent – to say, 'I don't immediately appreciate this, therefore it isn't any good.' And in trying to find a just compromise between the necessarily difficult and the wilfully inaccessible, the controlling vote must be with the writer. The inevitable arbitrariness of art, the way in which it is for so many writers – and perhaps for all writers of originality – the pursuit of a personal daimon, must not be legislated against. But anyone who tries to write will equally inevitably find himself or herself trying to learn control of that impulse to write. One of the key components of that machinery of control will be the maintained determination to make his or her writing as accessible as he or she honestly can, or the writer will have sacrificed integrity. 'Great problems are in the street,' Nietzsche says. I think writers should try as far as possible to put the words that seek to deal with them in the same place.

Of course, the question of accessibility has to remain an open one for every writer as he works. But for the critic it does admit of judgment, albeit difficult judgment. Whatever creativity is, it has much to do with achieved clarity.

It is difficult to arrive at any guiding principle for assessing how just, how earned the difficulty of a poem or a piece of prose may be. But I would think that fairness to the reader has to be a relevant criterion. No matter what private beliefs in the sanctity of art or divine inspiration or the priestliness of his task a writer may draw his initial energy from, he had better remember what he is trying to do when he applies it. He is trying to communicate with others. To do that effectively, he will be concerned not only to declare where he is but to direct that declaration towards where they are.

Where they are most significantly, if he reaches them at all, is reading his work. This means that any serious difficulty he presents them with should be resolvable within the terms of the work itself as it relates to their intelligence and experience. This doesn't mean that no work should make allusions to any other work. Almost all poetry does so, however indirectly. What will matter is that such allusions shouldn't be necessary to give the new work coherence, to justify its existence. Otherwise, it has no significant existence. The allusions may be a kind of incidental decoration or they may, more importantly, be so subsumed in the whole that they achieve a new and independent life in it.

That respect paid to the active and present intelligence of the reader – as opposed to the hypocritical 'respect' of assuming that he or she must have read what you have read or must at least want to – is one guide to the difference between necessary difficulty and wilful obfuscation.

198

It is a sign of dynamic intelligence to work for mutually meaningful confrontation with all other intelligences, not wilfully to choose forms of expression which preclude such confrontation. The latter is often no more than a ploy to establish intellectual status, to elicit from others a habit of intellectual respect your use of your intelligence doesn't justify.

Instead of taking on the burden of the communal experience more determinedly, instead of addressing itself to the problem of finding renewed relevance, of finding how to speak to, about and for the lives around it, poetry has often pursued a sterile aestheticism. For many people the most important criterion in measuring the development of a poet has become how fully he has explored his own technical virtuosity. How far he may have spoken relevantly to the times, how far he has contributed to the community's understanding of itself outwith the hothouse culture of the universities or the oxygen-tent conditions of a poetry-reading will be of less significance.

'He exercises neither of the tools of the critic, comparison and analysis' (*Imperfect Critics*). As far as I have been able to determine from my reading of *The Sacred Wood,* what Eliot means by the tools of the critic is 'comparison with his own other work and with the work of other writers' and 'analysis of linguistic effects'. We are back to poetry as 'poetry and not another thing'. But it is several other things: 'poetry as certainly has something to do with morals, and with religion, and even with politics perhaps, though we cannot say what'. That being the case, how can 'comparison and analysis' be justifiably or even meaningfully limited in these ways?

It may, of course, create problems we cannot satisfactorily solve immediately to push the critical intelligence beyond these invented limits, but, according to Eliot's own principles, that should surely not deter us: 'And the free intelligence is that which is wholly devoted to inquiry'. That's fine. It presumably means that such inquiry will not confine itself to questions so carefully limited as to be merely molten answers. Yet the questions Eliot's critical intelligence sets itself are in a very real sense 'rhetorical'. They are about words in self-containment, considered as a self-governing body. As such, they don't make poetry more alive for us, they embalm it. To do more than this, 'comparison and analysis' would have to be made to extend their application, no matter what difficulty or trepidation that involves for the applicant. 'Comparison' would centrally involve 'comparison with apprehended experience' and 'analysis' would most importantly include 'analysis of the honesty of the work's relationship to experience'.

Eliot's reverential contemplation of the past is, I have suggested, morbid. It is so determined to achieve what looks like a literary equivalent of transcendental meditation that it mortifies the present, rendering its poetic potential anorexic. Hence, perhaps, *The Waste Land*, that impressive echo-chamber poem, where, to achieve dramatic stature, his own times have to be buskined in old quotations, masqued in allusions. I don't think Eliot is significantly describing the post-war world so much as he's describing his own culture shock. I see the deeper, accidental meaning of *The Waste Land* as being not that things were so different before but that the ability to pretend that they were is on the way out. The stature of the past and of the men of the past was always a myth. By the time Eliot wrote *The Waste Land* it was a disintegrating myth. His poem is one of poetic idealism's last stands, and for me not a particularly heroic one. Instead of trying to look steadily through the hole history had blown in the pretensions poetry had for so long allowed itself, he papered it over with nice quotations, and jacked up those pretensions even higher.

What I think Eliot is reacting against in *The Waste Land* and in his criticism is what much modern poetry has reacted against. They may call it 'decline in standards' or 'loss of values' or just plain 'philistinism'. Not a few modern artists and appreciators of the arts see themselves as standing out against the vulgar tastelessness of so much modern life. Poets, I suspect, are particularly prone to this romantic misconception. (Consider the first words quoted in this essay from *The Sacred Wood*.)

Like *The Waste Land*, what they are holding out against is, I believe, the most significant literary event of this century. This event isn't a series of novels or the career of a great writer or a school of poets or a critical theory. It's only 'literary' in the sense that it affects drastically and probably irrevocably the status of literature in our culture. The event is simply that our society has become culturally open.

The relative importance of the various factors contributing to this condition is debatable; even what these factors may be could be debated: international upheaval; social emancipation 'crawling' abroad; a decline in the intellectual status of religion; perhaps even the way in which Marxism has tried to arrange a shotgun wedding between Western society and the idealistic philosophy it had maintained for so long as its mistress – that has certainly been one traumatic experience. What I would have thought isn't seriously debatable is that poetry, obliged to live in the midst of such a cultural hubbub, such a jostling and unresolved confusion of cultural values, renders any contribution it might make largely invalid by entrenching itself in purely aesthetic criteria, by defining itself as 'a superior amusement' (Preface to the 1928 edition).

Surrounded by change, faced with the emergence of new modes of communication, bewildered by the now much more openly acknowledged varieties of life as it is lived, confronted with the collapse of its own spurious idealism, finding the closed assumptions of its past no longer tenable – what should poetry do? Eliot's answer is chillingly simple. It should close those assumptions further. Since the public is such an unappreciative rabble, poetry should not concern itself with them. Let it develop the sensibilities of the few.

'Individual sensibility' is, he would say, what poetry is for. And what is individual sensibility for? It is for itself, its own 'pure contemplation'. Perhaps it could hardly be for much else, since it is so rare. It is, of course, the appreciative counterpart to that creative man 'The Arts' insisted should 'dispose of all that he has, even of his family tree, and follow art alone'. (You will remember that 'the two directions of sensibility are complementary' and that sensibility is 'rare, unpopular, and desirable'.) It all makes for a rather romantic spiritual scenario: rare and lonely artist meets rare and lonely critic and from their union come rare and lonely 'pure contemplations'. And that sterile marriage is the hallowed 'end' of poetry? I'd rather not be a guest at that particular wedding.

But is sensibility in either of its complementary forms necessarily such a limited phenomenon? I think a lot of significant art *does* have its origins in the kind of loneliness Eliot implies. I think a lot of serious writers do suffer in something like the way that Eliot suggests. But I also think that 'The Arts insist' is a rather hazily romantic explanation to append to that loneliness and that suffering. A harder look might yield a less Eleusinian response.

First of all, I don't think that isolation of the artist is something that he will work at, as if it were part of his craft. Or if it is so cultivated, he will be a poser. The lonely suffering the artist undergoes is inevitable, if it is there at all. It's the thing about himself he can't avoid. If it is 'insisted' upon, it can't be real. It's as likely to happen to him if he's holed up in the Hilton on an expense account as anywhere else. It's presumably what found Descartes in Amsterdam, what pursued Kafka from Prague to Berlin.

I am not saying it's some birthmark of the Muses. I should think it's an acquired characteristic. I just don't think that it is ever successfully acquired deliberately. And although its acquisition isn't achievable under laboratory conditions, I don't think where it comes from need be any great mystery. It comes, I believe, from an individual's compulsive need to codify his own experience for himself without intermediaries, to shape it for himself into a comprehensible para-experience, to recreate reality into a unity his actual experience didn't achieve. The artist suffers because he is trying to effect a painful rebirth. He is lonely because his compulsion precludes him from merely accepting who he is and sharing it with others. That is a very practical loneliness.

And why should the compelled nature of his isolation not make him seek as wide a communication as possible through his art? Perhaps only a dilettante of that isolation would be happy to extend it into his art by wilfully and complacently excluding people from it. His isolation will be how he earns his gift; his ability to share it will be how he expresses it.

And if the quality of sensibility in the artist needn't be judged by how patricianly dismissive he is of the importance of wide appreciation, why should the quality of sensibility in the critic be judged by how incommunicable it is to most other people? Critical sensibility is also acquired in loneliness, it is true, because it develops in a vigorous eliciting of your own responses, in a refusal to pretend to feel or think merely what you ought to feel or think, in a censoring in yourself of mimicry or imitation, in a discovery of honesty to self. But the very quality of that honesty will depend on how far you succeed in bringing to that confrontation between you and the thing read the sense of others who are not present, even of those who are incapable of being present (like the illiterate), by how far you can make the privacy of your head as public as possible.

Sensibility can be a growing capacity to identify emotionally and intellectually with more and more people. If it is so far what Eliot says it is, it might be a good idea to find out how to change it.

It is very difficult to achieve any just sense of what poetry is. I can think of a couple of reasons for this. The first is that its dominant characteristic is its variousness. Like a kaleidoscope, it fulfils itself by not staying the same. You may describe the structure and the principles of a kaleidoscope but the essence of it is that you don't know what it will do, what will be there when you look into it. The second is that, like so many of the arts, poetry gives rise to some terrible nonsense, boastful ravings of no ascertainable substance. With the possible exception of sex, the arts are perhaps the area where most lies are most glibly told.

These two reasons are not unconnected. The very vagueness of the boundaries of poetry, the volatility of any attempt to define its 'function', the inevitable uncertainty of judgments passed as to comparative quality in it, all conspire to make it a potentially happy hunting-ground for ideas that aren't always reputable. Like a small independent state the laws of which are vague and the customs of which are not notoriously stern on contraband, it welcomes to its bosom some strange theories whose papers of identity look distinctly home-made. These we can find sojourning in the land of poetry and sometimes living on fake currency.

Given that problem, it's perhaps understandable that an intelligence as fastidious as Eliot's should withdraw behind a structure of lofty principles, admitting only those whose credentials he regards as unquestionably authentic. He had, after all, the rhyming gossip of Georgian poetry to react against. (Perhaps one way to see *Prufrock* is as a marvellously ironic extension of that poetry, trivia in overdrive.) But more important than any understandable motivation seems to me the effect Eliot has had on subsequent attitudes to poetry by making himself, through the formidable force of his intelligence, a kind of Pierpont Morgan of the word.

The lingering effect has been, I believe, to intensify the splitting of poetry into the private and the public sector, as it were. There have been good 'popular' poets since the impact of Eliot and Pound ('popular' in relation to poetry being a word we should use tentatively, since it connotes a ghetto of popularity within a large indifference). But such guerrilla outbreaks don't seem to me to have very significantly repaired the division between 'serious' poetry and 'popular' poetry.

I think a kind of intellectual hangover remains, a fog of assumptions: that the very best poetry is probably beyond the appreciation of all but a very few people; that the ultimate quality of poetry is perhaps measurable by this very fact; that for poetry to be finally serious it has to be first of all solemn; that obscurity is perhaps a prerequisite of depth; that immediacy of impact might be rather vulgar. Such assumptions would be pernicious enough if their total effect were to confine a lot of creative energy to what I have called the 'private sector'. But their effect goes further, I think. They damage the potential development of a virile popular poetic tradition.

One way in which this damage is done relates to my suggestion earlier that to define sensibility as such a rare, rare thing is a demand for philistinism in others. The kind of impossibly high-minded aesthetic Eliot puts forward can have the effect – by cutting all but the most 'serious' poetry off without a cultural penny – of relieving popular poetry of its responsibilities to meet any significant aesthetic standards at all. A 'popular' movement like the 'Beat poets' seems to me a demonstration of this effect. You don't need to have the severity of vision of T. S. Eliot to see their poetry as generally pretty bad – not because they haven't studied the tradition of the medieval troubadours but simply because when they come to the page they use words vaguely and lack form. I don't think they're an isolated phenomenon. I think some of what passes for popular poetry today patronises its potential audience.

That, it seems to me, is not to combat those assumptions mentioned previously, but to condone them. It is to make a kindergarten of the possibility of a popular poetry while the grown-ups get on with the real stuff. I think any attempt to move towards a healthy popular poetry would involve the reader in real effort. But, hopefully, the effort would bring rewards because the poetry wouldn't be an expression of lofty indifference towards most readers but an attempt to engage in a dialogue, even in an intermittently complicated dialogue, with the lives of the people around it. It wouldn't seek to be merely a 'superior amusement'. It wouldn't accept the inevitability of Auden's statement: 'poetry makes nothing happen'. (*In Memory of W. B. Yeats*, a good poem which for me makes several things happen.)

For, surely, poetry does make something happen. The problem is that it isn't easy to define what poetry makes happen and impossible to legislate for how it makes it happen. For these things happen in the sensibility of the reader or listener. They are insights, illuminations, pleasures, sympathies, unexpected recognitions, understood griefs, new awarenesses, changed ways of seeing, confirmations of the half-felt, wonder at the familiar, renewed possibilities. There is more but this already seems to me quite a lot for poetry to make happen. It is exactly this capacity of poetry to intensify our awareness of being alive, to sharpen our sense of our shared humanity that makes its use as some status symbol of an élite so unacceptable.

To fulfil effectively the things it can do, I should have thought poetry has to try to make itself relevant to and accessible to the 'sensibility' of as many people as possible. It shouldn't fear the compromise of its principles. In giving itself a function alongside television or cinema or rock music, it would remain itself. For literature still contributes to the development of individual sensibility – and therefore to the potential development of communal sensibility – an element that no other medium of communication can supply. Literature remains a do-it-yourself phenomenon for the reader, demanding exercise of the imagination, acknowledgment of complexity, honest thought, education of feelings. And poetry especially involves these.

I can't see anything sacred about poetry. But the structure's there with all its facilities and, as always, there's a cultural war on. It could perhaps be commandeered for more practical purposes. If it's no good as a temple, it might make a useful field dressing-station.

I'm aware that such an essay as this is like Caesar running all the way to the Capitol, especially when what it precedes is in part an experiment in trying to appropriate for poetry some of the techniques of the novel and the cinema. But I believe in the attempt.

Farewell to Polkemmet

IT USED TO BE THAT FROM THE ROAD OUTSIDE THE hospital, you had a clear view of how it loomed on the skyline, overhanging the village. It was sombre and ugly, a burning hill. Gashes of red appeared along its flanks from time to time. It looked like something out of Tolkien country.

But there was nothing fantastic about its origins. It was the amassed waste of years of working Polkemmet colliery, a huge memorial to numberless man-hours, a sweat-mountain. Its shifting weight, letting in air haphazardly to oxidise some remains of the coal, made of it a nest of shifting fires. The fumes from those fires often hung in a pall over the village of Whitburn. Depending on how the wind moved, anyone in or around Whitburn was liable to catch the sulphur of the bing's breath and be reminded that for a long time coal had ruled here.

If you travelled the countryside around Whitburn, you would find the past supremacy of coal in the lives of the people unmistakably confirmed. Going to or coming from Whitburn or Fauldhouse or Longridge or the Forth or Breich, you would see coal's monuments to itself, like a Pharoah not content with one memorial. There are large tracts of land given over to the nursery forestation that marks the worked-out sites of open-cast mining. There are abandoned drift mines. There are the burial mounds of old pits.

These once had names. There was Northfield and Southfield, the Knowes, Knowtoun, Kiltrigg and Benhar (East and West). Some retain their legends. Falla Hill is where, they say, a man going back for his graith before the pit closed was lost in the fall and never dug out. These were coal's lesser monuments in the area.

But Polkemmet was for a long time the big one. The sinking of the pit began in 1913. There were delays in the work during the First World War and the new pit-workings were nicknamed the Dardanelles because local people said that about as many lost their lives at the industrial site as at the military one. The first coal began to be brought up in 1919. The pit is closed now. During the miners' strike of 1984–85, the longest in British history, striking miners had withdrawn safety cover from the mine because coal was being brought out. The National Coal Board retaliated by stopping the pumps and flooding the mine. At the end of the strike, the Coal Board said it wasn't economically viable to reopen the mine.

The last time I visited Polkemmet, on a winter day of shallow snow, there was little to be seen but flat whiteness and frosted rubble and, I remember, an old, forlorn, abandoned working-boot. It was good to see that the tip, with its malignant breath, had gone. But I felt sad. What else had gone?

For mines have always meant more than themselves. They have always produced more than greater or lesser tonnes of coal. They have spawned very special communities, a distinctive ethos, an intermittent radicalism, a way of life. To the outsider, probably the most striking aspect of the mining tradition has been the interdependence of miners, their solidarity. Stories are told of families from dead mining villages being rehoused together in their new place because they refused to be separated. It isn't surprising they kept close. History had taught them the value of doing so. The miners were in their origins bond-slaves. Being rejected by many other people, they responded as strong people will to rejection. They took a pride in it. They held together and they made a community of their isolation. Could that community still stand?

The time before that when I had gone to Polkemmet was after the 1984–85 strike. The pit had already been sentenced to death. Diggers were dismantling the massive landmark of the tip, men working round the edge of the burning bing, like labourers in hell. The position was that about 50 men were still being employed in the rundown of Polkemmet. From the rest of the work-force, the older men were being forcibly retired, given redundancy notices that read 'no option'. Some of the younger men had been moved to another colliery, Bilston Glen. Others had refused to make the move and had taken their redundancy. Bilston Glen was not a popular place among Polkemmet miners, since they regarded many of its workers as 'scabs'. A young Polkemmet miner who had transferred to Bilston Glen was asked on Whitburn's main street what he thought of his new pit. 'Complete pish!' he said and walked into a pub.

For a more detailed expression of feelings in the area, I went to the Miners' Welfare Club in Whitburn. It is an old battered building which looks a bit like the meeting-hall of one of the less popular religious schisms, some not very clearly identified group of close brethren. Inside, it is friendly. There is a snooker room. There are the ubiquitous fruit-machines. There is a bar. There is a large lounge with many tables and chairs and a stage, waiting that weekend for a country and western singer.

In the committee room of the club I met with seven ex-miners of Polkemmet. They were a varied group, disproving the not unpopular delusion that miners are all of a piece, as if they have all been howked from the one seam of humanity. They were an under-manager, a couple of developers, electricians. One spoke in a carefully measured way, like a slow-motion teleprinter, seeming to check that a sentence was going to work before he finished it. Another hardly spoke at all. One was a staunchly active member of the Labour Party. Three had retired early before the strike, one to nurse his wife, who had since died. Of the other four, two had been given compulsory redundancy and two had chosen redundancy rather than go to Bilston Glen; two had stayed out throughout the entire strike while two had gone back early.

What they had in common was their tolerance. Miners can give and take rough talk among themselves without dislodging their smiles. It can leave a bystander wary, how a remark that seemed thrown like a knife is played back like a shuttlecock. You get the sense that this game may be private and doesn't extend to strangers. It is as if the mutual dependence that is central to working down the pit has created a measure of play in their natures towards one another. You don't reject a man up here when you may be needing him down there.

Yet their tolerance extended to me. I was an interloper, questioning them after the worst year of their lives with the pain of it still raw. Sometimes, too, my questions were less than tactful, emerging from my own pained disbelief in what had happened. I had my moments of investigative impertinence. But they took any questions I asked and answered them as honestly as they could.

It was a long session we had. As the empty glasses marched across the table, we covered and re-covered ground, digressed, debated, disagreed, confessed we didn't know. In making my own wilful minutes of that meeting, I must inevitably be writing as much about my own beliefs as theirs. The generosity of giving was all theirs. The dubiety of what has been made of the gift is mine.

Money was obviously high on the agenda of our discussion, although money wasn't what the strike had been about. The strike had been about jobs. It had been a determined refusal to accept the closure of pits as purely a decision of management. It had demanded immediately no pit closures and subsequently no pit closures without full consultation with the work-force. But defeat of that purpose had left them counting their money. 'Everybody lost,' Bill Russell said. The compensation for that loss was their redundancy money. That money seemed to have an ambiguous feel to some of them. The three men who had retired early had made a private peace with themselves, though for one of them it looked troubled. The other four appeared not yet to have adjusted to their circumstances.

Not one of them complained about the amount. More than one man in the room had received over £25,000. The uncertainty perhaps related to what the money stood for and to the changes it was bringing into their lives.

Some men in the village had already exhausted their funds, some women were already struggling to hold the house together without ever having seen much of the money. There were stories of alcoholism, of ex-miners in flashy Italian suits that seemed to be bought with a fancy woman attached to the arm, of marriages breaking or broken. One of the men I sat with, an honest and committed socialist who had been active throughout the strike, admitted to having sunk £15,000 in investments, because he dreaded happening to him what he saw happening to others. Their response to my unsubtle suggestion that they were being turned into mini-capitalists were shrugs and nods.

The sense of displacement in the room was almost palpable. These men were no longer where they had been and they hadn't worked out yet where they were. Redundancy money can operate like a prolonged anaesthetic. For them the anaesthetic hadn't yet worn off but they had already begun to notice the pain of others for whom it had. They sat together yet were strangely dispersed, divided amongst themselves, not quite sure where each other was. If you're not certain where you stand any more in your own scale of values, you're not likely to have a clear sense of where anybody else is. It was as if the money had bought each of them out of the social contract he had had with the others.

At the house of John and Margaret Tumbler, where I later had a meal, John offered a simple explanation for what had happened to them. He was a passionate and articulate man, forced out of the pits because of his health and then working at the British Leyland plant in Bathgate, another place doomed to close soon and add to the unemployment in an area where it already ran at 26 per cent. 'They're no' the men their feythers were,' he said.

He meant it as a moral judgment. I respect his right to make such a judgment but I don't have that right, nor do I want it. These men were impressive enough for me. But, in a neutral sense, I could agree with him. They were different from their fathers in that they no longer had the sense of solidarity of their fathers. Perhaps the hurt which even the miners' gift for laughter out of darkness, much in evidence as we talked, couldn't quite allay, related to that loss. They had been brought to a place where they were given 'no option' but to cash in a tradition. Like an aristocrat obliged to sell his hereditary estate, each had had to settle for the money that was going. The sale was made the more painfully ironic because the estate in question had never been measurable in purely material terms. It was an inheritance of hard truths earned over generations, of values money couldn't buy, of continuing belief in the ability of people to care as much for one another as for themselves.

Given the working-class heritage associated with the mining industry, it isn't difficult to see why a lot of people who have no connection with mining felt an almost personal sense of loss at the defeat of the miners. The miners have been seen by some as one of the last fortresses in working-class life against the devastating intrusion of materialism. They have been understandably concerned with money, it is true. But that financial concern has tended to be inseparable from the shared, harsh reality of the conditions in which they have worked. (The slogan for the General Strike of 1926 maintained that connection: 'Not a minute on the day, not a penny off the pay'.) They have seemed less susceptible to an individual sell-out of shared values than the rest of us.

That is partly a romantic view of miners, but only partly. The element of romanticism in it can be demonstrated by pointing to Nottinghamshire, where a rich and comparatively easily mined coalfield has created for several generations a 'Fuck you, Jack' philosophy. But once the eyes have been rinsed of romanticism, there are still strong reasons for seeing the miners as staying largely loyal to a fierce sense of community many of us have abandoned.

A couple of years ago, while it was still working, I went down Polkemmet. I was invited by Yvonne McEwen, medical sister there at the time, who had used an extract from *Docherty* in a paper she had written. I was glad to go. I wanted to check my past experience of miners against some sense of the current situation. I had to pay my dues as a tourist. Tam Birkley, my guide to the nether regions, was happy not just to lead me but sometimes to lead me astray. At one point he said, 'We'll no' waste oor legs walkin' back, Wullie. We'll use the belt. Just do what Ah do.'

He jumped effortlessly onto the conveyor belt in a oner and began to recede, waiting for me to follow. I did what I thought was the same and finished on my back, slithering dementedly with my helmet bouncing behind me, my arms and legs waving like an insect, my hands grasping at the sides of the belt. I decided, with a bruised nonchalance, to sit the journey out. I had hurt my hand but I felt the protocol would be to avoid mentioning the fact. I think I passed the initiation test, for we got on very well after that and I ended up singing Burns songs in the showers with some other miners. Membership of the glee club in one day can't be bad.

It was an acceptance that mattered to me. George Orwell suggested in the 1930s that miners were the most impressive men he had come across. I don't think he would find much change. These men are no parvenus of the spirit. They have serious substance and they know it. They have to confirm it daily. Every day they bring out the coal, they bring out with it a reaffirmation of themselves. They have a sense of their own worth that could never be measured against the weight of a pay-poke. Some of them down that pit had eyes as steady as I have seen. They rarely pre-empted my questions, just watched them coming patiently. For what could I ask them that they couldn't honestly answer?

The source of their effortless self-assurance didn't seem to me hard to locate. I was a guest on a diminishing territory that belonged to them. We were standing in one of the last places in British industry where the quality of the man as a man is daily paramount. The work remains hard and dangerous, as it is, for example, on the oil rigs. But in mining, the technology, though it has made considerable advances, is less dominant. The day I was down, I visited a face where the machinery had broken down and I watched men stripped to the waist and shovelling coal on their knees. While miners exist, no imaginable technology will be able to diminish their pride in themselves. The only way to make coal-mining safe and easy is to devise a method of mining from the surface by pushing buttons.

Miners remain among the most dramatic representatives of the nature of labour, its harshness and its risks. Remove a man from an assembly line and his replacement will be accepted in the couple of days or so it takes him to learn his basic function. Remove a man from a pit and whoever replaces him will have to earn his way into the estimation of his workmates. You don't travel down there and show them how to do it in a day or two. You will learn slowly and sharing will be involved in the learning and so, perhaps, will courage.

It was maybe their awareness of that vanishing complex of traditions that made the seven men in Whitburn sad in spite of the money. There was a slightly baffled sense among them of having been swindled. The government hadn't just bought their individual jobs. It had broken up the heritage of generations and sold it, literally in job-lots. It was as if the men had been obliged to sell what they suspected wasn't entirely theirs to sell.

Nobody should blame these men. Let no armchair radicals judge them. They had spent a year as part of the only group in our society to offer determined and sustained opposition to the policies of a government which reduces human beings to economic ciphers. They had declared that their work was a part of them as people. They had maintained that they weren't statistical digits in a work-force but members of a community. Given the way the utterly spurious but vigorously reiterated certainties of Margaret Thatcher had intimidated coherent opposition, the miners' stand was a lonely one. The inadequate support they received contributed to their defeat.

The full cost had yet to be counted, both financially and psychologi-cally. A lot of debt had been incurred. I was told of a former Polkemmet miner who now worked in Bilston Glen. After paying off some of his outstanding debt each week (including double rent for his NCB house, since he had a year of rent arrears to make up), he took home £40. Consider that as a week's remuneration for working down a mine.

210

Also, to stay away from a pit for a little while is to want to stay away from it for longer. Miners don't work inside the concept of the importance of mining to the maintenance of working-class values. They work in a pit, and that's a bad place to work. During the miners' strike, some miners decided they were staying up for good, no matter what the outcome was. Fresh air is habit-forming.

It is true that the majority of miners have formed some kind of affection for working in the pits. Why else would they do the job? The quality of that affection came out in the stories that punctuated our talk in Whitburn. Miners have a great love of anecdote, the moment that typifies a man or crystallises a style. So they told me of a legendary pit-manager, a hard man who had come up through the ranks. Involved in an accident for which he blamed another man, the manager got to his feet and faced him. They cursed each other elaborately for about a minute before the manager walked away. It was only later that the other men discovered that he required fourteen stitches in his arm. Another time, a miner came to ask him for a line to get a duffel jacket from the stores. The manager wrote out the line, folded it and gave him it. When the miner reported to the stores and passed the line over, he was equipped with a Number Ten shovel. Going back to the manager to see about the mistake, he was told, 'Use that an' it'll keep ye warm. Ye'll no' need a jaiket.'

A lot of mining stories seem to travel underground from pit to pit and surface almost simultaneously in different places, like ancient myth, with only the names and unimportant details changed. In Whitburn I heard two stories I already knew from Ayrshire. In Ayrshire it was two canaries vanished from a cage, in Whitburn it was two rats missing from a piece-tin – that must have 'ett each ither'. In Ayrshire it was a miner's bottle of lemonade that went missing three days running. In Whitburn it was a bottle of Barr's Irn Bru that was stolen two days in a row. In both places, the aggrieved miner, a man of formidable physique, sat at the piece-break, scanning faces and waiting patiently 'for the first bastard that rifts'. The mutual borrowing of stories is understandable. Just as myths tell us more about the myth-makers than anything else, so the overlapping of mining stories is a means by which miners identify with one another in the specialness of what they do, an anecdotal freemasonry. That tradition has never quite eroded.

It's not surprising, then, that miners retain a deep emotional attachment to the fact that they are miners. When you take on the job, you are issued with the legend. But it is a complicated affection. Just as any deep love, because of the amount of yourself you have invested in it, tremors sometimes close to hate at the prospect of betrayal or the thought of the risk you are running, so miners can hate the pit like a woman they are hopelessly involved with and are not sure they can trust.

'A pit's a great thing as long as ye're no' doon it,' one of the men in Whitburn told me. He was right, of course. It is *having been* down it that is great. Listening innumerable times to miners and ex-miners talk of working in the pit, I have often caught an echo of the way people talk about another area of experience – the war. This isn't to suggest that coalmining is remotely equivalent to fighting in a war, merely that it offers, to a much lesser degree, an intensification of the sense of ordinary life. That is perhaps why the Monday shift has always been the hardest shift to ensure is fully staffed. Who wants to go back from a furlough? That is perhaps why miners have long been manic lovers of the countryside and wildlife. That is perhaps why mining families have a long tradition of trying to keep their sons out of the pits. That is perhaps why an Ayrshire miner, asked by the pit-manager why he was only turning out for three shifts a week these days, replied, 'Because Ah canny leeve oan two.'

The temptation to get out of the pits is something that confronts a lot of working miners every other day. Add to that a year of hardship on strike, the continuing threat of redundancy and the offer of more money than he has ever had in his hand before and it is a wonder that so many miners have had to be forced to accept redundancy money. The reluctance to take the money was still strong in that committee-room even though the deed was already done. Bob Ronald said, 'If they gave me ma job on Monday, Ah'd pay them back every penny of their money. Ah miss the work, Ah miss the men, Ah miss the laughin'. Ah run the wife to her work in the mornin'. Ah come back an' clean oot the fire. An' that's me for the day.' The money was compensation for defeat and therefore remains not a contradiction of it but a confirmation of it.

Yet they refused to be glib about ascribing reasons for that defeat. 'It's all very well with hindsight,' one of them said. But once something is over, what else do you have but hindsight? The question of Arthur Scargill's leadership of the year-long strike was much discussed. While every man in the room thought he had made mistakes (the refusal to condemn picket violence, for example) only one of them attacked him, saying his father had brought him up to undermine the structure of our society. The others pointed out that Arthur Scargill didn't call the strike alone nor sustain it alone. One saw him as being spectacularly unlucky: 'If Arthur Scargill went to Lourdes wi' a humph on his back, he'd come back wi' two.'

The acceptance had a kind of stoicism to it. But I regretted it. I sat among people who had as much right to anger at the moment as any group of us I could think of and there was no serious anger, just bafflement that dulled the eyes and the stillness of despair. I came away respecting them – what else could you do? – but mourning what was lost.

I remember hearing the voice of Archie Wilson, an ex-miner in his 80s, a man who had spent all his working life in the Lady Victoria mine. He wasn't speaking to me. He was speaking to Elizabeth Partyka, producer of a radio programme called *The Image o' God* (a title taken from Joe Corrie's poem), for which I wrote the commentary. I listened to him a lot as I replayed the tape, looking for words that would help to contextualise the story of mining. Archie Wilson had the earned articulacy of experience. He didn't say too much but what he said he meant. He used one phrase to describe himself – 'proud but bitter'.

If you want a phrase to encapsulate the stance miners have traditionally adopted towards their own experience, those words seem to me to serve. In the village of Forth, I was casually told, 'Proud people in the Forth.'

'Proud but bitter.' The pride is from the ability to endure hard conditions that cannot be avoided and survive them. The bitterness is from having had to endure hard conditions that were a human invention, a wilful imposition on their lives. Necessary suffering is everybody's birthright. Unnecessary suffering, suffering that is socially engineered for profit, is an obscenity for which our society has always had too much tolerance. The history of mining has been to some extent the people's voices raised against that obscenity.

The memory of Archie Wilson's voice clarifies for me what I suspect I was witnessing in that committee-room in Whitburn. There was little anger because anger can only come from a sense of your own identity. In order to be outraged, you must know who you are. There must first be pride in selfhood before there can be bitterness at society's abuse of that selfhood. The mining community had for generations earned that pride. They had maintained it throughout the strike. But, now that the strike was over, they realised that they had found no reflection of it in the society around them. They were looking in a broken mirror and could see no coherent image of themselves. They were left to wonder who they really were.

The Labour movement, that should have been their mirror-image, had fragmented. Where was the just reflection of their pride? Where was the just reflection of their anger?

There was no anger. That was strange. When the most reactionary government this century, which dissociates its economic policies from the human wreckage they cause, grinds to unjust defeat a group of people among the most impressive to be found anywhere in contemporary society, anger is not an indulgence. It is a necessity. It is what is left of the kind of vision socialism once had before it became paralysed by expediency, senile with theory and myopic with self-absorption. Faced with a government that showed contempt for every aspiration beyond the material, which offered us a nation where each family would function like a private company, the Labour opposition could do no better than indulge in an I-told-you-so discussion of the tactics of the strike.

Past defeats had at least yielded a cauterising anger, a purifying reassertion of basic purposes. This one had yielded mainly a criticism of the miners' leadership. Arthur Scargill was due plenty of criticism but none of it should obscure the failure, once the strike was happening, of the Labour Party and the TUC to support it effectively. What the strike told us about Arthur Scargill was less important than what it told us about the serious ill-health of the Labour movement. To confound these issues was like accusing the technician who takes the X-ray of causing the cancer.

The men and women (very notably the women) of the mining communities, who took socialism back on to the streets during the miners' strike, evoked no accurate or supportive reflection of their stand in political terms. The splinters of the Labour movement were reflecting nothing but themselves. The mainstream of the Labour Party appeared to have decided that expediency is principle and seemed not to want the miners to damage its electoral image. On the other hand, Arthur Scargill's leadership was an intellectual radicalism superimposed on circumstances, not elicited from them. In purely intellectual terms, that radicalism is understandable, even seductive. But without subjecting itself rigorously to a realistic understanding of the historical and popular context it is obliged to inhabit, it becomes like a brain under the influence of LSD. It begins to hallucinate. It starts asking bodies to fly.

The intellectual premise of the strike was acceptable. But the burden it imposed upon the miners was impossible. Divided even among themselves, they were denied significant support from the TUC or the mainstream of the socialist movement. Since 1926, the Nottinghamshire coalfield has been a fissure in the miners' solidarity. In the 1984–85 strike, that division provided a lot of socialists with an excuse for not standing determinedly on either side of it. Most of us stood by and watched a diminishing and beleaguered section of the population try to lift the entire country out of apathy into action. It was like asking one person to move a mountain. Cheering didn't help.

The miners' strike crystallised a recurrent socialist dilemma. Like a Protestant faith, socialism is dependent upon the integrity of its adherents. That integrity is a difficult thing to legislate for. It goes too hard or too soft very easily. There is a problem in maintaining an honest tension between attempts to realise the vision and the circumstances that obstruct that realisation. That tension tends to oscillate between uninhabitable puritanism and lip-service careerism. Between the prophet, contemptuous of visions more ordinary than his own, and the careerist, contemptuous of everything but the techniques of power, live most of us. In socialism it is that majority that matters.

Yet, certainly in Scotland, the Labour Party seems to be out of touch with many members of that majority. On the streets it can feel as if the establishment of the Labour Party and the extremists operating on its edges have both decided that they know best. What the first group know best is what has to be done to gain power, what boats must not be rocked, what dangerous impressions must not be given. Their pragmatism seems an inadequate representation of what people in Scotland want. What the second group know best is what we all need, what dramatic measures must be taken if we are to be saved. Their theories frequently fall on the ears of the people they purport to be saving as if they were in Sanskrit. The rest is baffled silence.

Somehow, that silence has to be articulated for socialism to rediscover a consensus. I think it was the absence of any such consensus that let Polkemmet die and left the men in that committee-room in Whitburn puzzledly bereft, like people staring into a mirror that offered no reflection.

In the summer of 1991, I attended the Miners' Gala Day in Edinburgh. It wasn't a big event. There were still some banners and some bands but you could understand why they decided to make it an occasion involving other unions besides the miners'. That way, it might feel less like an ill-attended funeral.

In the march from Waterloo Place to the Meadows, I walked beside Yvonne McEwen and May Russell, who live in Whitburn. Their latest report on the village was bleak. They told of aimlessness and inertia, of once-proud ex-miners hunkered at a corner, passing the wine-bottle and bumming cigarettes.

I thought of other places besides Polkemmet – places in Yorkshire and in Kent and in the Welsh coalfields – where communities had been ravaged and hard-earned values subverted. I thought of other industries – like shipbuilding and steel – where the same thing had happened. It occurred to me that this had been achieved not by taking the votes of people and trying to turn them into the practical realisation of their wishes but by taking their votes as a licence to deny those wishes, not by eliciting from human behaviour the circumstances that would most effectively fulfil it but by wilfully creating circumstances that would programme that behaviour and predetermine it, make us predators one upon another.

It will be a long way back from the Meadows that day. But I believe the journey will be made. It will have to start back among the people who began it in the first place by the humanity of their concern for one another. The industries are going but I think their legacy will remain. The just pride in the decency they maintained among hard conditions enabled those people to complain with dignity against social injustice.

215

The dignity of just complaint must never be lost. Without it, we accept what we shouldn't accept. Social injustices are endured as if they were the will of God. We lose our sense of ourselves and become about as self-determining as straws in the wind.

Polkemmet is dead. Long live its spirit.

A Shield Against the Gorgon

In any street an epic, any room
Strange stories never told, testaments dumb.
The richness overwhelms. A chance remark
Can touch new land, unload another ark.
Transactions of small change will sometimes yield
Coins of a minting you have never held.

Break any casual stone and find strange veins.
The colours blind. The anecdotes will range
Through wild geographies of spirit, form
Plain men with unknown flowers in their arms.
In each face new horizons, any day
An archaeology more rich than Troy.

I REMEMBER AS A BOY BEING ALONE IN THE LIVING-ROOM of our council house in Kilmarnock. I would be maybe 11 years old. I was lying in front of the coal fire with my head resting on an armchair. It was, I think, late on a winter afternoon. The window had gone black and I hadn't put the light on, enjoying the small cave of brightness and heat the fire had hewn from the dark. Perhaps I was a far traveller resting by his camp-fire. Perhaps I was a knight keeping vigil for the dawn when wondrous deeds would be done. For I could be many people at that time, as I still can.

Maybe controlled fantasy is everybody's natural habitat and it's just that some of us lose the vulnerability to admit it, even to ourselves. We hardly go shopping without blessing the bread with half-formed thoughts of what else we might be doing, without some vague sense of who might be eating it with us. Ghosts of the past, ghosts of the future haunt our daily lives.

I remember that ghost of me at my hearth of small, butterfly dreams but I don't know how I came to be alone at that time in that place. In our house, with six not unnoticeable presences, it wasn't an easy trick to be alone, even without counting the cavalcade of aunties and uncles and cousins and friends who seemed to be constantly passing through. I wonder if I had come home from school to find the house empty. But that seems improbable. My mother was a ferocious carer who had an almost mystical capacity to conjure solid

217

worries out of air that to the rest of us looked untroubled and clear. Maybe somebody else was supposed to be with me and had gone out briefly.

I don't know. I am simply aware of myself there. The moment sits separate and vivid in my memory, without explanation, like a rootless flower. Whoever I was being, traveller or knight, I must have been tired. For I fell asleep.

The awakening was strange. I think I must have been aware of the noise of people entering the house, one of those slow fuses of sound that sputteringly traverses the unconscious until it ignites into waking. My consciousness and the room came into the light together. My eyes were bruised with brightness. What I saw seems in restrospect to have had the shiningness of newly minted coins, all stamped unmistakably as genuine, pure metal, the undepreciable currency of my life.

What I saw in fact was pretty banal. My father had his hand on the light-switch he had just pressed. My mother was beside him. They were both laughing at what must have been my startled eyes and my wonderment at being where I was. Around them was a room made instantly out of the dark. It was a very ordinary room. But it was wonderful. How strange the biscuit barrel was where my mother kept the rent-money. How unimaginable was the image of Robert Burns with the mouse, painted on glass by my uncle. How incorrigibly itself the battered sideboard became. The room was full of amazing objects. They might as well have come from Pompeii.

And at the centre of them were two marvellously familiar strangers. I saw them not just as my mother and father. I knew suddenly how dark my father was, how physical his presence. His laughter filled the room, coming from a place that was his alone. My mother looked strangely young, coming in fresh-faced from the cold and darkness, her irises swallowing her pupils as she laughed in the shocking brightness. I felt an inordinate love for them. I experienced the transformation of the ordinary into something powerfully mysterious.

The compulsion to write is fed from many tubers, most of them blessedly untraceable. For if we could find the roots and subject them to rational analysis, who is to say we could make them grow again? Creativity occurs in the heart as well as the head. It is passionate intelligence. It demands for its appreciation the mind, of course, but that mind must come dressed in body and suffused with feeling. Mere intellect comes to fiction like a day-tripper, capable of appreciating the scenery but not of emotionally sharing the life that fills it. When emotion and intelligence fuse in appreciation, they recreate the work in a way that is almost as mysterious as the source of the work itself.

But, if it is impossible to trace any work effectively to all its origins, I'm convinced that that moment in the living-room at St Maurs Crescent is one of the experiential paradigms from which *Docherty* (and perhaps everything I've written) grew. It was a moment which has had many relatives in my experience. When I consider them, I realise that they have several features in common. In those shared features can be glimpsed the genealogy of the compulsion from which *Docherty* was born.

One of them is a belief in the grandeur of the everyday, the conviction that for experience to be significant it needn't be masked in exoticism or buskined with social status. The ordinary is just the unique in hiding. As it says in *Docherty*, 'messiahs are born in stables'. That being so, as a boy I kept finding Bethlehem round every corner. So many things amazed me.

There were the stories surrounding me, for a start. *Docherty*, I should think, began its gestation in the mouths of the people all around me. Our house was an incredible talking-shop. As the youngest of four, I seem to have grown up with an intense conversation going on endlessly about me as my natural habitat. By one of those casually important accidents of childhood, the two youngest of us had to sleep in a fold-down bed in the living-room. Lack of space has its advantages. This meant that from a fairly early age, I could be involved, however marginally, in these debates, often going to sleep with the sound of disputation as a lullaby.

As time passed, I didn't want to sleep at all until the issues had been resolved, if only by exhaustion. I remember when I was 15 and attending Kilmarnock Academy, there was an earnest man in his late 20s who had decided that my life would be enriched if I joined the YMCA. He pursued my conversion quite assiduously. One night he came to the door about 11 o'clock and expressed some shock that what he called 'a three-language student' wasn't in bed yet. The slight prissiness of his attitude and my dismay at it were expressive of the cultural distance between us. He was a social missionary who knew what was good for me. I was a native who believed that my life had more going for it than the missionary's. Who wanted to go to sleep when new ideas and unimagined facts were going off all around in the room like fireworks? Leaving him, I went back to the fray. I didn't join the YMCA.

To this continuing seminar on life and the strange nature of it came many visiting speakers. Our house often felt to me like a throughway for talk. Relatives and friends were always dropping in. They brought news of local doings, bizarre attitudes, memorable remarks made under pressure, anecdotes of wild behaviour. Most of it was delivered and received with a calmness that astonished me. I vaguely sensed early on the richness they were casually living among, rather as if a traveller should come upon the Incas using pure gold as kitchen utensils. The substance that would be *Docherty* was beginning to glint for me in fragments of talk and caught glimpses of living.

But writing is not experience. It is what you make of your experience. The processes involved in the making are many. They include observation and perceptiveness and the skill of honesty towards both feeling and thought and the developed ability to comprehend your experience fresh for yourself, the earned right to recreate it justly into what it means to you. The unifying factor in all these processes is, of course, words – their seductiveness, their treachery, their capacity for freezing the flux.

Cognate to my awareness of the rich and largely uncommemorated life around me was a fascination with language. Given my background, I was lucky to be in a house where books were part of the practical furniture, not there as ornaments but to be read and talked about. My mother was the source of the activity. My sister and my two brothers had established reading as a family tradition by the time I was old enough to join in. Only my father, someone – it has always seemed to me – educated spectacularly below his abilities, was never to be comfortable with books. His presence on the edges of our immersion in reading became, I think, in some way formative for me. I wanted him somehow to be included in the words.

The scene in the film *Viva Zapata!* where Marlon Brando hesitantly and vulnerably acknowledges that he can't read and asks his bride to teach him has always had a special and moving resonance for me – like seeing a variant of your personal life made public and enlarged into the fictive. For, soon after they were married, my mother spent a long time improving my father's literacy. My awareness of the partially stifled intelligence in him convinced me that users of words should use them in the service not just of those who have them but of those who don't. Writing, I decided, you should be including not just those who will listen but those who can't. Otherwise, literature becomes the complacent activity of a cultural clique – this cliqueyness is perhaps inevitable to some extent but it should never be self-satisfied. It should find forms that give expression to the absent. This principle of mine was of particular relevance to the writing of *Docherty*, which is in part an attempt to articulate in the context of a book on behalf of those who may be inarticulate in a literary way. Hence, the central paradox of the book: it is written for people most of whom will never read it.

Love of reading led naturally, it seemed at the time, to efforts at writing. If books were not the most sought-after domestic adjunct in our housing scheme (depraved orgies of poetry-reading behind closed curtains), the desire actually to write the poetry could have been construed as proof of mental aberration. But this was my next move, one I effected without being ostracised by my peers because, perhaps, I was also very good at football. Having successfully undergone my masculine rites of passage in the West of Scotland, I could indulge in a little limp-wristed scribbling.

Here again the family situation helped. No one – least of all my father (despite being uninterested in books) – ever questioned the validity of the time I spent arranging words on pieces of paper. I took such tolerance for granted. It was only much later I realised how different it might have been for a working-class boy with ambitions to write. A woman writer-friend told me some years ago of a man she knew who came from a background similar to my own. He was bedevilled by a longing to write plays, much to the embarrassment of his relatives. On one occasion an older brother beat him up severely in an attempt to bring him to his senses and get him to stop inflicting shame upon the family. Such an attitude had been unimaginable to me in my boyhood. If I had met opposition, though, I think I would have withstood it, for, besides reading, there was another strong family tradition, this time from my father's side: 'You never shite on anybody else and nobody shites on you.'

I first wrote what I called a poem when I was 14. It was a Sunday, I remember, one of those Scottish ones that feel as if you've wandered into the antechamber to a featureless eternity. All external life is monochrome and any colour will have to be self-mixed in the head. I wrote a poem. It came with amazing ease. I stared at it in wonder. Can such things be?

Like a person who has found a piece of some extra-terrestrial substance in the living-room (which is where I was writing), I had to check it out against someone. I took it to my brother Neilly, eight years older and – the choice wasn't accidental – enormously charitable to my slightly feverish imaginings. He read it over very carefully. I waited to find out what it was that I had done. He looked up slowly. 'You,' he said, shaking his head, 'didn't write that?' I was tremendously elated. My subsequent realisation that his response could be taken two ways (the second being 'God, I hope you didn't write that') didn't trouble me for long, because I knew which way he had meant it. I sometimes think all my books should carry the epigraph: 'Neilly's to blame'. It was all the encouragement I needed.

My uncertain vision of the lives around me and my hesitant attempts to express myself in writing were on course to converge at some point. This is, I would imagine, the experience of most people who are trying to write.

What you want to express and the verbal skills you are seeking with which to express it will wander in mutually exclusive terrain for a long time and it is only when they meet at some unexpected border that you will witness them mysteriously merge into the one entity and you will discover that the voice you are speaking with is yours and no one else's.

That is certainly how it was with me. My early efforts at writing had scant connection with the pressing reality of the experience about me. That first poem demonstrates this. I can still remember it word for word but, feeling charitable, I shall restrict myself to paraphrase and minimal quotation. It's a poem ostensibly written by a man who is simultaneously committing suicide with a knife, presumably making sure that the blood doesn't obliterate his words. He has, it seems, killed his friend and his guilt ('I have sinned 'gainst God and man') makes him rather hard on himself. I suspect the shadow of a woman somewhere in the poem, too. The poem ends on the knife-thrust: 'I drive the blade my body through and all is calm within me.'

The archaisms and the inversions and the alien subject-matter are what strike me in retrospect. The borrowed forms echo the borrowed content. Suggested adultery, murder and suicide weren't exactly the staple diet of a 14-year-old in Kilmarnock in the '50s. But they were testing things to write about. In a way, the initial separation from myself of what I was writing about was essential. If you wish to engage as effectively as you can in a contest, you don't just walk into it. You train. You develop yourself in imitation conflict with yourself before you take the real risks. And writing *is* a conflict, an endless lovers' quarrel with the word. Some readers may miss this because what they are reading will be the terms of the truce.

This dichotomy between what I was actually writing and what I wanted to write persisted for a long time. There were lapses, of course, times when – instead of wandering like a tourist into some established writer's sanctum and listening to my mimic echo – I would stumble unexpectedly into my own and find myself, awestruck, writing not towards what other people had written but directly out of where my compulsion lay.

But mainly I spent my time being an ancient Greek or Shakespeare or William Saroyan or Ernest Hemingway (despite the dearth of big-game hunting in Ayrshire). I continued trying to write poetry and short stories. I don't know how long my experience and my writing might have continued living apart and flirting with each other but circumstances arranged a shotgun wedding between them. When I was 18 and in my first month at university, my father died of lung cancer. The impact of that terrible event was indescribable and I was compelled to try to describe it. My love of words had come upon a personal reality it must try to confront.

But the effect on my attempts to write was hardly immediate. Creativity works by indirections. At university I read countless writers and no doubt ventriloquised many of their voices. But at the same time I kept returning to struggling with my own necessity, which was to make an understanding of my father's death.

I worked on it over several years, winning found fragments of meaning from the pain. The result was to be a long poem called *Initiation*, not published until 15 years after the event which it described. Four years before that, *Remedy is None* – a novel to which the experience is also central – had been published.

The poetry and the novel and the second novel, *A Gift from Nessus*, had – besides simply being written for themselves – brought me nearer to an understanding of my boyhood experience and heightened the confidence I needed to attempt the finding of a form to express it. Other things had helped to prepare me as well.

One was my reaction to being the first of any branch of my family to go to university. After the initial awe, I became progressively unimpressed. Later, I would give to Laidlaw, in the book that carried his name, some of my feelings: 'I took acres of fertile ignorance to university. And they proceeded to pour preconceptions all over it like 40 tons of cement.' With some very honourable exceptions, I couldn't accept the mechanistic shallowness of much that was on offer.

I remember one moment that haunts me still. Between the second year and the third year, we had to submit an essay to the English Language Department on some aspect of Anglo-Saxon. On my first day in Junior Honours, I nervously entered the lecture-room, wondering what was ahead of me. It didn't take long to find out. A lecturer I had never seen came in and dumped his leather case beside the lectern. When he opened his mouth, he was, it transpired, a very bluff Yorkshireman.

'Mucklevaynee,' he said. 'Where is 'e?' For a country boy in academe, still occasionally wondering when he would be found out, it was a tense moment. I raised a palsied hand. 'Stand oop,' he said. I unravelled myself slowly among 30 or so students. The lecturer stared at me as if he was viewing his first Martian. 'You, lad,' he said. 'Use words ah can oonderstand. Siddown.'

I sat down into a disillusionment that had two more years to grow. Part of my discontent was to crystallise into an anger at the absence of the life I came from in what was called literature.

Also, when I was in my early 20s, I had written a long blank-verse play about working-class life – a kind of *Hamlet* in jeans. This was a bizarre enterprise called *Actions in Generic Tense,* a title not calculated perhaps to have them queueing round the block. But that misguided endeavour was very important to me. It made me try to express the resonance and importance of the lives around me in words that made no concessions to their assumed lowliness. That, too, brought *Docherty* nearer.

The third novel I started to write was called *Tribute to the Minotaur*. I had written over 20,000 words when I stopped, never to return to it. The reason wasn't so much a revulsion away from that book as an overwhelming compulsion towards another.

I wanted to write a book that would create a kind of literary genealogy for the people I came from, the people whose memorials were parish registers. Since their history was largely silence, I would be constructing a communal fabric of myth. That didn't bother me since I had long looked on history itself as being a form of decadent mythology. I wanted the sort of feeling I had experienced in the living-room at St Maurs Crescent, an almost mystical conviction, to be given flesh.

I began to write *Docherty*.

When Perseus wanted to confront the Gorgon, he had a problem. He knew that if he looked on her directly, he would be turned to stone. But, borrowing a burnished shield from Athene, he was able to approach Medusa through her reflection, survive her lethal stare and claim her head. He came off whole. The Gorgon can be seen as the incomprehensible nature of experience. You cannot capture experience raw. Try that and your endeavour becomes lifeless. Experience is too multiform. You can only reflect it, in more or less coherent fragments. You need a shield between you and the annihilating variousness of experience. The shield is art.

Every writer of originality makes his or her own shield. Some shields are more elaborately original than others. And you will find people who regard themselves as connoisseurs of shields making whole careers out of praising the designs along the edges, the unimaginable patterns chased out on the metal. I think they miss the point. These are dilettantes of experience who think that such shields were made just to be hung on walls and reflect nothing but themselves.

To realise the serious but not solemn purpose of creativity, you only have to consider its origins. When the people huddled in the Lascaux caves made their pictures on the rock, it may have been a kind of play but they knew it was a game with mortal consequences. They were trying to magic the animals they depicted into meat to sustain them. Catch the image, catch the creature. Understand the beast or die.

Our need to understand the beast in its ultimate form – the nature of experience – continues. 'We have art,' Nietzsche says, 'in order not to die of the truth.' While I can see what he means, I think I would prefer to say that we have art in order to die of the truth. Mortality is incurable. The most that we can ask of our lives is that when we die, it is not – as it was for Joseph K – 'like a dog' but that the awareness with which we meet death will transform its emptiness into a meaning of our own, that it will not negate our living merely but be obliged to fulfil our living in some way against its will, by the cunning and the art of our approach. To comprehend our life justly is to overcome our death because we will make its meaninglessness just the backdrop to our meaning. We will write a meaning on the void.

That is why for me the shield of artistic technique is so important. It is one of the means by which we determine the justness with which we approach our dying, the validity of the terms by which we live. That is why I think that many of the criteria currently in vogue for judging the efficacy of the shield are frivolous and irrelevant. Mere novelty is often confused with originality. The more wilful and arbitrarily different the shape and pattern of the shield, the more likely it is to offer a distorted reflection. And the reflection is all. The criteria that matter most will be the accuracy, the justice, the intensity and the comprehensiveness (how far the pieces justly imply the whole) of the reflection of experience that is given.

Each new book is to some extent a newly structured shield. If the experience it is hoped to reflect is working-class experience, Perseus has another problem. He had better make the shield himself. There is no sustained tradition of such craftsmanship.

In the writing of *Docherty*, I was aware of this loneliness. I had precursors, of course, from Langland's 'field full of folk' to Robert Tressell and the work of Zola and Lawrence and Sillitoe. But, though they helped, they didn't answer my purposes. One reason for this is, I think, that people writing about working-class experience have tended to approach from a pre-determined angle, perhaps because they have never known it as a given reality that surrounds them from birth (and therefore their reason for coming to it in the first place has an ideological bias) or because, having been born there and left it, they are rationalising the nature of their departure.

Zola, for example, writes in his work-notes:

> The bourgeoisie betrays its revolutionary past in order to safeguard its capitalistic privilege and remain a governing class. Having conquered power, it does not want to pass it on to the people. . . . I must express the important, decisive idea, that the bourgeoisie has played its part, that it has gone over to the reaction to preserve its power and riches, and that all hope for the forces of tomorrow lies with the people.

I have no quarrel with this as a political analysis of Zola's time as I understand that time to have been, but it seems to me a patricianly simplistic way to view a vast and complex area of human experience. It is yet another example of how those who see themselves as part of a revolutionary agenda have always been eager to patronise working-class people out of their present into a future they did not ask for, rather like the bestowing of a knighthood by a king in exile, the status to become effective come the millennium. Given that tourism may be noble, this is noble tourism. But I think I understand and believe in the nature of working-class experience too much to endorse this attitude.

D. H. Lawrence, on the other hand, was part of this experience and escaped. His version of the experience is largely a justification of his getting away from it. His literary career can be seen as offering some parallels with David Livingstone's life as a missionary. I find the irony of Livingstone heading for darkest Africa, while apparently not noticing the squalor of the darkest Blantyre that he was leaving behind, is echoed in the way D. H. Lawrence abandons the significance of his earlier life to explore the wilder and most abstract shores of visionary theory.

Sons and Lovers is for me mainly a libel on the nature of working-class experience. It is the vision of a man in flight and that is inevitably a distorting perspective, since it will reflect the significance of going rather than the significance of staying. It shows positive moments in that way of life, it is true, for Lawrence was a writer who tried to practise a kind of desperate honesty, but I believe it offers a vision so essentially negative that it could only seem just to those who have never known that way of life or are glad not to know it any longer. Being, like so much that has been written about working-class life, a kind of gospel according to Judas, it is a testament of some value but of a limited value in trying to obtain a just sense of the nature of working-class experience, its richness and its dynamism.

In trying to arrive at the vision of working-class experience I was hoping to reflect, therefore, I had to begin by knowing what I couldn't use, by discarding what would distort the image I felt to be true. It would not be the familiar story of the boy of abilities and sensitivity winning his way out of an underclass into a more enriching form of life, for this is to presuppose the comparative shallowness of the life he is leaving – an assumption with which, having experienced the old life left and the new life found, I have never been able to agree. There is a simple reason for the consistency with which this erroneous assumption has been maintained: it is that to judge working-class culture, once you have left it, by the standards of the established literary culture you have entered is to judge it by terms which were created to deny it.

You have no option but to impoverish your own past. The rules are made to work that way.

For one of the keys to working-class life is precisely that it lives along the edge where thought and feeling keep fusing in experience and are not formally 'culturised' into separate entities. Both live in dynamic interrelation, as I believe they should. In my sense of it, working-class life is rich in an intelligence that re-earns itself constantly on the pulses of life and doesn't abstract itself into mere intellectuality, which is then able to pursue ideas for their own sake, regardless of how they may fail to relate to the realities of experience. Therefore, I believe that to judge the passion of working-class life by the clinical procedures of middle-class culture is like assembling the data of an autopsy and calling it a life-story.

It was for that reason that I was determined that *Docherty* wouldn't be an escape story with the escapee patronisingly looking back on the lives of those who were still inmates. The vision would be from within, frontal not tangential. In this connection, Conn's instinctive refusal to seek an alternative life to the one he has is central to the book.

Also, the book would not be conceived through the lens of an ideology, would not be angled and selected to support a specific political stance. I believe this would have been wrong on two counts. Firstly, I think that good writing is a report from some kind of front line of experience. You find out what is happening, you don't pre-decide it. If you want to understand the nature of experience, you had better let it tell you. To go simply looking for the data that will support your thesis is the ultimate insult to experience and she won't forgive you. Your complacent perceptions will be cuckolded by reality. Secondly, working-class experience is especially recalcitrant to the intellectualism of an ideology, as many frustrated revolutionaries in their visionary cabals have found to their despair. Its reality keeps proliferating spontaneously, overgrowing the conceptual borders the theorists would set for it. Lenin understood this problem and, being, like all good revolutionaries, capable of theorising to the point of denying his own humanity, he came to the conclusion that theory should subordinate spontaneity. But it can't. Theory may stifle spontaneity for a long time but it cannot control it permanently. If it could, humanity would be over.

So, I knew what I wasn't after. That's important. It means you can discard the reflective devices that seem to offer distortions. But what *was* I trying to reflect accurately about the nature of working-class experience? A poem I had written some years before, called *Eugenesis*, gave me one of the clues.

> On the first day They eradicated war.
> Nations were neutralised. In desert places
> The cumbered void rusted with defused bombs,
> The gutted chambers. In random heaps
> The rockets lay, like molar monuments
> To brontosauri sentenced to extinction.
>
> On the second day They fed the starving.
> The capsules gave immunity from hunger.
> Faces filled. The smiles were uniform.
> The computers had found a formula for plenty.
>
> The third day ended work. With summer
> Processed to a permanence, the sun-
> Machine in operation, every day
> Would be as long as They desired it.
> Season-chambers were erected. The nostalgic
> Could take a holiday to autumn if they wished.
> The computers thought of everything.
>
> On the fourth day death was dead.
> Synthetic hearts, machine-tooled brains,
> Eyes and limbs were all expendable.
> Immortality came wrapped in polythene.
> Every face was God's you saw upon the street.
>
> By the fifth day crime was cured.
> Mind-mechanics, they located every hatred,
> Extracted it, and amputated angers.
> Each idea was sterilised before its issue.
> The computers fixed a safety-mark for thinking.

The sixth day saw heaven's inauguration.
Benignity pills were issued. Kindness meetings
Were held on every corner. They declared
Love as the prerogative of all.
That day became the longest there had been.
But as long as there was light the people smiled.

On the seventh day, while They were resting,
A small man with red hair had disappeared.
A museum missed a tent. Neither was found.
He left an immortal wife, the changeless years
Of endless happiness, and a strange note
In ancient script, just four historic letters.
The Autotongue translated: 'Irrational Anger'.
The Medic Machine advised: 'Rejection Symptoms.
Source Unknown. Primordial and Contagious'.

It was too late. The word ran like a rash
On walls and daubed on doorways. Cities emptied.
In panic They neglected Their machines.
The sunset was unauthorised. Its beauty
Triggered the light-oriented metal cocks
That crew until their mechanisms burst.
Fires twinkled in the new night, shaping mattocks.
On the dark hills an unheavenly sound was heard.
The Historometer intoned into the silence:
'Ancient Barbaric Custom Known as Laughter'.
Seizing up, the computers began to cry.

The small man with red hair would help me construct my shield.

In the process of constructing the shield that is your book you will catch
reflected fragments of the creature you are after. Such moments can be
encouraging. They convince you that the beast you seek is out there all right.
What its exact configuration will be you still don't know but you are already
catching pieces of it. For the writing of a book is the process of discovering
what it is about. The thing you are trying to ambush is constantly ambushing
you. You keep glimpsing it among the foliage and its observed nature keeps
surprising you. You realise that in getting so close to it you must have been
doing something right and you try to remember what it was. In this way, you
gradually learn the habits of the beast you want to trap, the manner of
approach that won't disturb it, the lures it will respond to. Such devices may
be very simple, even banal, but, handled with skill and tension, they may
bring you an expression of life not quite seen before. (This in no way means,
of course, that commentators will appreciate its rarity, for critics tend to be
like the tourists at the end of *The Old Man and the Sea*: seeing only

the bones, they find it hard to tell a shark from a marlin. Show most critics a unicorn and they will see a deformed horse. They're also quite good at thinking deformed horses are unicorns.)

Working on *Docherty*, I learned and forgot and relearned the habits of my quarry, what presumptions frightened it off, what methods encouraged it to come nearer. That methodology is now a thing of the past: it belongs to the book that made it. For a while, I lived with it almost daily. But when it has fulfilled itself, it is over and you must move on.

A new book is a new risk or it is nothing. As Rilke says, you begin again. Any past achievement is mainly valuable in providing the terms of the bet you can hazard on the future. You first renew your wonder. Then you relearn the techniques to express it.

A writer's greatest gift is a continuing capacity to try to achieve more. After completing the vastness of *Moby Dick*, Herman Melville could write to Nathaniel Hawthorne: 'As long as we have more to do, we have done nothing. So, now, let us add *Moby Dick* to our blessing, and step from that. Leviathan is not the biggest fish; – I have heard of Krakens.'

But, if I can't recreate the endless tensions and shifts of perception and the number of occasions I was knocked off my horse to discover that Damascus had never been my destination in the first place, I can remember some small awarenesses of the time that helped me towards the making of *Docherty*. They're just small pieces of scoria that hardly suggest the reality of the eruption, but maybe they're better than nothing.

I knew I was after a book that would make no concessions on the truth I believed I saw to anybody, not to the people I was writing about, not to the people most likely to read it, not to the intellectual 'supporters' of the people I was writing about – not to anybody. This made for an appropriate loneliness, which is for me where creativity begins.

It meant that, while I was writing partly on behalf of people many of whom didn't read much, the prose would in no way make obeisance to that fact. It would express my vision to the limits of my own articulacy, not pretend to imitate theirs. The most basic premise on which I was writing was that their lives were full of an immanent significance which, not being made explicit in literary form, was often regarded as not existing at all. The only way to demonstrate its existence was to express it as fully as I could.

This in turn meant the risk of alienating some readers by expressing the unspoken experience of characters to a level beyond their own achieved articulacy. But such a risk was central to the endeavour. Without it, there would be no book. Writing for me involves isolating the area where you must take your own risks, not the risks already taken by others. To me this risk was inescapable. Besides, I did have precedents. It was just that it had not been deemed appropriate to apply them to working-class life. What prince of Denmark or Roman general or Scottish king ever spoke like Shakespeare?

Elizabethan blank verse brings poetry often from the mouths of ruffians – high-class ruffians, maybe, but ruffians. What kind of snobbery would allow a convention of heightened articulacy to them but not to a narrative of working-class experience? And where did that rough seaman, Ishmael, get all his allusions if not from Melville?

This, of course, was an offence not just to those whose effete snobbery would disenfranchise the ferocious energy of working-class experience from entry into the salons of culture. It was an offence also to those self-appointed guardians of the significance of working-class experience, those weekend intellectuals who – like ideological social workers – patronise a reality dynamic beyond their own capacity for living by dressing it up in second-hand ideas. I wanted to create working-class people who were so fiercely themselves, whose collateral was not in houses or career or erudition or in the future but was what they walked about in, who were so strongly present that they could walk into any room in any time in any place and forbid condescension.

As I wrote, I knew that *Docherty* would be a seriously subversive book (whether anyone happened to notice the fact or not). I sensed the hard place it was trying to go towards. Today, I'm not sure many have followed it there. A Paris graffito once said, 'When a finger points at the moon, the fool looks at the finger.' It's maybe just your average authorial paranoia, but I suspect a fair amount of critical finger-watching in relation to my books (though not from lay readers).

Docherty can be said to be the story of a working-class mining family in the West of Scotland in the first quarter of the 20th century. That's what it is, all right. But that's not what it's about. That's what the shield is made of but what it was built to reflect is something much bigger. Whether it successfully does so or not is another matter.

For a start, it has for long seemed to me that the essentials of working-class experience form a kind of esperanto. By this I mean that working-class people in any given country are liable to have more in common with the working classes of another country than with, say, the middle classes of their own place. I remember reading Steinbeck's *The Grapes of Wrath* as a teenager and being amazed, in my naïvety, at how Scottish the Okies were (even down to some of the terms they used, like 'redd' for 'clear up'). I suppose what I really meant was how Okie working-class Scots were. I remember the numerous *frissons* of recognition I felt in reading about Hardy's yokels, often relating to how similar their sense of community was to the one I had been taught – their ability to appreciate the communal as a means not of strangling the eccentric and the individual but of letting it flourish in mutual tolerance. I remember the joy of discovering Albert Camus' essay *Summer in Algiers* and realising that he was talking about my own people, with great insight and compassion. Such generously shared perceptions from other places and times were like finding out that what you had thought was a dialect was, in fact, a language and one spoken in many parts of the world. It gave me the confidence to believe that, while I was writing out of my own experience, I was also writing towards the experience of countless others. The accent might be Scottish. But the message, whether they wanted it or not, was for everybody.

What that message was only emerged for me slowly in the writing. All the shifts and adjustments and failed endeavours and altered structures were moving towards the catching of a central image. Often I wasn't sure myself what that image was. It was only when the book was finished that I thought I knew. (The way in which the book was finished, incidentally, illustrates the kind of creative dementia I was working in. I had already written some 30,000-odd words past the point where the book now ends. My editor was becoming slightly despondent of ever seeing an end to it and he was beginning to suggest that we might have to sell the book through a building society, when I realised suddenly and surprisingly that the book was over. I had been going on with the writing of a novel that was finished.)

By the time I had finished the book, I thought I at last knew what it was about. Like any novel, it has its confusing variety of pointing fingers (novels being a process first of discovering understanding out of experience and only then of inventing experience out of understanding) but, if you can see beyond them, it seems to me, they are all pointing generally towards the same core of significance. The shield may be made up of many facets but they combine for me in offering the same coherent central reflection, which is the subject of the book. *Docherty* is essentially an attempt to democratise traditional culture, to give working-class life the vote in the literature of heroism.

The obsession that fuelled me in the writing of it did not have its antecedents, as some commentators have suggested, in Galt's *Annals of the Parish* or George Douglas Brown's *The House with the Green Shutters* or Lewis Grassic Gibbon's *Scots Quair*. This seems to me about as perceptive as listening to the common accent of two voices and concluding that the content of what is being said must be essentially the same. I have read and enjoyed these books but knew, even as I read them, that my obsessions were elsewhere. Of course, since these books all grow out of Scotland, some similarities will be found. There may be heard in the corner-standers of Graithnock, for example, an echo of the 'bodies' of Barbie. But it appears a pretty thin echo, not yielding any very fruitful comparison. To see any great kinship between the books on this kind of basis seems to me cultural myopia. After all, the device was hardly discovered in Ayrshire. The Greeks, too, had their choruses.

And the Greeks had more effect in determining what I was after than any previous Scottish novels. The three areas of my reading which have had the greatest impact on me are Greek myth, Greek tragedy and Elizabethan drama. The nature of heroism lies at the centre of them all. But it has always been a heroism based on an implied premise: social status. It has been a commonly enough remarked element. But it was A. C. Bradley in *Shakespearean Tragedy* who first emphasised it for me. It was one of many illuminatingly simple observations I found in him. (He has been often mocked subsequently for his intellectual naïvety in treating Shakespeare's characters as if they were real – 'How many children had Lady Macbeth?' – but I find his intelligent innocence a truer approach to the nature of literature than much of the etiolated intellectualisation that came after him.) That required social status of the hero or heroine troubled me. From Gilgamesh onwards, it was there. But while it was established as a historical fact, it did not seem to me a philosophically necessary ingredient of heroism. It blocked my path towards what I wanted to write, like a Gordian knot I had to unravel to get where I was going.

To do that, I had to come to my own understanding of the nature of heroism. I had to break it down from its achieved and assumed forms into its elements and see if it was possible to reconstitute it successfully without the dimension of social status. This meant, first of all, purifying the idea of heroism of some of the debased modern accretions it has acquired.

Heroism in its origins is a way of living, the definitive actions of a life. It is a story, not a gesture. So the contemporary tabloid debasement of heroism as a single act of courage will not serve. This is not to say that heroism will not be found in lives reported in the tabloids, just that it won't be expressible in such terms.

Nor does calling the main character in a book or play the 'hero' or the 'heroine' clarify things. They need exhibit none of the characteristics of heroism and yet assume its name. This is to abuse a word to the point of making it meaningless.

In trying to crystallise my own perception of heroism, in trying to arrive at my meaning of the word, I tried to relate its derivation to its contemporary usage. The ancient hero occurs in myth and myth was a precipitate of past experience. It was an endeavour to illuminate in human terms the darkness of the past. The ancient hero comes bringing with him the religious mists from which he emerged. He begins as superhuman, god-descended and sometimes god-becoming.

Much of the mythology that tends to define the modern idea of a hero, it seemed to me, is born of our fears, ignorance and half-knowledge not of the past so much as of the future. It is prospective, not retrospective. It is born less out of the darkness of the past than out of the darkness of the future. Made credulous by the technological advances of the past, we look forward in trepidation to those that can only be imagined and to their effects.

In such an atmosphere of the comparative loss of the importance of self, it is perhaps not too surprising that a modern cult hero like James Bond and many of his cinematic descendants, should move among pointless and spectacular carnage in which human life spins, aimless as an orange in a fruit machine. We are offered as hero a robot stylisation of the individual virtues, man evolving to the demands of his environment, surviving by adapting himself into an imitation of the machines around him, stripped to a few standard reflexes that emerge when circumstances push the appropriate button: self-protection, gastronomy, copulation. His bible is an unarmed combat manual. His sacrament is not love but sex. His only comprehension of the 'good life' is a gourmet's. This is the hero as less than human.

Between these two impossibilities, ancient origin and current distortion, superhuman and less than human – neither of which we should try to be – I was looking for the possible hero. I thought I found him between the two. The key for me lay in the realisation that the greatest thing we can be is definitively human. The hero celebrates humanity above all dogmas, codes, ideas. He becomes remorselessly and undeniably himself, against all proferred chances to imitate mere social mores and evade his own identity. (Hence, the importance of events, of happenings, those things that take us beyond thoughts or ideas and make us occur in fact. Heroic narrative is the record of humanity learning to be itself.) In this way, true heroism does not lie in eccentricity but in concentricity. It is individuality in essence. And those who are most individual are most other people. Individuality is the confirmation of other people's nature through your own. A hero is someone who is more ourselves than we are because, by rejecting the compromises of our nature that we accept, he shows us our potential to be more than we pretend to be. He is our unacknowledged self.

From this central dynamic of liberating us into our own humanity emanate all his virtues. Like Prometheus, he steals the secrets of the gods to enrich our living here and now. Like Antony after Actium deciding on 'one more gaudy night', he says, 'Go out as you choose, not how they tell you to go. Your life is not just what they tell you it is. It is also what you say it is.' Because, like Oedipus, he demands fully to know, he says to us in the meridian moment before his fall, 'Know, too, who you are. You are falling anyway – loud or quiet.'

But what he demands is also to be known, not just to know. One source of the effeteness of much modern literature, I believe, comes from the fragmentation of the hero's quest. The down-market modern hero seeks to be, without knowing. He will function effectively without having to know, insight and wisdom reduced to cunning and competence. The up-market modern hero will often seek to know without the responsibility of being his knowledge (which Oedipus had to endure) – literature as some kind of abstract science that need never be applied. One is soulless experience, the other experienceless soul.

The complete hero encompasses both dimensions. He will know as far as he can in his understanding, which is at least variable and at most won't take him far. Hercules was no sage and Gilgamesh no philosopher. But they were heroes. For who will judge a hero by his intelligence alone? His intelligence, in its variable limitations, only matters in how honestly and uncompromisingly it leads him into the further knowledge of how to be, most fully and most justly. Beyond the failure of his understanding, the hero must endure Keats's knowledge of the pulses, Kafka's physical inscription of 'In the Penal Settlement'.

The hero liberates us into the possibilities of our own nature because he enacts the subjective victory over objective circumstance and in doing so can teach us that we may do the same. Having a vision beyond his given horizons and the courage to live by the vision, he defeats those imposed horizons. His achievement is the transformation of experience through spirit. That is why his ultimate challenge is death, the final experienceable border of human nature. He will die, of course. But in meeting death he will transform its significance. He will fill its emptiness with his own humanity. His spirit will survive his dying, a part of us that diminishes death.

In *The Epic of Gilgamesh*, Gilgamesh, ruler of Uruk in Babylonia, loses his great friend, Enkidu. Faced for the first time with death not as concept but experience, Gilgamesh wishes to find how to live forever. From Utnapishtim, a variant of Noah, he learns of a rejuvenating plant at the bottom of the sea. Acquiring the plant, he is on his way home when he decides to bathe in a pool. The plant is left on the bank and is eaten by a snake, thus explaining how snakes can slough their skin and renew themselves. Gilgamesh's search has failed. Immortality reverts to nature beyond man. But there remains the stature of the quest, a quality of spirit endlessly renewable to match the endlessness of death.

Having worked out my definition of heroism, I believed that I could see how the social position of the hero was irrelevant. That quality of engagement with living could be practised daily anywhere. It seemed to me, for example, that many of the disadvantaged and the handicapped, creating to the point of death lives defiantly fuller than their circumstances offered, were living, in the most stringent terms, heroically. I had often thought that subsumed in *The Odyssey* was a *Eumaeid*, the story of Eumaeus, the swineherd who never leaves Ithaca during the 20 years of travel of Odysseus.

Heroism was, of course, in this sense a literary convention. But what I was suggesting to myself was that some of the trappings of that convention were unnecessary, that the convention could be purged of anachronistic elements and made to work again. The hero need not be socially important or exceptional in terms of his experience. These appeared to be historical deadweight, carried over from outmoded social structures, descriptive not so much of the essential nature of the hero as of the disguises he had to wear to meet the social assumptions of the time. Indeed, these factors seemed to me ways of diminishing the liberating power of the image of the hero. His social importance could be seen as relating to his fall and a warning to most of society not to try and emulate him. If that's what happens when you put your head above the parapet, keep yours down. If his experience is seen as exceptional, his kinship with us is blurred. He becomes a scapegoat, leaving us to practise our repetitive compromises undisturbed.

I wanted to divest heroism of its incidental historical robes and put it on the street. It wouldn't be the impressiveness of the experience that made people heroic but the impressiveness of how they confronted it. I would try to express heroism through working-class life. If my belief was that heroism could be found anywhere, not just in arched chambers and among dissolving dynasties, I would locate it in the most unlikely place. I brought it into the family. In time, I thought it settled in quite well.

The material of *Docherty* is largely my own experience of family life, enlarged by what was going on around us. But the Dochertys are not my family. I start from the premise that you cannot render actuality in prose, only an impression of reality. No living person ever appeared in a novel. People are too various, too shifting, too much. To write is to create, more or less, well or badly. The most neutral reportage is a fictive form. Just to select – and the very act of perception is a process of selection – is to create your own reality out of the actuality.

Also, I deliberately moved the raw material of my experience back in time. In setting the novel in a time before I was born, I was obliged to pass it through the transforming agent of research, oral and written. The experience became not an end but a means. It was as if it belonged to other people and I had to recreate their circumstances and responses. The material became malleable and I could try to shape its various parts into a whole that would reflect a true image.

What I thought that image essentially was, I have suggested. But what is reflected remains outside the thing that reflects it. So, while *Docherty* was made to be about the nature of experience anywhere, its reflective surfaces belong to a certain time and a certain place. Precisely because you are claiming to demonstrate, as I was, that a heroic ability to engage life can be found anywhere, you cannot then import alien materials to prove your case. To do that is to undercut your own contention. *Docherty* remains imaginatively rooted in the West of Scotland in the first quarter of the 20th century, in its speech, its ethos, its conditions of living. The code, as it were, in which its wider significance is expressed, is very specific and needs patience if it is to be cracked.

This causes a couple of problems. The first is that a lot of people won't bother to read it at all. (I remember my agent showing me letters from American publishers, praising the novel and saying they wouldn't consider publishing it, since it wouldn't be accessible to an audience there.) The second is that sometimes those who do read it, it seems to me, breach the terms of the contract that is necessary between reader and writer. They demand a late 20th-century sensibility from early 20th-century lives.

For example, the social and political objections feminists might bring to the superimposed nature of Jenny Docherty's experience are understandable. But in lamenting the lost potential, it would be wrong to undervalue the achievement. That would be a slander on her heroism. Given the terms she inhabits, she is just as heroic as Tam Docherty. It is just that, there and then, the terms for her were different. Heroism, I was suggesting, lies in the quality of the subjective response to the objective conditions.

But then any idea of working-class heroism as a philosophically serious concept, outwith its usefulness as a source of simplistic slogans for political purposes, is bound to offend social reformers. It is an uncomfortable attribute for them to accommodate because it represents a form of human fulfilment here and now, in defiance of the circumstances. And if circumstances cease to be all, the question of social programming ceases to be all-important. The need for reform is not denied – how could it be, given the social conditions we live among? – but it is seen to be part of something much bigger and more complex. Zealots never like that. They might have to rethink their priorities.

That is why I have suggested that *Docherty* is a subversive book. It is subversive not just of traditional cultural attitudes but of many contemporary cultural attitudes as well. The idea of heroism as something belonging to now offends traditionalists because it diminishes the importance of the past and it offends reforming revolutionaries because it diminishes the importance of the future.

What *Docherty* is essentially offering as the definitive characteristic of both working-class life and of heroism is rebelliousness. That lies at the centre of what it is reflecting, the primal feature of the beast. That is why we are what we are. That is both what we die of and what defies our death. That is why heaven and Utopia are places on our mental map at which we can never arrive, because we would have to deny our nature to get there. We must improve the shared conditions in which we live, of course, but the essential purpose of that will be in order to inhabit more fully the necessary and unalterable terms of our existence. Take away the avoidable injustices of some lives that we may humanly share in the unavoidable injustice that is all our lives.

This rebelliousness is all that finally survives in *Docherty*. If you take away the terms in which I tried to identify it, if you transform completely the working-class conditions where I thought I saw it, it will still be there. I believe the small man with red hair will be there as long as we are. I'm glad. As long as he's around, our humanity may be saved. That is why *Docherty* is primarily a celebration of rebellion and a negation of revolution.

Rebellion is the discovery of a possible future through an argument between the present and the past. Revolution is the invention of the certain future through a denial of the past, or at least a definitive reading of the past, by the present. Rebellion is fitful, questioning, potentially all-inclusive. The rebel is potentially the saviour of the man he rebels against, by reminding him of the just limits of his own nature. Revolution is systematic, dogmatic, inevitably exclusive. The revolutionary is predeterminately the destroyer of the man he revolts against.

A rebellion denies categories, a revolution invents them. Rebellion is made by individuals, revolution is made by committees. The loneliness of a rebel establishes kinship. The kinship of revolutionaries creates loneliness. One proclaims individuals, one denies them. Whoever proclaims individuality establishes a fraternity with our own. Whoever denies individuality through a cause leaves us alone with ours.

Revolution is a bourgeois and essentially reactionary phenomenon because it deifies the establishment, the *principle* of the establishment. It is petrified rebellion. The revolutionary is the sophist and pharisee of our time. Sophistry is speaking from the mouth, pharisaism is living in the mind. That is why revolutions become messianic and murderous.

But rebellion is pragmatic and salvationary. It moves forward constantly in doubt. It tries to confront the simplifications and lies of ideology and dogma with experience, the reality of our living. It renews our sense of our own humanity. To be true to our own experience, to its multiplicity and its incompatibility with received preconceptions as to its nature, is to rebel towards a more just way of living.

That's why *Docherty* ends as it does, not neatly resolved. The 30,000 words I had written beyond where it ends were, I came to realise, a form of obedience to an aesthetic that wasn't the book's. The ending had to hang like an unfinished phrase in the air, to be continued by other lives. The novel is about the generosity of the individual dream being broken against the inadequacy of circumstances. That story doesn't end.

'There is no epiphany as yet in his prose,' one critic has said of *Docherty*. I would have thought there was. But if it is there, it's the epiphany of constant rebellion. The book was made to be that way. If it had a patron saint, he would be Spartacus, the slave who led a rebellion to the gates of Rome, which was there for the taking, then turned away and went back to Sicily, where his rebellion had started, and died – seeking to engage the opposing general, Crassus, in combat, refusing either to be crowned with what his enemies called success or to yield:

What news is there of Spartacus?
The slaves of time don't need to ask.
They simply go where he has been
And do not ask, 'What did he see?'
Rome is before them still today:

Still chosen hills, the in heat town
That says no and undoes the gown,
The gates that open wide like thighs,
The defences that are coquetry.

He turned away. And so they must
Who in the honest heart of action
Find victory a cheap seduction.

Where is he now? When will he come?
He can't who is already here.

His long descendants don't know where
But in their daily lives they find
The small, hard legacy he left,
A nub of truth, eyes lie-bereft,
A dreadful justice of the mind
That will not palter with success
And knows power lies and force, if just,
Seeks judgment on itself at last
That it may still have honour.

He is the timbre of the voice
That, trapped in time, makes human choice:
I will not be victorious
And I refuse to say 'defeat' –

Which is, of course, the best of us,
Who *are* the news of Spartacus.

No Land in Sight?

Stands Scotland Where It Did?

Speech to the Scottish National Party Annual
National Conference, Dundee, September 1987

I'M SPEAKING HERE TODAY AS A KIND OF SOCIALIST, NOT
as a card-carrying member of any political party, which I'm not, but as
someone who believes, maybe sometimes uncertainly, in socialism.

There are reasons why I want to make this clear at the outset. I think
socialism today is running scared. One of the sad things I've observed
over the past ten years is how many people appear simply to inhale
the political climate of the time, to have their attitudes determined by
the prevailing mood. Fifteen years ago I knew people whose stance was
vaguely egalitarian, and whose stance now is vaguely entrepreneurial. The
change has come about not because of some great ideological upheaval
in them but because in the present hard times for most people, they're
doing all right, thank you. They were imitation socialists then. They
are imitation monetarists now. I don't respect them. What you believe
in should not be for sale. I have never found anything more rationally
justifiable, more morally acceptable, more humane or more honourable
to be than a socialist. Until I do, I'm a socialist.

The second reason for declaring my affiliations relates to place. I'm
speaking at the Scottish National Party Conference; therefore, to a party
of which I am not a member but a party for whose limited but significant
achievement I have respect. Scotland over the past 30 years and more
owes the Scottish National Party a debt. The SNP have reminded not
only us of who we are – they have reminded Westminster as well. And
they are still doing it. When you respect someone, you should be honest
with them.

The third reason for declaring my affiliations relates to the times. I
spoke of honesty. Honesty was never more needed in Scotland than now.
We live in an era of remarkable double-talk. We live under a government
which has wiped out whole areas of Scotland and then cynically carved on
the headstones: 'Regeneration'. Aye. Maybe in the next world. And yet
behind all the economic gobbledygook, the policies of this government
resolve themselves into one basic premise, I believe: they are a licence
issued to the wealthy to exploit the poor. It seems to me an indication of
the political shabbiness of the times we live in that that licence isn't kept

hidden away like the dirty thing it is. It is worn as if it were a badge of honour. In such times, we had better try to be honest with one another.

One final introductory remark. I am not a politician. I can't speak to you as such. I'm an interested layman; and a thoughtful layman, I hope – as a lot of laymen are in Scotland. Maybe you should see me today as standing in for John o' the Commonweal: a non-professional voice among specialists. There's a validity in having such a voice represented at your conference.

Politics may be the art of the possible. But in a democracy the essence of that art is making the wishes of the people possible. I can't claim to represent the wishes of the people. All I can hope is that perhaps some of the things I have to say may reflect some of the frustrated feelings that are abroad in Scotland today. And there are a lot of those about, I can promise you.

So much for the Bernard Shaw preface. Now for the play.

And since my sermon today, dear congregation, will be more humanist than religious, I have chosen our text not from the Bible but from literature – the pagan scriptures. And if you're going to quote, it's as well to quote from the best, even if the source isn't Scottish.

Shakespeare has a scene in *Macbeth* in which Ross arrives at the English court where Macduff is hiding out. Rather like a constituent trying to get in touch with his MP. Strange how little things change. Anxious for news, Macduff asks:

Stands Scotland where it did?

When Ross replies, he could be speaking of Scotland today:

Alas, poor country. Almost afraid to know itself.

Strange how little things change.

'Alas, poor country. Almost afraid to know itself.'

Of course, Ross is talking about a very different Scotland from ours – a much less stable place, a much more violent place, a place much more dramatically volatile. His subsequent words prove that:

> It cannot be called our mother, but our grave; where nothing,
> But who knows nothing, is once seen to smile;
> Where sighs and groans and shrieks that rend the air
> Are made, not marked; where violent sorrow seems
> A modern ecstasy; the dead man's knell

> Is there scarce asked for who; and good men's lives
> Expire before the flowers in their caps,
> Dying or ere they sicken.

No, that's not our Scotland. Is it? We're nothing like that. And then the picture gets even further away from us. Malcolm asks: 'What's the newest grief?' And Ross replies:

> That of an hour's age doth hiss the speaker;
> Each minute teems a new one.

No. That's got nothing to do with us. And yet. If you were to change the references slightly? You know the sort of thing they do when they're modernising Shakespeare. You get those productions that transfer the Trojan War to the Somme or put Hamlet in evening dress. If instead of shrieks you had demonstrations, if instead of deaths you had redundancies, if instead of griefs you had the latest application of Conservative policy to Scotland . . . the comparison comes closer.

'What's the newest grief?'

'That of an hour's age doth hiss the speaker;

 Each minute teems a new one.'

Sometimes, reading the papers day by day, that's not so far from how it feels. For this government has worked upon the country by a numbing accumulation of measures. We haven't recovered from the shock of one closure before there is another. We're still arguing among ourselves about the significance of one cut-back when the effect of another cut-back overwhelms that significance. We are by now so shell-shocked, after eight years of it, that we nod in acceptance of something that ten years ago would have made us want to take to the streets in protest. We lose sight of what is happening to us. We lose any clear sense of what is being done to Scotland. Given that condition, it might be good for us to try to answer Macduff's question for ourselves.

Stand Scotland where it did?

We can all see where Scotland stands clearly enough in general terms. It has a government it didn't vote for. It stands among closing factories and decaying industries. It is ravaged by redundancies. It has many young people for whom the prospect of a permanent job seems as distant as a mirage.

But these are generalisations. Generalisations are abstract and to that extent comfortable. The individual experiences behind them are not. Let's take a pretty mild case of the effects of our present condition on one person. And let's remember that behind it lie thousands of much worse cases.

She is a divorced woman with two children. Her husband left her for someone else and she is now a single parent. I met her not too long ago when I was writing an article about being poor in Scotland today. Here's a little of what I wrote. (I'm writing of the feeling of helplessness her circumstances have induced in her.)

'That sense of helplessness is exacerbated by some of the attitudes of others and by a conscience about as awkward as a piece of heavy engineering. A friend has remarked to her, "You're nothing but a sponger". ("If that's what a friend thinks of me, what are other people thinking?") Feelings of amorphous guilt grow like a fungus in the secretiveness such reactions promote, choking off her natural sociability. Her only apparent indulgence, smoking, is something she's not keen to let other people see her doing.

The guilt that waits in ambush in some of the simplest actions has promoted in her a hypersensitivity to the complex and largely incomprehensible rules she feels governing her life. She mentions the thought of the police coming to her door, for a reason she can't and doesn't want to imagine, and the moment is like a child trying to contemplate the bogeyman. She is determined to obey all the rules.

That determination seems to imply her acceptance of being immured indefinitely in her present circumstances. She can see no significant alleviation of them in the foreseeable future. The children, at thirteen and twelve, are at that stage when the young grow like the Incredible Hulk in a bad mood, with a corresponding need for new clothes, unfortunately not supplied magically by the props department. She says she gets no clothing grant. It looks as if they'll be outgrowing their mother's purse for a long time yet.

Paradoxically, her ambitions for them threaten to lengthen that time. She is determined that if anything thwarts her daughter's desire to be a teacher or her son's desire to be a civil engineer, it won't be their financial situation.

Such long-term ambition by proxy seems to be the only kind she can afford to indulge. Talking of herself, she gives the impression she has a horizon of about six inches. She hopes to hold on to her part-time job. She hopes, by scrupulous managing of money, to be able to let the children go on such school trips as are on offer. Asked what her greatest ambition is for herself, she claims it is to have the house redecorated, "To get it the way I want it". She admits how badly the paint and the furniture need renewing, but she's too used to them for her embarrassment to be more than token.

She has had a long education in learning by daily rote the acceptance of diminished dreams. Her father died when she was 13 and she can

remember her partially blind mother going to collect her 13/6d a week
to keep them both. She expresses no bitterness about her circumstances,
as if even that were something the rules perhaps don't entitle her to.

She simply stays at home except for the few hours she works each
day and one night a week when the local amateur dramatic society is
preparing its pantomime. On those nights she and the children go along
to help in the rehearsals and perhaps get a small part. It's an economical
activity, involving only the bus fares and the price of coffees.

Her case is unremarkable. It is at least partly the result of personal
experiences no one could have legislated for, but its most definitive
element remains insufficient money to live anything like a reasonably
fulfilling life and no apparent possibility of getting more. She is one
of very many trying to fight a rearguard action of personal decency
against the economic odds in a society where the principles behind
the distribution of the available wealth have developed, it should be
acknowledged, beyond the logic of the fruit-machine and the morality of
a Monopoly board, but not far enough beyond them.

She and others like her are able to maintain a superficial appearance of
sufficiency and to do it successfully enough, in many cases, to convince
not only others but themselves. They may live in different types of
areas. They will have little sense of sharing a common condition with
one another. They will assuredly have no sense of a common voice.

They're rather like a reservist army of the poor, uniform only in a
discreet malnutrition of the spirit, not yet mobilised into an open
acknowledgment of their shared state. For many of them perhaps their
greatest pride is that they have not yet had to make such open
acknowledgment. In a truly caring society it would be made for them.'

Of course, you could say: what's so different about that? Scotland has had
a lot of bad times before and it has often been left to the strength of
character of individual people, very often women, to fight that rearguard
action of decency against overwhelming odds. The Scots have had a lot of
practice at it – as have working-class people everywhere.

So maybe in a lot of ways Scotland does stand where it did. But for
me there is one ominous difference at the present time. We have had bad
governments in the past. We have had governments whose awareness of
Scotland's problems seemed on a par with their knowledge of the other
side of the moon. But we have never, in my lifetime, until now had
a government whose basic principles were so utterly against the most
essential traditions and aspirations of Scottish life. We have never until
now had a government so determined to unpick the very fabric of Scottish
life and make it over into something quite different. We have never had a
government so glibly convinced of its own rightness that it demands that

one of the oldest nations in Europe should give itself a shake and change utterly its sense of itself.

Under this government, it is not only the quality of our individual lives that is threatened. It is our communal sense of our own identity. For this government is out to change it. The complex traditions and attitudes and ways of thought that have emerged from the Scottish people's long argument with their own experience – these things are to be pushed aside. In favour of what? The abacus morality of monetarism? Henryson, Dunbar, Hume, Burns, the ILP, John Maclean – these are to be drowned in a puddle?

For Margaret Thatcher is not just a perpetrator of bad policies. She is a cultural vandal. She takes the axe of her own simplicity to the complexities of Scottish life. She has no understanding of the hard-earned traditions she is destroying. And if we allow her to continue, she will remove from the word 'Scottish' any meaning other than the geographical. At such a time, we should at least consider what it is we are in danger of losing. What is distinctive about the word 'Scottish'? What would be losing? What is Scotland?

Many of us would have different answers, and those differences should be respected. I can only offer you my own. I can only tell you what I think the happy vandal at Number 10 is destroying that belongs to me.

I spent almost a year recently in Canada. I met there a lot of expatriate Scots. Where don't you meet them? I remember a black man in a poncho and sombrero in Córdoba. He was a Scotsman. I know of a small man giving knowledgeable conducted tours of Reno. He was a Scotsman. I sometimes feel that, if you opened an alligator's jaws in the Congo, a Scotsman would nod out at you. 'Aye. It's no' much o' a hoose. But ye're welcome tae come in if ye want.'

One woman I met at a special event in Vancouver was a second-generation expatriate. She told me she had the right to two tartans. I explained that as far as I was aware I had the right to none. She told me she was distantly descended from the Scottish aristocracy and said she was thinking of writing about that. I wondered what she was thinking of writing. A public disclaimer?

She was a nice enough woman but, as you may have gathered, hers was not my sense of Scotland. I met many expatriates I liked. But often their sense of Scotland depressed me. They were happy to be where they were, which was fine. But they also wanted to keep a simplified idea of Scotland. They used Scotland like a little weekend cottage of the mind, full of kitsch wee ornaments like Ben Nevis and Loch Lomond. That's not my Scotland.

I met another woman at an event in Halifax, Nova Scotia. She claimed to be descended from James MacPherson of *Ossian* fame. It's funny how so many Scottish expatriates in Canada seem to be 'descended'. You hardly meet anybody who was just 'born'. And nobody ever admits that she was just the coalman's lassie. But this was an impressive woman. She would be in her 60s with much travel and deep thought behind her. She had a very strong sense of Scotland, a sense which even a native Scot could only respect. Her forefathers had been Gaelic-speaking and she knew much about the history of the Gaels in Canada. She taught me a few things.

But she also, accidentally, reminded me that the people who have created the definitive image of Scotland in Canada were primarily Highlanders. They came mainly in the nineteenth century. They often transported with them a historically frozen and geographically limited sense of Scotland. It's an important sense, as far as it goes, but for me it doesn't go far enough.

It is how those who stayed in Scotland developed those old traditions that for me makes the essential, living Scotland. The past gave us those important traditions but it is how we have adapted them in modern life that, for me, makes us distinctive as a nation. The most nourishing roots of the Scottish identity, the roots that offer potential for continuing growth, have their soil not in the historically romanticised past but in the more recent industrial history of the nineteenth and twentieth centuries.

The Scots remain Scottish not primarily because of the Gaelic bards or the clan system or because Mary Queen of Scots and Bonnie Prince Charlie were briefly and disastrously among us – but because of the characteristic ways we found of responding to the industrialisation of our country.

We are Scottish because our history has been a distinctive struggle with serious issues the woman in Downing Street doesn't seem to know exist. Scottish history has been for centuries engaged on serious business. But it's obviously not Mrs Thatcher's business. Her type of business is the kind you put a name to and float on the stock market. Ours has been about human matters, like how to go about achieving a just society.

I've travelled a bit – not too much but a bit. And I know nowhere less defined by materialism than Scotland. I remember sitting in a café in Paris, talking to a French friend, François. After about an hour, he looked at me with an exhausted expression on his face. 'I like to meet you, Willie,' he said. Then he shook his head. 'But you are so Scottish. Always the moral issue. The demand for justice. The world is not like that.' Many Scots have always felt that it should be. I want to go on living in a country where we still feel that.

That's what is under threat for me. Scotland still has potential in that direction. The potential of Scotland is valuable because it has remained in a kind of stasis, is to some extend underdeveloped. It shouldn't seek to imitate more elaborately developed cultures but to offer an alternative way to the one they have taken. Given its early origins, it has roots deep enough to do that. It is as old as they are, older than most in the West. It holds, in suspended animation within itself, an alternative tradition. Politically and culturally, it retains dynamic choices many other countries have lost.

Let us make those choices for ourselves. Let us honour our own traditions. A long time ago, with the Declaration of Arbroath, our country and our culture set out towards a destination. There has been a lot of deep thought along the way. Will we allow that country and that culture to be hi-jacked by a woman who keeps her intelligence in her purse?

I hope not. I hope we will refuse to go where she is trying to force us to go, with the blunderbuss of her economic policies held to our head. I hope we have the courage to remove ourselves, at least some distance, from the bullying shallowness of her philosophy. I hope we have the wisdom to return to prospecting our own traditions once again.

There is a deeply ingrained tradition in Scotland that we will not finally judge one another by material standards. A country as poor as we have been for so long has at least learnt that there are more important measures of a human being than the financial – more significant assessments of the state of a nation than the stock market. We have a humane tradition to uphold second to that of no other nation.

If we wish to remain Scottish, we will honour that tradition. If we wish to remain Scottish, we will reject from the root the fundamental precepts of the present government in Westminster. If we wish to remain Scottish, we will refuse to be coerced into measuring the worth of one another on the Dow Scale. If we wish to remain Scottish, we will have contempt for judging a man by how much money is in his wallet or a woman by the cheques she writes.

We need to measure people? Do we? We need to judge performance? Do we? We need to assess significant contribution to society? Do we? All right, we can do that. But if we wish to remain Scottish, we won't use a system based on some crude scale of economic weights and measures: let's see how much his pockets weigh. We won't measure the floor-space of his house. We won't call in an estate agent to evaluate his acreage. We won't phone his bank manager.

No. We'll use another system – a system long established here; a system developed from the experience and the pain and the long thought and the deep humanity of the Scottish people. And that's not a hard system to apply. Its principles are simple enough. You want a measurement of people? Then, if you wish to remain Scottish, here it is. You will measure them by the extent of their understanding, by the width of their compassion, by the depth of their concern and by the size of their humanity.

There's a real system for you. And it has never been under greater threat than it's under now. For this government is trying to convert us, is trying to convert this nation, to another system. The conversion to decimalisation? You found that confusing? Wait till this one hits you. This government is trying to convert our very way of life, the way we think, into a contradiction of itself.

Make no mistake. The times we are living through now are witnessing a ruthless attempt to subvert the most fundamental traditions of Scottish life. If we let it happen, we deserve the result. And the result will be a piecemeal repetition of 1707 – only this time, one that is finally effective. It won't be as immediately dramatic as the Act of Union, of course. But that's maybe why it will be more effective.

In 1707, the rank-and-file of the nation saw clearly enough what was happening and many rioted in opposition to it. We have no such single focus to rebel against today. For this government operates a double standard: bland and meaningless reassurances like camouflage, within which is hidden the weaponry of ruthlessness. It is dismantling the spirit of this nation over a period of years, piece by piece.

This government doesn't waste much time opposing Scottishness in theory; it simply undermines it practically. It is, of course, a phased process. Garotte an industry here, starve out a small community there. The effects are already bad. Consider the mines. This woman takes the most important and the most deeply sustaining traditions of ordinary people and sells them, literally, in job-lots. She sells what does not belong to her. The effects are already bad? They will get worse.

If the Scottish people continue to accept what is happening to our country, if we continue to go about our private lives as individuals who have found no way of effectively unifying into a nation, we will all waken, not too many years from now, to find that we no longer live where we thought we lived. Some of us may well have prospered. Most of us may well be surviving more or less adequately. But the mental landmarks this nation has built over centuries, those ways of thought by which we know ourselves, will be gone.

No matter what the outward appearance of our country may be then, we will look around and know in our hearts that we inhabit a desert of dependency – a land of lost principles, of decayed traditions, of ruined ideals. What generations of our countrymen and women earned in the sweat of hard experience and the intensity of honest thought, we will have bartered in return for the facile statistics of monetarism. There will be no way back for Scotland from that place.

I honestly believe that time is running out for us if we are to try and realise anything like our potential as a people who have learned to love justice, who have learned to value the human above the material, who have persistently refused to give up our sense of our own identity. The traditions we have proudly inherited are, for the moment, still ours. But that condition carries no guarantee. If you want to hold on to good traditions, you must re-earn the possession of them. Tradition doesn't survive in a vacuum. It survives on living recommitment. Put it in the deep-freeze and it doesn't keep.

Let none of us make excuses at this time. We are at some kind of eleventh hour in our country's history. There is no noise of battle around us, right enough – no screams of the dying, no sound of guns. Just the rattle of a padlock on a factory gate that is closing for good, the rustle of redundancy forms. But even a nation can perish quietly. And that may be what is happening, unless we stop it.

So let's make no excuses for ourselves. If, later on in this country, we fail to recognise the place we knew, let's not pretend that we weren't there at the time or there was no way we could work out what was happening. It's happening now. We can see it all around us. We have a choice to make. Whatever we do with our awareness of what is happening to our country is that choice. If we strive for a Scottish Assembly, that is a choice. If we abstain from involvement in the whole business, that is a choice. If we can't see that there's a problem at all, that is a choice, too.

Stands Scotland where it did? Just about, but not for much longer. A crisis-point has arrived. We will either become more ourselves or less ourselves in the next few years. We cannot much longer maintain the ambiguity of our present situation: that of a people who retain a strong sense of themselves as a nation yet have no effective structure of government within which to develop and give expression to that sense.

Scotland's ability to maintain an identity of its own has, since 1707, been a miraculous balancing act. Without the machinery to govern ourselves, we have nevertheless remained distinctive – through our language, through our literature, through our churches, through our law, through our education, through the radicalism of our desire for social justice. We are not English. We are Scottish. We have earned the right to that distinction in the bones of our past.

But we will not much longer sustain that distinction in the circumstances we live in at present. We are now so threatened by a government implacably hostile to the ideas that have nourished Scotland's deepest sense of itself that we must protect ourselves. We will either defend our identity or lose it – no other choice. So alien to Scotland are the uncaring principles of the present government, we might as well be governed by Martians. And don't take refuge in the fact that this government won't be there forever. We can wait that long? A virus called look-out-for-number-one has been deliberately let loose in this country. In five years it could become an epidemic. We should protect ourselves.

And how do we protect ourselves? By establishing a structure of government that carries out the wishes of the people. When a government implements the wishes of the people, we have democracy. When it does not, we have something else. Effectively, at this moment, we do not have democracy in Scotland. Effectively, at this moment, the Scottish people do not have the vote. Oh, they can make wee marks on bits of paper, right enough. But we might as well write graffiti on them for all the effect they're going to have in Westminster under the present system.

Consider our situation as demonstrated at the recent election. Scotland was overwhelmingly for Labour. That was how we voted. But a vote is merely an individual gesture. For too long now, the sum of those individual gestures has not been translated into effective communal action. How could they be?

Scotland is a part – and a small part – of the United Kingdom. The government Scotland gets often has scant connection with the way Scotland votes. The gestures too often remain merely gestures made towards Westminster. You don't penetrate brick walls by waving your fist at them. In effect, the Home Counties rule Britain.

If there is one incontrovertible argument in favour of some kind of devolved power for Scotland, this is it. If a country, a group of people recognisably distinctive in its characteristics and aspirations, finds its democratically arrived at will thwarted by the system of government under which it lives, it should seek to change that system. It must seek to inhabit a political context where that will is no longer paralysed. For Scotland this can only mean some kind of power structure separate from Westminster.

That conclusion shouldn't be retreated from because of the threatening shouts of 'parochialism' it evokes. Nothing could be more politically parochial than Scotland's present position, that of a populous village of the United Kingdom, the residents of which wait virtually powerless, to be informed what changes in their lives will happen next.

Parochialism is not where you live but how you live. A man living in the Outer Hebrides who takes the trouble to be aware of what is happening in the world and to concern himself with it is less parochial than the most sophisticated Londoner who sees his club as the hub of the world. Scotland can only become less parochial by taking more responsibility for itself and, therefore, for its relationship to events in the world.

Nor, for Scottish socialists, should the old argument about dividing the movement carry much weight these days. The English Labour Party gives the impression of having suffered a kind of ideological stroke, possibly

251

terminal. The two sides of its body politic seem to function independently. The right side is close to paralysis, offering us a paper rose as its emblem – a nice, placative symbol. Radical? Us? Oh, no.

The left side is a jangle of disconnected nerve-ends from which no coherent policy could possibly emerge. It is a riot of schismatic phoney radicalism. Every other week the splinter groups splinter into splinter groups. Soon we can expect the emergence of a group to champion the rights of baldy men. They will demand shaven heads in public because bald people feel disadvantaged by the sight of hair.

Should Scottish socialism stay harnessed to a horse that is being flogged to death with feathers? The most significant move that Scottish socialists could make towards establishing socialism in Britain is to establish social-ism in Scotland. For socialism to survive it has to find new tactics.

And all of us in Scotland, socialist or not, had better find such tactics soon. For too long Scots have underestimated the power that government has in determining the way we live.

Government changes lives. I know that from my own experience. If the Labour government had not been returned in 1945, I – and countless others – probably wouldn't have gone to university. Without the experience of Labour in power, I would not have come as near to fulfilling myself as I have. Mind you, I've still a long way to go – but that's not Labour's fault or the university's. Conversely, the effects of the present Conservative government will be felt for generations to come. It isn't merely the damage to the present that breaks the heart – the wasted years, the rejection of the aged, the demeaning of the young. It is the incalculable damage to the future – the loss of belief in society, the anti-social tendencies encouraged, the lesson branded on thousands of minds that you are alone and your society doesn't care. We will live with the effects of this for years to come. Government changes lives.

I say this particularly to those people who are understandably, at the present time, battening the hatches and looking to the protection of their families. I will do what has to be done, they say. Whatever the rules of the game, I'll play it. My kids are there and I want the best for them. I'm sorry about those other kids but I've my own to look after. That is an understandable philosophy but, held in isolation like that, it is a very dangerous one.

To those people I would say: where will your children live? The planet Mars? They will live here. They will live in the society your blindfolded view of things has helped to create. They will inherit not only the education you contrive for them, not only the decent manners you teach, not only the job you help them to get, not only such money as you may manage to bequeath. They will inherit the streets of the inner cities. They will inherit membership of a generation the largest part of which has been systematically deprived of its most basic rights: to work, to feel a sense of belonging, to try to live a fulfilling life. That will be some inheritance. If you care for your children, care for the society they will have to live in.

I care for my children, too – too much, I hope, to want them to inhabit fortresses of privilege within a wasteland of deprivation. That is no gift to give your children. I don't want my children stunted in that way. I want them to live in a society where the potential richness of their nature is encouraged, a society where they are not narrowed into predators but enlarged into sharers, a society where they can see that giving is the measure of humanity, not taking.

Such a society, of course, will not arrive tomorrow. But it can be worked towards. It's the only kind of society worth working towards. Scotland in the past has at least had honourable ambitions in that direction. But that humanising thread that has run throughout its hard history is in danger of being cut. If it is, this country will lose the best of itself and it will never be the same again.

Government changes lives. And because it is trying to change our lives, finally and for the worse, we had better find a way to change government – and fast.